THE MUTUAL EFFECTS OF THE ISLAMIC AND JUDEO-CHRISTIAN WORLDS: THE EAST EUROPEAN PATTERN

EDITED BY

ABRAHAM ASCHER, TIBOR HALASI-KUN,
BÉLA K. KIRÁLY

BROOKLYN COLLEGE PRESS, BROOKLYN, N.Y.

Distributed by Columbia University Press
New York

1979

Copyright © 1979 Brooklyn College CUNY
Published by Brooklyn College Press
Distributed by Columbia University Press

Library of Congress Catalog Card Number 77–90629
ISBN 0–930888–00–6

Printed in USA

BROOKLYN COLLEGE

OF
THE CITY UNIVERSITY OF NEW YORK
SCHOOL OF SOCIAL SCIENCE
DEPARTMENT OF HISTORY

STUDIES ON SOCIETY IN CHANGE, No. 3.

BROOKLYN COLLEGE STUDIES ON
SOCIETY IN CHANGE
—Editor in Chief Béla K. Király—

To the memory of Jesse D. Clarkson

PREFACE

The present book contains the proceedings of the "Second Annual Brooklyn College Conference on Society in Change." It represents a first in our young series, entitled "Brooklyn College Studies on Society in Change," for it emerged in its entirety from scholarly discussions carried out on our own campus. The various chapters represent an already established tradition of these conferences and publications: they are investigations of major issues in modern society on the highest academic level; the research, presentations, and conclusions relate to the life of our generation and to our community; the studies combined represent an interdisciplinary approach; they concern our actual educational processes; and they utilize the talents and expertise of our own colleagues, those of the sister colleges of CUNY, and those of other distinguished institutions of higher learning.

This volume includes studies written by Ülkü Ü. Bates (Hunter College), Stephen Fischer-Galati (University of Colorado), Alan W. Fisher (Michigan State University), Peter B. Golden (Rutgers University), Tibor Halasi-Kun (Columbia University), Allan Z. Hertz (McGill University), Halil İnalcık (University of Chicago), Béla K. Király (Brooklyn College), William G. Lockwood (University of Michigan), Jaroslaw Pelenski (University of Iowa), Peter Pastor (Montclair State College), Omeljan Pritsak (Harvard University), and Dankwart Rustow (Brooklyn College). The several fields represented by these scholars include art history, anthropology, history, linguistics, political science, East Central European, Jewish, Medieval, Middle Eastern, Slavic, and Turkic studies.

The book, then, runs across a unique spectrum of scholarly fields of research, and the authors have come together, physically and in scholarship, from an impressive array of institutions of higher learning. The subject matter being vast, the book does not claim comprehensiveness, and that was not its goal. Nonetheless, publication will contribute to the better understanding of a complex issue, many facets of which continue to need substantial scholarly development.

With this volume, Number 3 in the series on Society in Change, the Brooklyn College sponsors of the annual conference and the publications, and their colleagues at other institutions, deserve recognition for their achievements. The series is new but its volumes have come quickly and excellently, the last despite the hardships through which the City University and Brooklyn College are passing. Hardship or not, we look ahead now to the next conference and its scholarly result.

September 1, 1976

Donald R. Reich
Professor of Political Science
Vice President and Provost

CONTENTS

INTRODUCTION

The volume introduced below is the result of a conference at Brooklyn College, May 3–4, 1976. The aim of the conference and of this volume clearly follows from the title: "Conference on the Mutual Effects of the Islamic and Judeo–Christian Worlds: The East European Pattern."

Although at first sight this title may appear rather general in meaning, at closer look it becomes evident that, with an indeed carefully selected wording, the program director, Professor Béla K. Király, a modern historian whose particular area of interest is Eastern Europe, wanted to focus attention on the cultural interchange that took place mainly in the Early Modern Period of our history. If his intent had been a more general study of cross-influences, or a study devoted, in particular, to the Middle Ages, the title either would have contrasted the three Worlds as separate entities, or would have spoken of mutual effects between the Judeo-Islamic and the Christian Worlds.

Accordingly, it is easily understood why, though given complete freedom in the selection of their particular topics in the outlined frame of the main theme, eleven of the twelve authors, as can be seen, chose to discuss questions pertinent to the Early Modern Period. Only one article reaches back into the pre-Islamic times of the area, furnishing a valuable and colorful background to the main theme of the volume.

Furthermore, it is interesting to see that, influenced by the subtle regional limitation expressed in the second part of the title, the articles, once again with one exception, all are concentrated on the Turkic segment of the Islamic World, the only Islamic segment that was directly in contact with, and played a major role in the history, in the development of the area under consideration. And even further, nine of the twelve articles deal with Ottoman problems, while two refer to the modern Islamized remnants of the Kipchak Turkic Golden Horde. These figures clearly underline the paramount importance of Ottoman source materials whenever East–West relations are concerned.

If one considers that the Ottoman Empire was splintered into about thirty-five successor states (Albania, Algeria, Armenia, Azerbaijan, Bulgaria, Cyprus, Egypt, Ethiopia, Georgia, Greece, Hungary, Iran, Iraq, Jordan, Kuwait, Lebanon, Libya, Moldavia, Morocco, the North-Caucasian States, the Persian-Gulf Emirates, Rumania, Saudi Arabia, Slovakia, Sudan, Tunisia, Turkey, Ukraine, Yemen, and Yugoslavia), one realizes even more the importance of the vast documentative material the Empire left for posterity. As any aspect of the Classic and Early Middle Ages of South Eastern Europe cannot be properly treated without reference to the Roman Empire and without a knowledge of Latin, and similarly the Later Middle Ages of the same area cannot be understood without reference to Byzantium and the Caliphate and a knowledge of Greek and Arabic, so the Modern Period of this region cannot be treated without recourse to the Ottoman Empire and rich materials in the Ottoman language. The same holds true for areas well beyond the scope of this volume. Thus, for instance, nineteenth-century Egypt or Yemen cannot be properly studied without a mastery of Ottoman. This means, of course, that Ottoman Studies form a sine qua non prerequisite for all serious studies entailing Near Eastern History. It is encouraging to see that, despite the difficulties inherent in Ottoman, the scope of Ottoman Studies in general is increasing with a reassuring speed. The bibliographies by A. Tietze bear the best witness to this development. In 1973–1974 some 1,418,[1] and in 1975 some 1,739[2] books and articles were published dealing with topics in Ottoman Studies. It is more than certain that among these publications there are many that, be it directly or indirectly, touch upon questions of interaction between the three major culture groups that still prevail in the area considered the cradle of Judaism, Christianity, and Islam.

Last but not least, we also have to point here to the importance of the Golden Horde in any study dealing with questions on Eastern Europe. This special aspect was, for the longest time, neglected by specialists of the field. But, we have now advanced to the point where the consensus holds that, as without the Khazar Empire no study of medieval Inner Russia or the Kievan State can be carried out effectively, so too no valid studies can be ef-

---

1. A. Tietze, "Turkologischer Anzeiger (*TA 1*)," *WZKM* 67, pp. 339-448.
2. A. Tietze, "Turkologischer Anzeiger (*TA 2*)," *WZKM* 68, pp. 297-485.

fected in the field of Russian history for instance without a deep probing into the history of the Golden Horde.

In conclusion, we are deeply indebted to Brooklyn College without whose support this volume would not have come into existence.

T. Halasi-Kun

I. EARLY CULTURAL INTERACTIONS

O. Pritsak

THE ROLE OF THE BOSPORUS KINGDOM AND LATE HELLENISM AS THE BASIS FOR THE MEDIEVAL CULTURES OF THE TERRITORIES NORTH OF THE BLACK SEA

The name *Bosporus* (Ho Bós-poros) is of Ancient Greek origin and has the literal meaning "ox-ford."

This term was used to refer to the straits between two seas.

Two such *Bosporus*es became known in history. The first was the Cimmerian Bosporus (Ho Kimmérios Bósporos), located at the point where, according to the classic geographic authors, Europe and Asia met. It corresponded to the modern straits of Kerch, which connect the Black Sea with the Sea of Azov.

According to the author of the *Odyssey* (XI, 13–19), the enigmatic Cimmerians, first mentioned by Homer, lived in a country of fog and darkness on the confines of the inhabited world (meaning Europe). Many archaeological cultures (*e.g.,* the "Catacomb," "Koban," "Thraco-Cimmerian") have been attributed to them, but without scholarly validity.[1]

The other Bosporus, the Thracian (Ho Thrákios Bósporos), was the strait that unites the Black Sea with the Marmara branch of the Mediterranean Sea. The Thracian Bosporus is well known from Greek mythology, in which Io, a maiden loved by Zeus, and given the form of a heifer by the jealous Hera, crosses the straits during her wanderings.

Our concern will be the first of these referents—the Cimmerian Bosporus.

Greek colonies of the *polis* type were established in that region in the eighth to sixth centuries B.C. The most important of these was the Milesian colony of Panticapaeum (present-day Kerč) located on the western side of the straits, at the extreme eastern tip of the Crimea. Ten miles to the south lay Nymphaeum. On the eastern side of the straits were the colonies of Phanagoria (near modern Taman'), founded from Teos, and Hermonassa, founded from Mytilene.[2]

The early history of the colonies is for the most part unknown. Panticapaeum is said to have been founded with the permission of the Scythians, the successors of the Cimmerians in Eastern Europe.

By 480 B.C. the first ruling dynasty of tyrants had been established in Panticapaeum. To judge by their names, the Archeanactids were probably purely Greek in origin. In 438 B.C. they were replaced by the half-Thracian Spartocids; the latter's history is fairly well known because of their close relations with the Athenians.

According to M. Rostovtzeff, "the semi-Thracian aspect of the new dynasty speaks rather for a native reaction against Greek domination, and this theory is corroborated by the title which the new rules assumed: 'archons of Ponticapaeum and kings of the Sindians and the Maeotians.' The fact that among the Sindian princes who ruled at the same period as the tyrants of Ponticapaeum, one finds Thracian names like Gorgippos and Komosarye, and that the two dynasties probably united shortly after the revolution of Spartocos, seems to show that the principal cause of the political change was the necessity of reconciling the interest of the natives, and especially the native aristocracy, with those of the Greek population of the polises."[3]

It is noteworthy that "this phenomenon was not peculiar to Panticapaeum. Similar conditions led to the establishment of similar forms of government, nearly concurrently, at Heracleia on the Pontus, at Halicarnassus in Asia Minor, and at Syracuse in Sicily."[4] "The same movement gave rise to the Greco-Macedonian monarchy in Macedonia, and later, to the combination of the city-state and monarchy at Pergamon."[5]

But it was only in the Cimmerian Bosporus that the form of government so produced proved stable: here it lasted from 438 B.C. until at least the fourth century A.D. (production of the coinage of the Bosporus kings ceased in 337 A.D.).[6]

The earlier Spartocids governed as archons; the royal title was not used by them until the Hellenistic Age.

The Sindian kingdom in the Taman' peninsula was then incorporated, so that Spartocid power extended further northeast, beyond the mouth of the Tanais / Don river (later the city of Azov).

The able dynasty of the Spartocids suppressed piracy on the Black Sea and through wise management were very successful in the trade of grain, fish, and slaves, as is shown by their fine coinage, vases, and jewelry.

Until her defeat in the Peloponnesian war (431–404), Athens maintained a monopoly over Bosporan trade: the tyrant of Panticapaeum was forced to accept the status of the Athenian commercial agent and agree to export all corn to Athens, alone.

Panticapaeum had received the right to trade freely, with the single condition being the guarantee of ample custom duties to Athens. The reigns of the kings Satyros (433–389), Leucon (389–349), and Pairisades I (349–310) were ones of great prosperity for the Bosporus. In Athens, Leucon was spoken of as the model of a virtuous tyrant; Attic historians wrote about him, as well as Panticapean. The statues of the three kings adorned public places in the Greek capital. The Scythians became resigned to the independence of the Bosporus state, which had organized a powerful army of mercenaries, a commercial fleet, and a regular traffic system.[7]

It was not until the second half of the third century B.C. that economic and political decay began to appear in the prosperous society.

The Spartocid dynasty survived until about 110 B.C.; the kingdom then came under the control of the kings of Pontus (Mithradates VI Eupator, 121–63 B.C.). At the beginning of our era a new dynasty of the Iulios was established, which ruled until at least the middle of the fourth century, or the time of the shortlived East European empire of the Ostrogoth Hermanarich.[8]

One might mention that the Gothic naval raids on the Black Sea (beginning with 256 A.D.) originated in the Cimmerian Bosporus; the Goths became sea-born only after they were able to arrest the Bosporian fleet.[9]

One might also note that—according to the Byzantine sources—the Ruś of the Grand Prince Igor used the Cimmerian Bosporus as an operational base in his campaigns against the Byzantine fleet.[10]

The famous Ruś trade and cultural center Tmutorakan' / Tá Tamátarkha was a successor town of the Bosporian Hermonassa.[11]

II.

1.

In the famous bibliographical work *Kitāb al-Fihrist*, the Arab scholar Abu'l-Farag Muhammad b. Ishāq al-Warrāq, called an-Nadīm, who finished his study before the year 377 of the Hijra (*i.e.*, 988 A.D.), presented some very surprising data which until now was unexplained.

In an entry devoted to the literary activity of the Abbasid Caliph al-Ma'mūn, the son of Harūn ar-Rašīd (813–833), one reads the following:

"Among his [al-Ma'mūn's] books were: Answers to the Questions of the king of the Burghar (Kitāb Jawāb malik al-burghar min umūr) addressed to him [al-Ma'mūn] about Islām and at-Tawhīd (Unity) . . . (al-islām wa'l-Tawhīd)."[12]

In another passage of the same work, some further details are given about the work in question:

"He [al Ma'mūn]"—we read—"wrote to the king of the Burģar a letter of over one hundred pages in length, but although he did not seek anyone's aid or quote any verse from the Book of Allāh, may this name be exalted, or any word from any wise man preceeding him, al-Gāhīz cajoled his tongue into saying, 'This letter we have regarded as being taken in a favorable way from a discourse of al-Gāhīz.'"[13]

Referred to here is, of course, the great Arab writer Abū 'Otmān 'Amr ibn Bakr al-Gāhīz (b. *ca.* 776. d. 869), who, like the Caliph himself, was a follower of the intellectual movement called Mu'tazila (lit. "Secessionists"), or "the people of unity (*at-tawhīd*) and justice (*al-'adl*)," a movement of liberal thologians studying the nature of the divinity.[14]

Certainly, we cannot dwell here on the question of whether or not the royal author plagiarized al-Gāhīz. Our concern is to understand why the learned caliph found it necessary to correspond with a Bulgar king, of all people, on subtle philosophical matters, especially strange because the Mu'tazila were among the first Muslim scholars to use the categories and methods of Greek philosophy in expounding their theological system.

It is well known that al-Ma'mūn founded a school of savants at Baghdād called "Bait al-ḥikmet" (House of Wisdom) in which the study and translation of Greek works, especially those in science and philosophy, was pursued with the utmost vigor. Translators engaged there were Syriac Nestorian scholars who knew both Arabic and Greek.[15]

But who were the Burghar / Bulgars who figure in our question?

The Bulgars first appeared in Eastern Europe after the fall of the Hunnic ruler Attila (453), as a new regrouping of the defeated Huns. Subsequently, in the sixth and seventh centuries, there existed a *Magna Bulgaria*/Boulgariá hê megálē, or new edition of the Bosporus kingdom.[16]

As mentioned above, during ancient times the basis of the Bosporus' prosperity were the three export commodities of grain, fish, and slaves. The first of these made the Bosporus the main granary of Athens.

The importance of the fish export is reflected as the late V. Minorsky noted, in that during the Khazar rule over the Bosporus, the primates (non-elected) of the cities Bosporus and Tamatarcha (Jewish Samkarč) bore the official title of *baligči*, a Turkish word meaning "fishermen."[17]

The official title of the king of the Bosporus Bulgars prior to 641 (the end of the Sasanian dynasty) was—according to Ibn Khurdadhbeh (the well-informed Arabic geographer of Persian origin during the period 840-880)—'King of the *Saqāliba*,' i.e., ruler over a territory recognized as a reservoir of potential slaves. It is probable that the very term *Sklav-/Sclav-*(*Saqlab-*) (later *Slav-*) was introduced to the sphere of Mare Nostrum from Bosporus sometime in the sixth century.[18]

One might add that Ibn Faḍlān, the Arabic missionary traveler of the Volga Bulgars in 922, used the same title, "King of the Saqāliba (*malik aṣ-Saqāliba*)" with reference to Almuč, king of the Volga Bulgars.[19] The latter were not Slavs, however, but were of Turkic and Hunnic origin; their dynasty descended from Kubrat of Bosporus Bulgaria, whom Ibn Khurdādhbeh (as mentioned above) addressed in the same way: *malik aṣ-Saqāliba*.

The idea of trade in human beings may give us some uneasy feelings today, but we should not forget that in the Middle Ages, as in the days of Athens' supremacy and during the Roman Empire, slaves were regarded as an important commodity (the source of energy). Concurrently, the importation of slaves was a highly respected profession, requiring experience, expedience, and proficiency.

Although the Turkic Khazars' drive for hegemony put an end to *Magna Bulgaria* as an independent political power *ca.* 660, so that many Bulgars migrated to either the Danubian Moesia, the Kama–Volga basin, or Italian Ravenna, the essential components of Bulgar society remained on their old territory. One should note that their ruler may have accepted Islām as early as the eighth century.

It is significant that during the ninth century the Bosporus Bulgar realm was the only cultural center to which the caliph, interested in Greek philosophy, could turn for help and discussion.

2.

Around 800 A.D., Charlemagne destroyed the once-mighty Avar realm. Originally a small band of young, enterprising adventurers from Inner Asia of both Altaic and Iranian origin, the Avars had appeared in Central Europe in the middle of the sixth century.

They consolidated their rule and chose the Slavs, until then a forgotten people, to serve two purposes. First, among them the Avars selected recruits for command posts who, after thorough training, became the so-called *fšu-pāna* (Slavic *župan*), literally "the shepherds of (human) cattle." Second, they used the Slavic masses as cannon-fodder, called *befulci* by the contemporary Frankish chronicler Pseudo-Fredegar, "because," he wrote, "they advanced twice to the attack in their war bands, and so covered the Chuni [meaning Avars]."[20]

The pacification of the Avars after their military defeat was not a simple undertaking. After some time, in the 860s, both Romes although on inimical terms (referred to here are Patriarch Photius and Pope Nicholas I) decided to fill the vacuum left by the dissolution of the Avar realm. Their plan was to elevate the former slaves of the Avars, the Slavs, and to give their barbaric tongue the status of a sacred language, alongside Hebrew, Greek, and Latin.

At that time, despite the Carolingian Renaissance, only Constantinople had scholars who could create a new literary language and eventually translate the Christian religious writings. The Thessaloniki brothers, Kyril and Methodius, friends of Photius, journeyed from that city to Moravia, a territory claimed by the Roman Pope.

But in order to proceed with their project, it was necessary that the brothers learn the art of translating and obtain a working knowledge of Hebrew, the sacred language of the Bible.

No one in ninth-century Constantinople knew how to write any language other than Greek, because for several centuries Greek had been the only medium for cultural activity. Therefore, everyone who held any position in the world of *literati* knew and used Greek. Knowledge of Hebrew did not exist in Constantinople for several centuries.[21]

Therefore, when one reads in the *Vita* of Kyril/Constantine about his undertaking a voyage to the Crimea (then belonging to Khazaria) to learn Hebrew and Syriac, one must conclude that the Crimea, or former Bosporus Kingdom, was the only place in Europe where both training in the art of translating and the opportunity to learn Hebrew were available.[22]

3.

From 1890 to 1910, Hungarians, Russians, Englishmen, Frenchmen, and Japanese undertook expeditions to the Oasis states of the Tarim Basin in Chinese Turkestan, as well as to North India (Gandhara), Mongolia, and Northwest China, there to uncover finds of written texts, art, and material culture. Here it will suffice to mention just three of the explorers involved in those expeditions: the renowned Scholars Albert von Le Coq (1860–1930), Sir Aurel Stein (1862-1943) and Paul Pelliot (1878-1945).[23]

The discovered texts were written in many unknown scripts and languages. But scholars—among them the ingenious F. W. K. Müller (1863–1930), working in Berlin—quickly deciphered them, and with the result that several new languages, including two Indo-European, the Tocharian and Khotan Śaka, were added to the realm of scholarship.

The monuments of art displayed a variety of styles, the most

significant of which bore the unmistakeable imprint of Hellenistic art (*e.g.*, the Gandhara monuments in present-day northern
Pakistan).[25]

Now it became apparent that the diligent peoples of the
oasis states, located on the "crossroads of civilizations," were
able to combine international trading activity with cultural and
religious affairs. For instance, all great world religions found
their ardent followers in Turkistan: thousands of manuscripts
and manuscript fragments with texts of Buddhist, Manichaean,
Nestorian Christian provenance, written in many languages, bear
testimony to that fact.

As the texts underwent philological scrutiny the astonished
scholars discovered an unusual type of religious tolerance in
Turkestan. For these confirmed the existence of professional
translators who specialized in several "sacred" languages and
were able to translate religious texts without discrimination.
One and the same translator (say, from Chinese into Soghdian)
could on one day translate a Buddhist text, and on the next
work on a Manichaean or Nestorian one. These translators seem
to have been primarily Iranian Soghdians.[26]

4.

"What, now, does Hellenism mean?"—writes W. W. Tarn—"To
one, it means a new culture compounded of Greek and Oriental
elements; to another, the continuation of the pure line of the
older Greek civilizations; to yet another, that same civilization
modified by new conditions. All these theories contain a truth,
but none represents the whole truth . . ."[27]

It was the German historian J. G. Droysen who, in the early
nineteenth century, first realized the cultural unity behind the
history of a number of European and West Asian states in the
period from 323 to 30 B.C., *i.e.* from the death of Alexander the
Great to the incorporation of Egypt into the Roman Empire.[28]

The word "Hellenism" derives from the Greek word *hellenizein*
"to speak [or to act] Hellenic," *i.e.* "like a Greek." It was used
especially in reference to non-Greeks who had accepted the Greek
way of life.

But the term is inaccurate, in that during the same period many
Greeks also accepted non-Greek, *i.e.* Oriental, ways of life,
whether Persian or Judaic.

There is no doubt that the Hellenistic world was created by the Macedonian Alexander, half-barbarian (*cf.* Bosporus Spartocos) in origin, whose unique discovery lay in his realization of the possibility for a world-wide "marriage of cultures."

"Alexander proclaimed for the first time"—writes W. W. Tarn— "the unity and brotherhood of mankind . . . Above all, Alexander inspired Zeno's vision of a world in which all men should be members one of another, citizens of one State without distinction of race or institutions, subject only to and in harmony with the Common Law immanent in the Universe, and united in one Social life not by compulsion but only by their own willing consent, or as (as he put it) by Love."[29]

If this worldview is accepted, then stress should be placed on what makes understanding between human beings possible: that is, on the realization that two religions can be true,[30] and that two different sacred languages should be regarded as equals, having the same *dignitas* in two respective cultures. By extension, attention should be focused on the birth of a foremost concept in human history—the idea of translating from one literary language, *i.e.*, one having *diginitas*, to another literary language, with equivalent *dignitas*.

Translations from one language into another began early in human history: they are attested to in Old Mesopotamia for the second millenium B.C. At that time translations from the enigmatic Sumer texts were made into Semitic Akkadian. From that time originates the international term *talami* (>>*tilmač*) "translator," which lives even today in the German *Dolmetsch(er)*.[31]

But in those early times until the period of Hellenism, the subjects of translations were primarily state documents and other official texts, in which the verbatim translation of words rather than ideas or sentences was the objective.

A translation in which all creative possibilities of one language were marshalled to render the ideas of another was first done in Hellenistic times. This fact alone assures that period a special place in the cultural history of mankind.

Two documents concerning this achievement have been preserved: these are the *Milindapañha* and the letter of Pseudo-Aristeas, both dating from *ca.* 100 B.C.[32]

The *Milindapañha*, or "Questions of Milinda" (referring to the

Indian king of Greek origin Menander, who lived during the second century B.C.), are preserved in a Pali version and, in part, in a Chinese translation of the fourth century A.D. Written in the form of a dialogue, they are a good example of that typical intellectual invention of the Greeks.

The dialogue, between King Menander and the Buddhist sage, Nāgasena, is about the basic aspects of the Buddhist doctrine.

A letter of Pseudo-Aristeas tells the story of an invitation extended to seventy-two Jewish elders by the Greek Egyptian king Ptolomy II (d. 246 B.C.) to journey to his capital, Alexandria. Ptolomy supposedly asked the elders to translate their scriptures into Greek—this being the legendary account of the origin of the Septuagint. It is not our concern to discredit the testimony of this letter, although it has been universally recognized as a propagandist work designed to commend the Jewish religion to the Greeks. However, the product of the Alexandrian effort—the Septuagint—has survived, and its existence is what is important to us.

It is now appropriate to state that the Septuagint represents the first successful translation of a highly literary text from one literary language into another.[33]

5.

The nomads, especially the Khazars, are credited with an exemplary religious tolerance. Here I use the term "nomads" in the traditional sense; this term, taken from anthropology, has no meaning as a historical concept, however.

If we read that between 550 A.D. and 740 A.D. the Turks of Central Asia were masters of a "nomadic" empire, and that the Ottomans, being Turks, *ergo* nomads, created an empire, the following question confronts us: was the Ottoman empire also "nomadic"? The answer is no, since the common denominator in this syllogism is not "nomadism," but "Empire."

The only permanent element in the so-called Eurasian "pastoral nomadism" was the idea of an empire, or *pax*, created to produce economic profit and therefore always resulting in the cooperation of the steppe aristocracy with the international trading elite, who in Central Asia were usually of Iranian origin. Kāšgarī, the Turkic philologist of the eleventh century, noted a Turkic proverb saying: *Tatsiz Türk bolmas, bašsiz börk bolmas,* 'There is no *Tāt* except in the company of a turk, just as there is no cap unless there is a head to put it on'—the word *Tāt* meaning an Iranian merchant.

When any ruling class of the steppe *pax* lost its charisma, it was replaced by another ruling class. Similarly variable was the third element of the *pax*, its territory, provided that a new territory had similar significance from the viewpoint of economic strategy.

In order to keep the empire running, it was necessary to maintain a standing army and a functioning bureaucracy. As was the case in contemporary Western Europe, it was impossible for the creators of the steppe *pax* to produce enough cash to pay for both these necessities. Until the thirteenth century the only alternative was to exploit the pastoral economy for that purpose— a solution reminiscent of Western feudalism.

The Ottomans, however, had no Eurasian steppe at their disposal. Their solution was, therefore, to create a huge bureaucratic machinery without individual allegiances that would produce cash from conquered territories. Both this machinery and the elite military units (*yeničeri*) were recruited from especially trained slaves under the *qulluq* system, an invention of the Iranian long-distance merchants of Central Asia, who were often absent from their homes.[34]

Historians of this time period usually focus on these so-called "nomads," although their role was only that of steppe "policeman" or "blackmailer." The intellects behind the so-called nomadic empires were the aristocratic long-distance traders, residing in the oases or towns, who knew several languages and had a keen interest in philosophical and religious matters. They formed a society similar to the Western bourgeoisie of the early modern, post-secularized civilization. It is this town-based commercial elite, rather than the nomadic generals and brigands, that should be credited with the alleged religious tolerance of the nomads.

6.

After the territory of the former Bosporus kingdom was incorporated into the Russian Empire (1783) and archaeology emerged as a scholarly discipline, many archaeological expeditions were sent to that area. Unearthed there were many Greek and Hellenistic cities (Panticapaeum, Phanagoria, Tanais, Hermonassa, Gorgippia, etc.) whose places of social and cult activities yielded epigraphical and other monuments.[35]

Although the epigraphic material discovered to date is only fragmentary (there were no sands in the Bosporus, whereas in Egypt and Turkestan sand-buried documents were preserved)—it is still possible to form a general picture, especially since the publication of academician Vasilij Struve's *Corpus inscriptionum regni Bosporani* (1965).[36]

Most of the inscriptions are written in Greek, but many of them, beginning with the first century B.C., are not Greek but Judaeo-Greek in content.

One of the most important inscriptions of this kind, originating from Panticapaeum and dated 81 A.D., reads: "I, Chreste (Khrêstê), the former wife of Drusos (Droúsou), have manumitted my homeborn slave, Heraklas . . . who may turn whithersoever he desires . . . he is not, however, to forsake the fear of heaven and attachment to the synagogue (proseukhé) under the supervision of the community (synagôgê) of the Jews."[37]

V. F. Gajdukevič assumes that Jews came to the Bosporus from Pontus, after it was incorporated into the Kingdom of Pontus.[38] But the possibility remains that some Jews migrated to the Bosporus from Egypt, since Bosporus corn-merchants maintained close relations with their Egyptian colleagues and even undertook some joint ventures in search of new markets.[39]

The Jews settled in the Bosporus Kingdom,[40] especially in its capital Panticapaeum (now Kerč) and the towns of Phanagoria (later, during Khazar times, called Samkarč al-Yahūd or the Jewish Samkarč) and Tanais. It appears that they lived in congenial conditions, developing well-organized communities and building synagogues which served as communal centers.

The typical feature of Jewish life in the Bosporus was its connection with Greek cultural and social organizations.

The Jews entered the Greek *polis* as the *metoikoi*, but soon they were recognized as comprising the typical hellenistic, quasi-autonomous organization called *politeuma* (corporation), having its own courts. Many Jews were granted "potential citizenship," or *isopolity*, by the Bosporus kings.

The Greek language and customs penetrated into the Jewish synagogues: the Jews accepted the *manumisia*-rite, or redemption from slavery; several of the preserved Bosporus documents (among others, that cited above) are such *manumisia*-charters.[43] Among the organizations of the Bosporus Jews one finds the typical hellenistic exclusive clubs, "Thiasoi,"[44] having a set hier-archy—that is, the hiereús for rites, the patêr synódou to preside at meetings, and the grammateús, or secretary.

Typical of this type of club was the harmonious co-existence of religious, commercial and scholarly interests.

In Asia Minor Yahwe had already received the Greek designa-tion, ho Theós hýpsistos, which appears very often in the Bos-porus inscriptions.[45]

Later, in Khazar times, one can detect the penetration of some Altaic elements into the syncretic Judaism.

In a Khazar Hebrew document from Kiev dated about 930 A.D. (discovered among the Geniza texts by Professor Norman Golb, who is publishing its text in cooperation with this author), Hebrew names appear alongside the Hunic-Bulgarian as mem-bers of the local Jewish community. Particularly interesting is the case of a man by the name of Gwstata bar Kiabar Kōhen; *Gostatā* referred to a member of the political Bulgar clan *Gostan; Kiabar* was the name of the ruling Khazar tribe. Their connection with the Jewish institution of *Kōhēn*, reserved for the Levites, is strange indeed.

Professor Golb and I propose the following hypothesis by way of explanation. Among the Old Turks the hereditary institution of *gāms*, or priests of the *Täzri* (God) religion, played very important roles, including those of medicine-man and rainmaker. Even after he became a Jew, the *Gostatā* from the charismatic clan *Kiabar* retained his important position, now within the new religion. One may add that the Menorah, the Jewish candelabrum that symbolizes the Jewish faith, had its origin in the Bosporus. The well-known Russian Hebraist, Daniel Chwolson, discovered and published their oldest documentations from the gravestones of Phanagoria.[46]

7.

In the history of Kievan Rus, the city of Tmutorokan' (Herm-onassa/Tamatarcha) plays an unusual role.

The first Kievan historical writer and editor of the first version of the Primary chronicle of 1072 was Abbot Nikon of Tmutoro-kan'.[47]

The history of Ruś until Jaroslav is known primarily in its connection with Byzantine and Bulgarian events: only after the death of Volodimer, in 1015, did the other aspects of the historical process become gradually recognizable.

Jaroslav's main rival for power was his brother Mstislav, who ruled in Tmutorokan'. During the rule of the Jaroslaviči, the sons of Jaroslav, the province they most desired was Tmutorokan': each tried his luck in conquering that city.[48]

Only ca. 1150 did the Byzantine emperor Manuel Comnenus occupy Tamatarcha; in his treaty with Genoa (1169) freeing that commercial and maritime center from all duties, it is stated clearly that the Genoese may enter any Byzantine port for commercial activities, except Tmutorokan'.[49] Therefore, one should not be surprised upon finding how important Tmutorokan' was to the author of the Igor Tale.

There existed an unexplicable, almost biological hatred between the citizens of Kiev, whose rulers belonged to the dynasty of Volodimer Monomach, and those of Černihiv, headed first by Svjatoslav and later by his son Oleg, a nephew of Volodimer Monomach. In 1113 when, according to the succession arrangement established by Jaroslav, the ancestor of the Rurikid dynasty, after Svjatopolk died in Kiev and Oleg was to ascend the Kievan throne, a revolution erupted in Kiev. An unprecedented happening occurred: because the Kievans disliked Oleg, then ruling Černihiv, they began to attack the Kievan . . . Jews![50]

This first mention of Jews in the Chronicle has produced a significant scholarly literature; nonetheless, the action of the revolutionaries of 1113 remains without plausible explanation.[51]

Every student of Eastern Europe knows that among the oldest monuments of the Slavic Ruś literature are the two collections (Izborniki) of Svjatoslav dating from 1073 and 1076. But Svjatoslav was prince of both Černihiv and Tmutorokan'; from the time of Mstislav Volodimerovič, the brother of Jaroslav, these two regions were united under the same ruler. Tmutorokan' was the port of Černihiv, as Novgorod was for Kiev.

Why, one might ask, was there no Izbornik for a Kievan Prince?

It may be supposed that the first center of Slavic literary

activity in Eastern Europe was not the then newly (about 800
A.D.) founded capital city of Kiev, whose inhabitants were just
beginning to learn how to write in 1036[52] and were even then on
—so to say—the primary school level, but the old Hellenistic
center of Tamatarcha/Tmutorokan', which had a long tradition—
over 1500 years—of uninterrupted cultural activity.

Some years ago, the Russian scholar N. A. Meščerskij argued
that some of the oldest Kievan Rus' literary works, such as *The
Jewish War* of Josephus Flavius, must have been translated in
the Bosporus-Crimean region, due to some specific glosses and
other criteria.[53] He proved that the author of the Primary
Chronicle had at his disposal a Slavic translation of Josippon,
made in the same region directly from a Hebrew version.[54]

III.

Now let us summarize. I am aware of the fact that no paper,
even if it is as long as the present one, can settle a set of very
complicated problems from the realm of cultural history, especially if they concern peoples and cultures like that of the
Bosporus kingdom, which have no direct successors or academies
of sciences of their own.

Despite the impressionistic method which inevitably results,
and was used deliberately in this paper, I propose, as conclusion,
the following set of hypotheses:

1. The distinctive feature of Hellenism was the marriage of
cultures, which found its realization in the idea and practice
of the art of translating.

2. Classical Mediterranean Hellenism may have ended with
the battle at Actium in 31 B.C., but in the Eurasian steppe, Hellenism—as it has been discussed here—continued to flourish
until the tenth-eleventh centuries.[55] In the east, it ended with the
triumph of Turkic popular Islam (the Empire of the Karakha-
nids), whereas in the west its decline was marked by the conquest of Tmutorokan' by the Ruś. The last service which that
former Bosporus city rendered to culture was the elevation of
the Slavic idiom to the status of a sacred and literary language,
with its obligatory *dignitas*.

3. In the history of the Eurasian steppe one must distinguish
two elements:

(a) The commercial, intellectual, and religious *pax* of the citizens of oasis-type settlements (among the barbarians / *in partibus infidelium*) who have been forgotten and ignored by historians;

(b) The military and political *pax* under the control of the Royal Hordes, who, beginning with the Scythians in the eighth century B.C., have wrongly been credited with being the only historical factor of Eurasia.

4. In the east of the Eurasian steppe, the true bearer of intellectual activity and of the idea of the marriages of cultures were the Iranian Soghdians, while in the west, they were in all probability the Bosporus Hellenistic Jews.

NOTES

1. On the Cimmerian problem *see* J. Harmatta, "Le problème Cimmérien," *Archaeologiai Értesítő* 7-9 (1948), pp. 79-132; and T. Sulimirski, "The Cimmerian Problem," *Bulletin of the Institute of Archeology* 2 (1958), pp. 45-64.

2. *See, e.g.,* J. P. Kallistov, *Severnoe Pričernomor'e v antičnuju epoxu* (Moscow, 1952); V. F. Gajdukevič, *Bosporskoe carstvo* (Moscow–Leningrad, 1949).

3. M. Rostovtzeff, *Iranians and Greeks in South Russia* (Oxford, 1922), p. 68.

4. M. Rostovtzeff, *Iranians and Greeks*, p. 68.

5. M. Rostovtzeff, *Iranians and Greeks*, p. 68.

6. Gajdukevič, *Bosporskoe carstvo*, p. 463. Production of the coinage did not end with the collapse of the Bospor realm. An inscription from the Taman peninsula dated A.D. 341 exists, and in 362 A.D. the Roman historian Ammianus Marcellinus, named the new capital, Constantinople, as the seat of the Bosporan embassy (*Bosporanis . . . legationes*). *See* V. F. Gajdukevič, *Bosporskoe carstvo*, pp. 464-465.

7. Gajdukevič, *Bosporskoe carstvo*, pp. 54-93.

8. *See, e.g.,* C. Brady, *The Legends of Ermanarich* (Berkeley–Los Angeles, 1943).

9. Gajdukevič, *Bosporskoe carstvo*, pp. 444-461.

10. Leon Diaconos, *Historiae Libri decem*, ed. C. B. Hase (Bonn, 1828), p. 105.

11. Gajdukevič, *Bosporskoe carstvo*, p. 209.

12. *Kitāb al-Fihrist*, ed. G. Flügel and J. Roediger, I (Leipzig, 1871), p. 111. Eng. trans. by B. Dodge, *The Fihrist of al-Nadim*, I (New York–London: 1970), p. 254.

13. Eng. trans. by Dodge, I, p. 400.

14. Concerning the literature on Ǧāhiẓ, *see* Ch. Pellat, "al-Djāhiẓ", *The Encyclopaedia of Islam²*, ii pp. 385-387.

15. G. E. von Grunebaum, *Medieval Islam* (Chicago, 1946), pp. 54-55; R. Walzer, *Greek into Arabic* (Oxford, 1962); F. Rosenthal, *Das Fortleben der Antike im Islam* (Zurich–Stuttgart, 1965).

16. Gy. Moravcsik, "Zur Geschichte der Onoguren," *Ungarische Jahrbücher* 10 (1930), pp. 53-90; K. Lambrev, "Legendata za kan Kubrat i negovite sinove," *Istoričeski pregled* 3 (1946-1947), pp. 350-359.

17. V. Minorsky, "Balgitzi-'Lord of the Fishes,'" *Wiener Zeitschrift fur die Kunde des Morgenlandes* 56 (1960), pp. 130-137.

18. Ibn Khurdādhbeh, *Kitāb al-masālik wa'l-mamālik*, ed. M. J. de Goeje (Leiden, 1889), p. 18. The editor introduces the "reconstructed" form *qn'z* to fit the later Slavic title *knjaz'* (<< *konung-r*). A new analysis of the passage in question is presented in this author's *Origin of Rus'*, vol. 4 (in preparation).

19. Ibn Faḍlān, *Risala*, ed. A. P. Kovalivs'kyj, *Kniga Axmeda ibn Fadlana o ego putešestvii na Volgu v 921-922 gg.* (Xarkiv, 1952), p. 344, 1. 2 (Arab. text).

20. *The Fourth Book of the Chronicle of Fredegar with its Continuations*, col. and trans. J. M. Wallace-Hadrill (London, 1960), p. 40.

21. See K. Krumbacher, *Geschichte der Byzantinischen Litteratur* (Munich, 1897), p. 122: "Die Kenntnis der *hebräischen* Sprache ging den Byzantinern ganz verloren; nicht einmal Photios war des Hebräischen mächtig." Concerning the Byzantines' loss of interest in Latin language and scholarship, see Krumbacher, *Geschichte*, p. 543.

22. On the Slavonic mission see F. Dvornik, *Byzantine Missions among the Slavs: SS. Constantine-Cyril and Methodius* (New Brunswick, New Jersey, 1970); I. Ševčenko, "Three Paradoxes of the Cyrillo-Methodian Mission," *Slavic Review*, 23 ii (1964), pp. 220-234; *cf.* also my inaugural lecture, *The Origin of Rus'* (Cambridge, Mass., 1975), pp. 24-28.

23. V. Thomsen, *Aus Ost-Turkestans Vergangenheit* (Copenhagen, 1918). A. von Le Coq, *Auf Hellas Spuren in Ostturkestan* (Leipzig, 1926); A. von le Coq, *Von Land und Leuten in Ostturkestan* (Leipzig, 1928); A. von le Coq, *Die Buddhistische Spätantike in Mittelasien*, vols. 1-6 (Berlin, 1922-1928); A. Stein, *On Ancient Central-Asian Tracks* (New York, 1964); A. Stein, *Serindia*, vols. 1-5 (Oxford, 1921); A. Stein, *Innermost Asia*, vols. 1-4 (Oxford, 1928); *Paul Pelliot* (Paris, 1946); E. Waldschmidt, *Grandhara, Kutscha, Turfan* (Leipzig, 1925); *cf.* also D. Schlumberger, "The Excavations at Surkh Kotal and the Problem of Hellenism in Bactria and India," *Proceedings of the British Academy* 47 (1961), p. 95, pl. XXIV.

24. *See* F. Weller and B. Schindler, "Professor F. W. K. Müller: Leben und Werk," *Asia Major* 2 (Leipzig, 1925), pp. I-XVI.

25. For general orientation *see* T. T. Rice, *Ancient Arts of Central Asia* (New York, 1965); A. Belenitsky, *Central Asia* (Cleveland–New York, 1968).

26. *See, e.g.,* W. B. Henning, "Mitteliranisch" in *Handbuch des Orientalistik*, div. 1, vol. 4, pt. 1 (Leiden–Cologne, 1958), pp. 20-129, esp. 55-56; A. von Gabain, "Alttürkische Schreibkultur und Druckerei," *Philologiae Turcicae Fundamenta* (Mainz, 1964), pp. 171-191. A. von Gabain, "Die alttürkische Literatur," *Philologiae Turcicae Fundamenta*, ii, pp. 211-243.

27. W. W. Tarn, *Hellenistic Civilization* (Cleveland, Ohio, n.d.3), pp. 1-2. *See* also n. 55.

28. J. G. Droysen, *Geschichte des Hellenismus* (Gotha, 1877, 2).

29. W. W. Tarn, *Alexander the Great* (Boston, 1959), pp. 146-148.

30. *Cf.* W. W. Tarn, *Hellenistic Civilization*, p. 339: "but another

20   ISLAMIC AND JUDEO-CHRISTIAN WORLD

movement, very typically Hellenistic, was a great expansion of syncretism, the equation or fusion of one god with another as being alike forms of the one divinity behind them."

31. P. Jyrkänkallio, *Zur Etymologie von russ. tolmac 'Dolmetscher' und seiner türkischen Quelle* (= *Slavia Orientalia*, vol. 8) (Helsinki, 1952); for an opposing view *cf.* J. Németh, "Zur Geschichte des Wortes *tolmács* 'Dolmetscher,'" *Acta Orient. Hung.* 8 i (1958), pp. 1-8.

32. See the excursus "The Milindapañha and Pseudo-Aristeas" in W. W. Tarn, *The Greeks in Bactria and India* (Cambridge, 1951²), pp. 414-436.

33. For the most important literature on the Septuagint, *see;* H. B. Swete, *An Introduction to the Old Testament in Greek* (Cambridge, 1914²); R. L. Ottley, *A Handbook of the Septuagint* (1920); J. Ziegler, *Die Septuaginta: Erbe und Auftraag* (Würzburg, 1962), 29 pp. S. Jellicoe, *The Septuagint and Modern Study* (1968); S. Jellicoe, *Studies in the Septuagint; origins, recensions and interpretations* (New York, 1974).

34. See my inaugural lecture, *The Origin of Ruś*, pp. 14-16.

35. *See, e.g., Drevnosti, Bosfora Kimmerijskogo*, vols. 1-3 (St. Petersburg, 1854); M. Ebert, *Südrussland im Altertum* (Bonn—Leipzig, 1921); E. H. Minns, *Scythians and Greeks* (Cambridge, 1913); M. Rostovtzeff, *Iranians and Greeks in South Russia* (Oxford, 1922); Gajdukevič, *Bosporskoe carstvo;* T. N. Knipovič, *Tanais* (Moscow—Leningrad, 1949); *Fanagorija*, ed. A. P. Smirnov (Moscow, 1956).

36. *Korpus bosporskix nadpisej*, ed. V. V. Struve *et al.* (Moscow—Leningrad, 1965), 951 pp.

37. *Korpus bosporskix nadpisej*, pp. 77-79 (no. 70).

38. Gajdukevič, *Bosporskoe carstvo*, p. 347.

39. *Cf.* Tarn, *Hellenistic Civilization*, pp. 217-222, and pp. 254-255.

40. Gajdukevič, *Bosporskoe carstvo*, p. 377.

41. See Ibn al-Faqīh al-Hamadhānī, *Kitāb al-Buldān*, ed. M. J. de Goeje (Leiden, 1885), p. 271, ll. 1-2.

42. Tarn, *Hellenistic Civilization*, pp. 21-238, esp. 219-223.

43. *Korpus bosporskix nadpisej*, nos. 69-74 (Panticapaeum); no. 985-986 (Phanagoria); no. 1021 (Zaporožskaja); nos. 1123-1128 (Gorgippia).

44. Gajdukevič, *Bosporskoe carstvo*, pp. 431-438. The Thiasoi inscriptions are included in *Korpus bosporskix nadpisej*, nos. 75-108 (Panticapaeum), no. 870 (Mirmekij), no. 898 (Zenonov Xersones); no. 946 (Kimmerik), no. 967 (Ilurat), nos. 987-988 (Phanagoria), no. 1016 (Axtanizovskaja), no. 1054-1055 (Hermonassa), nos. 1129-1136 (Gorgippia), nos. 1230-1231 (Kuban region), nos. 1259-1292 (Tanais).

45. Gajdukevič, *Bosporskoe carstvo*, pp. 434-435; Tarn, *Hellenistic Civilization*, pp. 224-225.

46. Details are presented in N. Golb and O. Pritsak, *An Original Document of the Khazarian Jews* (in press).

47. M. D. Priselkov, *Očerki po cerkovno-političeskoj istorii Kievskoj Rusi X-XIIvv.* (St. Petersburg, 1913); M. D. Priselkov, *Istorija russkogo letopisanija XI-XV vv.* (Leningrad, 1940), pp. 31-33; D. S. Lixačev, *Russkie letopisi i ix kul'turno-istoričeskoe značenie* (Moscow—Leningrad, 1947), pp. 82-93; A. N. Nasonov, *Istorija russkogo letopisanija XI-načala XVIII veka* (Moscow, 1969), pp. 34-52.

48. *See, Povest' vremennyx let*, ed. D. S. Lixačev, i (Moscow—Leningrad, 1950), pp. 110-111; *cf.* A. N. Nasonov, "Tmutorokan' v istorii Vostočnoj Evropy X v.," *Istoričeskie Zapiski* 6 (1940), pp. 76-99; V. A. Mošin,

"Nikolaj, episkop Tmutorokanskij," *Seminarium Kondakovianum* 5 (1932), pp. 47-62.

49. A. P. Každan, "Vizantijskij podatnoj sborščik na beregax Kimmerij'-skogo Bospora v konce XII v.," *Problemy obščestvenno-političeskoj istorii Rossii* (= Festschrift M. N. Tixomirov) (Moscow, 1963), pp. 93-101. G. G. Litavrin and A. P. Každan, "Ekonomičeskie i političeskie otonšenija Drevnej Rusi i Vizantii v XI-pervoj polovine XIII v." *Thirteenth International Congress of Byzantine Studies*, Main Papers, iii (Oxford, 1966).

50. *Povest' vremennyx let*, ed. D. S. Lixačev, i, p. 196; *cf.* the more complete version in V. N. Tatiščev's *Istorija Rossijskaja*, iv (Moscow–Leningrad, 1964), pp. 179-180.

51. I intend to propose a new analysis of the sources in another publication.

52. See my inaugural lecture, *The Origin of Ruś*, pp. 26-28.

53. N. A. Meščerskij, *Istorija iudejskoj vojny Josifa Flavija v drevnerrusskom perevode* (Moscow–Leningrad, 1958), pp. 1-164, esp. 97-121.

54. N. A. Meščerskij, "Otryvok iz knigi 'Josippon' v 'Povesti vremennyx let,' " *Palestinskij sbornik* 2 (1956), pp. 58-63; Meščerskij, *Istorija iudejskoj vojny*, pp. 132-153

55. The differences in assessments of Hellenism's duration are attributable to the perspectives of individual viewers. In this respect it is important to note the following statement of S. D. Goitein: "We normally apply the term *Hellenism* to the period between Alexander and Augustus, between the establishment of the Macedonian empire and the final replacement of its heirs by Rome. This is Hellenism as seen from Greece and from the point of view of political history. However, from the standpoint of cultural history and the peoples affected by the Greek heritage, we have to extend this period far longer, well down to the seventh century A.D. when the study of Greek finally had come to an end in Latin Europe and when the countries of the eastern and southern shores of the Mediterranean were conquered by a new language and a new civilization, Arabic and Islam." (*Studies in Islamic History and Institutions* [Leiden, 1966], p. 56). But significantly enough, "Hellenism found a refuge precisely in the civilization and the language which had replaced Greek [i.e., Arabic] and Greek culture [i.e., Islam] in most countries which it had dominated for centuries" (Goitein, *Studies*, p. 1966). One should here recall that the eminent scholar C. H. Becker even declared that Islam *is* Hellenism, although, to be sure, an Islamized Hellenism (*Islamstudien*, I [Leipzig, 1924], pp. 24-53). Concerning the ensuing controversy (especially between these views and those of E. Troeltsch and H. H. Schaeder) *see* Goitein, *Studies*, pp. 65-66.

II. COMMUNAL AND NATIONAL RELATIONS

SERVILE LABOR IN THE OTTOMAN EMPIRE

The long prosperity of the slave trade in Islamic lands can be attributed to conditions peculiar to Islamic culture.[1] First of all in medieval Islam from the time of the Abbasid caliphs on slaves were employed in large numbers in the militias of Muslim rulers. Slaves were also used as labor force in the urban crafts and on the big estates belonging to the state or to large land owners. Furthermore, following the example of the palace, the upper class and even the well-to-do among the non-Muslims, had extended households with large numbers of domestic slaves.

In the Service of the State and Military Class

The *ghulām* or *kul* system,[2] in which slaves were trained as loyal servants to be employed primarily in implementing the central power of the sultan as agents and soldiery, had an unprecedented expansion under the typically military centralist sultanates of the Mamluks of Egypt and the Ottomans in the period of the thirteenth–sixteenth centuries. With the rise of their centralist state, the Ottoman sultans were faced with a growing need for men for their *kapı-kulu,* palace servants and divisions of the standing army at the Porte,[3] and, since war did not bring slaves in sufficient numbers, they had to resort to the unusual method of the *dewshirme,* a levy of boys from among their own Christian subjects, the *reāyā'.* In general the Ottomans did not regard the *dewshirme* as enslavement, but rather as one of the extraordinary services imposed by the state in an emergency.[4] The levied boys, attached to the Janissary corps, were first employed as labor in a number of public works (construction work, transport works etc.) in the capital and in Gallipoli before they became Janissaries.[5] In the classical period between 1300–1600, the Sultan's *kapı-kulu*, recruited from the *dewshirme* boys as well as from among prisoners of war and slaves bought for the Sultan, increased in number considerably: 15–20 thousand under Mehmed II (1451–1481), 60 thousand in 1568 and about 100 thousand in 1609. The absolute power of the ruler, we are told in contemporary Ottoman sources, rested upon his having slaves in his service in the army and the administration.[6]

That the members of the Ottoman ruling class, the Sultan in the first place, took special care to increase their slave retinue can be related to the fact that, in the frontier society of the early Ottoman state power rested on the ability to muster as many *ghāzī* fighters as possible from tribal companions, adventurers from outside, or slaves. It was true the use of warrior slaves was not confined to the state. The grandees also tried to maintain households and retinues as large as possible since this meant, through their patronage rights, *walā'*,[7] an extension of their influence and power, in-as-much as many of their slaves were destined to get important offices in the Empire later on.[8] These patrimonial factions were not infrequently the real actors in political feuds in the Ottoman Empire. In Istanbul, capital of the Empire, at least one-fifth of the population was estimated to be *kul*'s of the Sultan and of the grandees.[9] In other cities *kul*'s though in smaller proportions, made an important part of the urban population.[10]

The demand for warrior slaves in Ottoman society was intensified by the fact that members of the *tīmār* holding army in the provinces, from the *beglerbegi*, governor general, down to the simple *sipāhī*, cavalryman, were required by regulation to train and to bring to the Sultan's army a certain number of cavalrymen in proportion to the amount of their *tīmār* revenue (for a *sipāhī*, one for each 2 or 3 thousand *akče*, for *beg*'s, one for each 5,000 *akče*).[11] These auxiliaries were in their origins mostly slaves captured during the raids in Christian lands. A *beglerbegi*, governor general, was required by regulation to maintain a military retinue of at least two hundred men[12] in addition to his household slaves employed in domestic services. The *begs* strove to increase the number of their retinue beyond the regulation since that brought special favor from the Sultan.

However, the ruling class did not own as many domestic slaves as military. On the basis of a list of estates belonging to members of the ruling class[13] kept in Edirne between 1545 and 1659, the following data was collected: out of 93 estates, 41 had slaves.

Those with 1 slave			14
"	"	2 slaves	7
"	"	3 "	8
"	"	4 "	2
"	"	5 "	3
"	"	more than 5	7[14]

The total number of slaves in the estates was 140, 54 female and 86 male. 134 of them bore Muslim names, 5 were not defined, and 1 was a Christian woman. Some of these slaves appear to have been employed on farms.[15] In conclusion, the ruling class, because of extensive use of warrior slaves and because of its own high purchasing capacity, was undoubtedly the single major group keeping the slave market alive in Ottoman empire.

In the Crafts

Concerning the slave labor employed by the crafts in the cities we have valuable evidence from the records of the estates of the deceased kept by the judges, *kāḍīs*, in the Ottoman cities. The following observations are based on such records of 721 estates from the second half of the fifteenth century in Bursa.[16]

It was an exceptional case for the rich not to have slaves either in domestic occupations or employed as labor in certain crafts. (The rich composed 15.9% of the cases studied.) Slaves formed the third most important component of the estates, in value, after cash and properties. In the estates of the silk weavers slaves frequently represented the most important part since slave labor was extensively employed in the weaving of gold brocades, velvets, or fine cottons in Bursa.

Slave labor was organized under the system of limited service contract known as *mukātaba* in Islamic jurisprudence. Here are two examples of such a contract:

"In our presence Maḥmūd b. Seyyidī Aḥmed, weaver of taffeta, asserted that he agreed to emancipate his slave İskender, of Circassian origin (with the described features) upon the completion of one hundred pieces of taffeta equivalent in value to ten thousand *akčes*, and the said slave accepted the contract." (*Sher'iyya sidjilli*, no. A5/5, p. 276 a, *Bursa, Archaeological Museum*).

"Khwādje Sinān had previously agreed to emancipate his slave Shīrmerd son of 'Abdallāh (a convert), of Slavonian origin, upon the completion of the weaving for him of ten brocades known as *kemkhā-i gülistānī*. Now that he has completed the work he has become free, Muḥarrem 899 (*idem*, p. 21 a).

Here is a case of a slave weaver who was emancipated and rewarded by his master upon his death:

"Yūsuf B. 'Abdallāh (a convert) previously slave of Al-Hādj Tanrıvermish, asserted in our presence one day before his death to the effect that he emancipated his slave Ayās b. 'Abdallāh (a convert) of Russian origin, weaver of velvet; and declared in his will that Ayās be given in his possession the loom of velvet with silk and other pertinent things. 10 Shawwāl 890" (*idem*, p. 422 a).

This kind of *mukātaba* meant actually to allow the slave to exercise certain rights such as to work independently and to own his earnings so that he would be capable of ransoming himself. Another kind allowed emancipation upon work for a certain period of time without specifying the work. Example:

"Mawlānā Seyyid Meḥmed of Konya asserted in our presence that he agreed to set free Lutfī b. 'Abdallāh (a convert) of Bosnia (of the described features) upon service for him for four consecutive years; and the slave accepted the terms, date Djumāda I, 891" (*idem*, p. 95 a).

Mukātaba was widely practiced in the Ottoman Empire, as demonstrated by the *kādī* records. It is recommended by the Coran. It consisted in the master's granting his slave his freedom in return for the payment of mutually agreed upon sums of money. According to some legists it was ransom by the slave of his own person. As an interesting historical example, mention can be made of Meḥmed the Conqueror's allowing the Greek prisoners of war to work at the repair of the walls of Istanbul to ransom their freedom. The person subject to *mukātaba* is set free only when his payments are completed. Toward the end a rebate was normally accorded.[17]

Mukātaba was a contract binding both sides so that the owner could not change its conditions at the expense of the slave. Since emancipation was considered a charitable act, the owner might make modifications favorable to the slave, such as to shorten the period of service or to give up the work due. Of course at the same time the owner derived certain advantages from *mukātaba*. It guaranteed good and profitable service for a certain period of time since, as a rule, lifetime slaves tended to run away or to be indolent. It was particularly profitable in the silk industry as this required continuously careful expert work especially in brocade and velvet weaving. Wage laborers were not really suited for this kind of work, which demanded a long period of time on the loom for the production of a single piece.

Noteworthy also is the fact that the silk industry in Bursa had developed to such a point that it exported its costly gold brocades and velvets, not only to meet the growing demand of the upper class in the empire, but also to meet orders from Italy, Poland, Russia and other European countries. There were silk weavers in Bursa having forty or more looms at one time who can rightly be considered as capitalist entrepreneurs, organizing a domestic silk industry for export with slave labor: Al-Hādj Aḥmed with five looms and fifteen slaves, Hadjdjī Badr al-Dīn Isḥak with seven looms and eight female slaves, al-Khʷādje Sinān with six looms and twelve male and three female slaves, were all active in the middle of the fifteenth century.[18] Twelve of the slaves of Al-Hādj Aḥmed had a value estimated at 36,000 *akčes*, median price for a slave being 2,000 *akčes* or 50 gold ducats, a rate equal to or below contemporary average prices of slaves in Italy or Egypt.[19] Since slave labor was not cheap it was only in the crafts making high priced luxury goods in great quantity that slaves were employed. Our Bursa documents refer to no slaves in other crafts. In the weaving of cheap cotton goods, another Ottoman export item, peasant labor in the countryside and widows and children in the towns were used throughout Anatolia as the cheapest labor available.[20]

Finally, hiring out slaves was legal. H. Dernschwam, a German visitor to Turkey in 1555,[21] relates the widespread practice in Istanbul of hiring out slaves: Many people made a livelihood out of hiring out their slaves for 7 or 12 *akčes* a day as day-laborers (then 60 *akčes* equalled one gold ducat; a slave's daily expense was estimated at 1½ or 2 *akčes*).

In Commerce

Bursa documents of the fifteenth century also tell us how the freed slaves, 'atīk or ma'tūk, occupied an unusually important place in the economic life of Bursa as rich silk manufacturers and merchants engaged in distant caravan trade, in money exchange, in usury and in tax-farming.[22] In that city in 1477, 61 out of 402 persons whose estates were recorded in the *kādī* registers after death (34 male and 27 female) were freed slaves.[23]

Slaves and freed slaves were often employed as commercial agents by merchants in distant trade ventures. Special guarantees under the stipulations of Islamic law of *walā'*, patronage rights of the former master, must be emphasized in this connection.[24] The following is an interesting instance:[25] In 1480 Balıkdjı-zāde of Bursa and Khʷādje Meḥmed, freed slave of Khadjadjī Koči, made a partnership investing equal shares with capital in the amount of 545,000 *akčes* (approximately 60,000 gold ducats) for the purpose of an import-export trade with Egypt and Syria. The operation was conducted mainly through their slaves who made several trips via Antalya (Satalia) between Bursa and Egyptian and Syrian cities. In his will Balıkdjı-zāde emancipated upon his death three of his slaves whom he had used as commercial agents (in addition one eunuch and one female slave were to be emancipated with grants of money, while three female slaves with children, *umm al-walad*, from him were to be freed automatically at his death. On page 31 is a list of some other businessmen of Bursa owning slaves (the end of the 15th century). Of course, as in the case of Baklıkdjı-zāde most, if not all, of these slaves were employed in domestic occupations. The peculiar stipulations of Islamic law gave rise to a paternalistic type of master–slave relationship which fostered strong social ties especially where domestic slaves were involved.[26]

In the Agricultural Sector

Here slave labor became predominant on the big estates, which were in the form of *čiftlik*s belonging to the state, the wealthy, or powerful members of the ruling class, or in the form

Owner (first six all weavers)	total fortune in akče	slave	value in akče
Yūsuf, freed slave of ʿAlī	14,331	2 male 1 fem.	5,600
Al-Hādj Meḥmed	82,841	5 fem.	9,800
Mawlānā ʿOsmān	11,820	4 fem.	9,800
Hadjdjī Hamza	59,079	7 fem.	—
Sheykhislām	13,760	1 male	2,000
Hadjdjī Mūsā	29,021	4 fem.	9,500
Merchant Khwādje Meḥmed	73,250	5 male 4 fem.	23,000
Merchant of mohair, Mukbil, freed slave of Saltuk	224,900	3 male 2 fem.	7,600
İskender, American merchant of mohair from Ankara	227,348	4 fem.	21,666
Money exchanger Yūsuf, freed slave of Hoshkadem	58,713	2 male	—

of awkāf, pious endowments.[27] The main reason for this was that the reʿāyā, free peasants registered in the state survey books for taxation in a defined area, could not, under the law, be used in the newly established farm lands. The majority of the privately owned čiftliks and many of the state farms and trusts were formed on the uncultivated waste-lands, pastures, and uninhabited lands with servile labor. Furthermore, such čiftliks were market oriented, set up essentially for the purpose of profit. Cattle and crops were sold to nearby peasants in need or shipped to the ports for export or for provisionment of the Ottoman cities. As in the Western plantation system, maximum rentability was the main concern of the čiftlik owners or trusts; slave labor, free of any of the restrictions to be observed under the law for the reʿāyā was found to be the most suitable. Slaves besides were comparatively cheap and readily available during the period of Ottoman expansion. It should also be pointed out that organization of production on the čiftliks adjusted itself to labor conditions: stock raising became predominant on most of the čiftliks as it required a minimum amount of labor for the

highest rate of profit. Ortākdjılık/sharecropping with equal shares
between the owner and slave was a general practice on the *čiftliks* while if cultivated by a peasant of the *re'āyā* status, the
owner's share could not exceed as a rule one-eighth of the
produce. Lastly slaves constituted a capital investment which was
easily, and most of the time profitably, convertible into cash.
It should be noted that in all this members of the Ottoman ruling
class were following practices long established in the Islamic
world.[28]

Under the first Ottoman Sultans servile labor appears to have
been employed to form extensive cattle and sheep ranches in By-
thinia.[29] Big farms thus formed by the grandees were mostly
turned into pious endowments.[30] As an inalienable part of the
farms slaves were entered in the endowment documents often by
their names. In transactions they are treated in the same way as
other properties. In some endowment deeds it is made clear that
slaves settled in the farm or village were prisoners of war captured by the founder.[31] Over time some of the farms thus formed
developed into villages and the descendants of the slaves in them
were always separately registered as sharecropping slaves
(*ōrtākdjı kul*). In some other cases it is reported that slaves
ran away and farms or villages were left in ruins.[32]

The best example of the state's use of slave labor in reclaiming
an abandoned agricultural area is Mehmed the Conqueror's
attempt at settling with slaves a large area called *Khāṣṣlar* encompassing 163 villages around Istanbul and Pera between 1453
and 1480. Actually it was a part of his larger plan for the recon-
struction of Istanbul. By placing under state ownership the arable
lands under cultivation in this area he intended to contribute
to the provisioning of the city, to create new sources of revenue
for the treasury, and to keep the neighborhood of the capital
in order and safety, as is pointed out in the regulation made in
1498. Mass deportation of enslaved peasants from enemy territories was used for this purpose. This was not only because the
Conqueror planned a rapid recovery of the area but also because
settlement of *re'āyā* deportees, *sürgün*, from his own territories
proved to be difficult to carry out and ruinous for the areas from
which the deportation was made. It was impossible to go too
far in this operation because it violated the basic rights of the
re'āyā, Muslim and non-Muslim, by forcing them to stay in

their new settlements.[33] It should be added that shortage of agricultural labor was a general phenomenon in this period.

Actually, in the *Khāṣṣlar*, on land that belonged to the imperial treasury, the enslaved Greek population, as well as slaves from newly conquered Bosnia, Serbia, and the Morea, made up the majority of the population, along with the deportees, *sürgün* of *re'āyā* origin, sedentary or nomadic, and the group of the ordinary *re'āyā*. In 110 villages out of 163, slaves were in the majority. In 1498 there were altogether 1974 slaves left in these villages.

Since it was the prime concern of the administration to maintain the productivity of farm units, changes leading to the freedom of slaves (even in cases permissible in the religious law) were not tolerated in the *Khāṣṣlar*. There were however, many examples of slaves who became freedmen by illegal means, the principal one being the bribing of the *emīn*, or official in charge of administering the *Khāṣṣlar*. The money paid to emancipate a slave, *aghırlık*, appears to have originally been a compensation defined by the regulations but diverted by the *emīn* to his own pocket.

In the survey book of 1498 there were many who claimed to have been freed but who could not establish their emancipation by any evidence acceptable to the surveyor-inspector. As an occupation other than agricultural work actually made easier a change from slave status, in 1498 slaves were forbidden to engage in jobs such as fishing or carrying wood or lime in carts to the city, profitable occupations in the neighborhood of Istanbul.

There were greater opportunities for the female slave than for the male slave to change her status. Marriages with the *re'āyā*, free peasants who paid an *aghırlık* to the agent to obtain his consent, frequently occurred. In 1498 the government inspector observed that this widespread practice and the unwillingness of the female slaves to marry the *khāṣṣ* slaves, inhibited the continuation of slave families and the proper cultivation of the farm units in the *Khāṣṣlar*. Under religious law the children of a free man were to be free. Even if male slaves married free women their children were to be free. Apart from the decrease, in the long run, of the slave population there was also a disruption of the agricultural work, which was based on family labor on farm units. These points were stressed by the inspector in his report to the Sultan. In the new regulation of 1498 marriages of slaves with free men were forbidden and forced marriages between the slaves, which were provided for under the religious law,[34] were enforced. Exceptions were made for the widow whose son was able to maintain the agricultural work and for anyone who had an acceptable excuse for not wanting to get married. License for marriage with a free man was given only when there were more female slaves than needed, and when the free man agreed to undertake to continue the sharecropper's work on the land. For such marriages a specific license of the Sultan, sureties, and payment of a marriage due called *aghrlık* were demanded.

Comparable in its basic features to the Western colonate system, the use of war captives in agriculture, however, had a limited application in the Ottoman Empire. Under Süleymān I (1520–1566) in the central part of Rumeli encompassing Thrace and Macedonia, the slave agriculturists numbered only 6021 men, including those in the *Khāṣṣlar*, about 2 percent of the whole population of the region; and, in the province of Anatolia 1981 men.[35] The number must have been somewhat larger in the previous period since the state had to change slave status of some communities into that of *re'āyā*—a change which seemed to take place as a result of the great difficulty of keeping under control these slave colonies, which constantly dwindled away through marriage and intermingling among the overwhelming *re'āyā* majority around. In fact, in the subsequent surveys in the sixteenth century, the slaves in the *Khāṣṣlar* are referred to merely as sharecroppers.[36] Over time slave agriculturists everywhere in the empire were to be identified with the *re'āyā* masses and disappear.[37]

Slavery, it can be safely said in conclusion, was an institution of vital significance for Ottoman society. Not only the state organization but also various segments of the economy—the silk industry, *čiftlik* agriculture, distant trade, as well as the extended household-type family of the upper class—all rested upon slavery. It must be emphasized however that all were dependent on a regular large-scale supply of slaves from outside, since slavery in a Muslim society could maintain itself only with importation.

Islamic jurisprudence recognized only one category of slaves—those born in slavery or captured in war. Those Muslims born in slavery or converted while slaves could remain in slavery, but no free Muslim or *dhimmī*, non-Muslim subject of the Sultan could be reduced to slavery.[38] When a slave woman had a child by her master the child was born free. Islam also encouraged emancipation as a work of piety. The children of a female slave are free on her emancipation. A grant of enfranchisement taking effect at the master's death, a practice called *tadbīr*, favored by religious law and widely used as the Ottoman *kāḍī* records and testaments[39] demonstrate, was perhaps the most important factor in eroding the slave population. Also contractual enfranchisement as seen above was widely practiced in the Empire.

Supply of Slaves

In the period extending from about 1260 to 1390, the age of the great expansion of the Anatolian Turks into Byzantine territories in western Anatolia and Thrace and into Macedonia and Bulgaria, captives flowed into the Ottoman lands in great numbers. It can even be added that during this period the great demand for slaves from the Islamic hinterland and rising prices played an important part in the extension of the raids and consequently the rise of the prosperous *ghāzī* principalities in Western Anatolia. Paradoxically enough not only for the slave markets in Italy but also for agricultural labor in their Levantine colonies, Venetians and Genoese too became regular customers of these principalities.[40] As a result of its growing need for slaves, especially during the periods of rapid growth such as experienced under Bāyezīd I (1389–1402) and Meḥmed II (1451–1481), as well as when internal crises slowed down the flow of slaves, the Ottoman state experienced shortages in slaves, and as explained above, had to resort to extraordinary measures, such as the levying of boys from the non-muslim *re'āyā*, and the conducting of mass enslavements and deportations from the newly conquered lands.

On the other hand the rise of the Ottoman Empire affected the international conditions of slave trade in the Mediterranean in general. The slave traffic to Italy from the Balkans through Dubrovnik stopped.[41] Due to the strict control of the traffic through the straits after the Ottoman conquests of Istanbul (1453) and Caffa (1475) and the prohibition of traffic in Muslim slaves, mostly Turco-Tatars of the steppes north of the Black Sea, the slave trade between the Crimea and Egypt slacked off or changed its early character. As is well known, this trade, first in importance in the commerce of the Black Sea, was a Genoese monopoly. The new circumstances resulted in the ruin of the Genoese prosperity in the Black Sea, caused higher prices for slaves throughout the Mediterranean, and the replacement of Turco-Tatar slaves with Caucasian and Russian slaves.

The impact on the Mamluk system has not yet been the subject of a proper study.[42] What is certain is that the Mamluks now offered unusual prices for Caucasian slaves which greatly encouraged the trade in Circassians and other Caucasian peoples.[43] On the other hand, the new situation caused the prices to treble in Italy, and seems to have reinforced, among other factors, the anti-slavery feeling in Western Christendom, and undermined slavery as an institution in sixteenth-century European society.[44] Now the only exception in Europe was the great need for galley slaves, who were provided mostly by European corsairs from the territories under Ottoman rule.[45]

In the fifteenth and sixteenth centuries, before the Crimean Tatars became the main suppliers of slaves, the Ottoman ghāzīs or akındjıs, raiders, on the frontier areas in the Balkans and Central Europe met the huge demand for slaves in the Ottoman market. Süleyman's reign (1520–1566), the zenith of Ottoman power, witnessed also the great extension of raiding and enslavement activities by the Ottomans.[46] Capture and sale of slaves usually brought to an individual akındjı or Ottoman soldier a sizeable income—a strong incentive for him to join the raids or campaigns. It also furnished an important source of revenue for the Sultan's treasury, since, as we know, one-fifth, pendjik, of the captives or of their market value belonged to the Sultan. The captives always brought a good price in the cities' slave markets, which were organized originally and constantly supervised by the state.[47]

An eye witness, Konstantin Mihailović, gives the following description of raids organized in a frontier center in the fifteenth century:

"The Turkish raiders are voluntary—of their own will they ride on expeditions for their livelihood.... They live by means of livestock and raise horses.... If any of them does not want to go on a foray himself, he will lend his horses to others for half (of the spoils); if they win some booty they accept it as good, but if they bring nothing, then they say 'We have no gain, but we have great works of piety, like those who toil with us and ride against the Christians, because we support one another.' And whatever they seize or capture, whether male or female except for boys, they will sell them all for money. The emperor himself will pay for the boys."[48]

The slave merchants, *esirdjis*, working in the frontier centers or following the Ottoman armies, bought captives quite cheaply and brought them to inland markets, the most important of which were in Üsküb (Skoplje), Edirne, Bursa, and Istanbul.[49] By the end of the fifteenth century the Bursa slave market appears to have been the liveliest as demonstrated by the *kādī* records. Even the Sultan sent slaves to be sold at Bursa where, obviously the best prices were expected. Persian silk merchants were among the best customers. Apparently Bursa replaced Sivas in the slave trade in the Middle East during the Ottoman period. Edirne appears to be the main slave market in the Balkans. B. de La Brocquière on his journey in Rumili in 1432 saw such a train of 25 captives led by slave merchants to Edirne.[50] Later in the peace treaty with the Ottoman state Austria made the Porte agree not to allow the slave merchants to roam about the borders and buy slaves captured in violation of agreements.[51] Not only European visitors who met trains of slaves on their way to the Ottoman capital, but also Ottoman historians and epic literature furnish a vivid picture of this activity. It should be noted that the Holy War, and distribution of booty, *ghanīma*, played a major part in early Islamic history, and were regulated in every detail by Islamic law.[52] The Ottomans followed these regulations closely, as they did those on slavery in general.

Despite the fact that the Ottomans themselves used most of these slaves, there is documentary evidence that captives taken by Turkmens of the principalities of western Anatolia and by the Ottomans in the period fourteenth–sixteenth centuries became subject of an export trade to Egypt and Italy. In Venice's Levantine possessions, for instance on Crete, slaves of Balkan origin were employed in agriculture,[53] and in Italy (Florence, Milan) in certain specialized crafts. Italian notarial documents[54] demonstrate that slaves from the Balkans, Greeks, Wallachians, Albanians, and Serbians, appeared in Italy in the fifteenth century (with the exception of the Bosnian slaves who appeared

earlier). The same observation is made in the Mamluk kingdom in Egypt.[55] An Ottoman customs register in Antalya
(Satalia),[56] on the southern coast of Anatolia, dated 1560, also
tells us that while white slaves were still then exported to Egypt
and Syria in quite substantial numbers, in return black slaves
constituted an important part of the imports from those countries.

It should be noted that particular ethnic groups among the
slaves in the Ottoman empire or among those purchased by
foreigners became dominant at given periods of time depending
on where Ottoman raiding was then intense. In the fourteenth
century, Greeks and Bulgarians; in the fifteenth century, Serbs,
Albanians, Wallachians, Bosnians; and in the sixteenth century,
Hungarians, Germans, Italians, Spaniards and Georgians.

In the second half of the sixteenth century none of these
sources of supply could compete with the Black Sea, the importance of which grew in proportion to the decline of the Ottoman *akındjı* organization in the Central European frontiers
mainly as a result of the stiffening of Austrian resistance.[57] Now
the Crimean Tatars supplied the larger part of the Ottoman market, specializing, so to speak, in the business. Raids and expeditions into Poland, Circassia, and Russia became a regular
occupation of vital economic importance for the tribal aristocracy
of the khanate, so much so that often their relations with their
khans or with the Ottoman Sultans were determined by their
policies on this fundamental issue.[58] Muscovite lands became
the main field of operations from the time of Muhammed Girey
I (1514–1523); and large scale expeditions became regular after
1534 when the legacy of the Golden Horde in the Volga basin
was the subject of a long struggle between Muscovy and the
Crimea. The Crimeans naturally considered their actions as a
Holy War against an enemy who occupied the sister Muslim
khanates in the Volga basin and threatened the Crimea itself.[59]

The slave trade was indeed the foundation of the Crimean
economy. Essentially it was the economic pressures resulting
from immigration or from drought and famine, a frequent occurrence in the region, that thrust thousands of men, tribal
warriors as well as commoners, into Russia and Poland for raids.
Revenue accruing from the sale of slaves, contemporary observers
asserted,[60] constituted a real relief for the country at such times.
Nogays, pure nomads of the steppes outside the Crimea, were

absolutely dependent on the slave trade, selling their captives wholesale to the merchants coming to their headquarters. Most of the slaves were exported to the Ottoman market, but an important part of the captives was employed by the Crimean tribal aristocracy itself as agricultural slave labor to grow cereals for the city of Istanbul. Obviously that was the reason why they sometimes tried to capture and move whole families in their raids. If Evliyā Čelebī's[61] statement can be trusted, there were 400,000 slaves in the Crimea as against 187,000 Muslims (100,000 of the latter were, he added, commoners and 87,000 military) in 1667.

Raids by the Crimeans into Russia or Poland, usually in small parties from 200 to 1000, were continual occurrences irrespective of the formal peace between the Crimean Khanate and those countries. During their raids, the Crimeans avoided as much as possible the line of defenses which consisted of a series of the fortified towns with garrisons on the frontier. Scattered along an extensive frontier line, the Russian forces were often powerless before large scale Tatar invasions carefully organized under the chiefs of the tribal aristocracy or members of the Girey dynasty. In these raids slaves were considered as real booty, and their safe transport was always the chief concern of the raiders: they usually tried to avoid fighting, and doing anything which might lessen the value of their human chattel.[62]

As under the Genoese, Caffa (Turkish Kefe) and Kerch were the principal trade centers for slaves in the Crimea. The other less important centers in the region were Azov (Azak), Taman, Copa and Sokhum where Tatar, Circassian and Ottoman slave merchants met. Slave trade and taxation in the Crimea and Azov were regulated under special laws which apparently were made on the Genoese models.[63] The slave tax, taken as a rule at Caffa, was quite high: 210 akče, per slave, and with some additional dues reaching 255 akče (about four gold ducats at the end of the fifteenth century).[64]

At the height of the Crimean raids into Russia and Poland between 1514–1654 captives are reported in unusually great numbers. In 1578 annual customs revenue from the slave tax at Caffa was estimated at 4,463,196 akče.[65] Divided by 255, the highest tax rate, the figure 17,502 slaves per year is obtained. In 1614 following the large-scale expedition of Djanbek Girey Khan each Tatar soldier came, according to Russian sources, with five to ten slaves and prices at Caffa went down as low as 10 or 20 gold ducats per adult male slave,[66] while average price was over forty gold ducats in Edirne during this period (*see* appendix I-3). About thirty major Tatar raids were recorded into Muscovite territories between 1558-1596. And calculation made from the Russian sources of the seventeenth century on the number of captives gives us the following figures:[67]

Year	Captives
1607-1617	100,000
1632	2,660
1633	5,700
1637	2,280
1643-1645	10,000
1645	6,200
1607-1645	126,840

Whenever a peace with Muscovy, unpopular though it might be, was imposed upon the tribal aristocracy they often forced the khan to lead them in expeditions into Circassia, the second important region for slave raids during this period. Excuses were easy to find since the majority of Circassians were pagans at this time, and their chieftains refractory to the Crimean suzerainty. Sāhib Girey Khan (1532-1551) who intensified the anti-Muscovite policy of the Khanate was also responsible for large scale expeditions into Circassia which resulted in mass enslavements. In the 1530s Kansavuk, Circassian chieftain of the Jana agreed to send a yearly tribute of one thousand slaves to the Ottoman Sultan and five hundred to the Khan. Upon his failure to keep his promise, Sāhib Girey led an expedition against him in 1539, and took, according to his court chronicler, 50,000 captives. We learn from the same source that in his subsequent expedition against Kabartay (Caberda), the Tatars captured 10,000 Circassians, and in that against Pjedukh (Bjaduk) and Aliyuk 40,000 or 50,000. Circassians then came to exchange their captured noblemen for 20 to 100 common slaves.[68]

Let us conclude this rapid survey by asking the question whether the Ottoman society can really be defined as a slave society in the sense that its basic socio-economic structure was dependent for survival on an absolute control of labor or servile labor. We tried to show that the need for control of labor in Ottoman society varied in degree depending on the requirements of different segments of the society and economy. Slave in its classical sense, a person legally reduced to the nature of thing and subject to absolute possession and use by its owner, was something urgently needed in this traditional society in such enterprises as required large-scale, sustained and regular manpower—not only for an imperial army and navy, colossal construction works, the elevation of large number of transport animals or large-scale agricultural production for the army or palace, but also in certain crafts, large estates and extended households in the society at large. However, even in these segments which, as a whole, constituted a limited area within the general socio-economic setup of the Empire, servile labor, with the exception of the kōnāk (the extended household), and the large estates, disappeared over time especially from the end of the sixteenth century on when imperial laws were discarded and centralized power declined. We have already seen how in the second half of the fifteenth century the imperial government had great difficulty in maintaining its slave colony in the Khaṣṣlar. It became evident that servile labor was something extraneous within the Islamic agricultural system, and was exposed to constant and rapid erosion. The basic Ottoman organization of agricultural production rested upon the re'āyā–čiftlik system, that is to say, agricultural production was organized on the basis of small agricultural units (čiftliks) on the state owned lands placed in the possession of free peasant families (re'āyā)— Muslim or non-Muslim—who were under the sole obligation to cultivate it and pay taxes regulated by the state laws (kānūn). They were free (ḥurr) as defined by Islamic Law. No other person could force them to work or surrender the fruits of their labor without compensation. Even the restrictions such as the interdiction of abandoning the čiftlik land or the imposition of certain public services, such as mandatory work in mining or guarding the mountain passes, were not absolute, and were always mitigated by certain exemptions granted by the state. The imperial government was alert in preventing developments leading to the creation of personal ties of any sort over the re'āyā, and from the beginning made it a general policy to abolish serfdom or any other kind of personal tie over the *re'āyā* wherever it extended its rule. Of course, such a policy aimed first of all at weakening the power of the local lords in favor of the central authority. The Ottomans were aware of the fact that it served the expansion of their rule, and they utilized it as a propaganda device among the peasantry subject to serfdom in neighboring countries.

The *čiftlik–re'āyā* system was the dominant regime in the Ottoman Empire covering an overwhelming majority of the rural population along with most of the arable lands. It was not originally an Ottoman invention, but it was rather the re-establishment of an old system which had replaced servile labor as the major form of agricultural labor, economically the most advantageous and socially the safest under the demographic and economic conditions which prevailed during late antiquity. It can even be said that the Islamic Caliphate and the Eastern Roman Empire owed their enduring imperial existence to the fact that they embraced and became the champions of this regime which favored the continuance of independent peasant family units on the land.

At any rate what is known for sure is that this was the basic social and economic structure of the Ottoman Empire, carefully watched by the imperial government. Moreover, the Ottoman administration was ready to change the slave status of certain groups and eventually identified them with the *re'āyā* when overall developments began to lead toward the disappearance of servile labor—the difficulties in keeping a slave community within a majority of free peasants, the erosion of this community by frequent runaways and marriages with free men, and, perhaps the most important of all, the fact that slave labor became unprofitable under the new conditions of rising prices. But still, whenever private ownership under the *Sharī'a* stipulations was in question, especially on large estates and *kōnāks* any government disposition was excluded. It was only under the pressure from Western nations in the nineteenth century that the Ottoman government officially abolished slavery of any kind in its territories.

APPENDIX I

Slave Prices in the Ottoman Empire

Sale Prices from the registers of the *kāḍīs* of Bursa

1. From the Register of Estates dated 1464 (no. A 1/1 *Bursa, Archaeological Museum,* Sidjills).

Slaves of al-Hādjdj Aḥmed	in *akče* (one gold ducat = 45 *akče*)
Gülsine, female	3400
Benefshe, "	2400
Gülčiček, "	2400
Faṭma, "	1000
Kadem, "	8000
Nevrūz, "	3000
Isḥak, male	2400
Ismā'īl, "	1600
Shāhīn, "	1000
Of Khodja Turhan:	
3 female slaves	6000
12 male "	30000
Of Khodja Abdurraḥīm:	
2 female slaves	2200
3 male "	5400

2. From the register of transactions dated 1481–1486 (no. A 4/4, *Bursa, Archaeological Museum*).

	in *akče* (at this date official rate of one gold ducat is 45.5 *akče*)
Sold by the Sultan's agent in the slave market at Bursa by auction, one Hungarian male slave	2100
Runaway Bosnian slave sold to slave merchant Muṣṭafā	1000
Sold by Aḥmed Pasha, governor of Bursa, to Bathhouse Keeper Khalīl an Albanian male slave	7000
Sold to Jew Azrael a Circassian female slave	3000
Sold to Pīrī of Bursa a female slave	4500

Sold to Maḥmūd, slave merchant, two slaves	4600	
Sold to Bali Beg two eunuchs	4300	(100 Egyptian gold)
Sold to Bali Beg three male slaves	5590	(130 Egyptian gold)
Runaway Bosnian boy sold at auction	1430	
Sold by the Sultan's agent, boy from Jajče (Bosnia)	2000	
Runaway Bosnian old man	1000	
Sold by slave merchant Maḥmūd two slaves	5600	
Runaway Bosnian boy sold at auction	850	
Female slave sold at	5500	
Two female slaves sold at	4300	
Two male slaves sold at	9000	

The slave tax, calculated as one-fifth of the value of an average slave, was 240 *akče* in 1479 and 250 in 1485. In the capitulations granted to Venice in 1513 the compensation for a runaway slave was fixed as 1,000 *akče*. Living expenses for a female slave were reckoned as 40 *akče* a month around 1500 (the register, no. A 8/8, 33, *Bursa, Archaeological Museum*). Thence the price of an average slave was equal to his maintenance expenses for 2 or 2½ years. Wage of a worker in Bursa was one *akče* a day in 1478 (Bursa, Sidjill A 4/4, p. 58b) and an average sheep was worth 35 *akče*.

3. Average slave prices according to the data in the Register of the ḳassām in Edirne, 1545–1659 (published by Ö. L. Barkan, *Belgeler*, 3 1968).

	Period
1500 *akče*/25 gold pieces	1500s
2000 *akče*/33 gold pieces	1540s
2500 *akče*/40 gold pieces	1550s
4000 *akče*/66 gold pieces	1560s
5000 *akče*/41 gold pieces	1600s
8000 *akče*/66 gold pieces	1630s

Minimum price on the list is 700 and maximum 30,000 *akče* (60 silver *akče* were equal to one gold piece until 1584, fluctuation in the following period between 120 and 220).

APPENDIX 2

Slave Prices in the Mediterranean World, 1200–1453

Date	Egypt	Italy	Dubrovnik	Turkey
1200–1250	—	10 *dinār* (Genoa)	—	—
1250–1350	60 *dinār*	25 *dinār* (Genoa)	2–10 Gold pieces	—
1350–1400	50–70 ducats	30–70 ducats	—	—
1400–1453	70–140 "	45–70 " (15–20 in Caffa)	40–70 ducats	25–50 ducats (in Bursa in the second half of the 15th century)

Sources: F. Ashtor, *Histoire des prix et des salaires dans l'Orient Médiéval*, Paris, 1969.

C. Verlinden, "Traité des esclaves et traitants italiens à Constantinople (XIIIᵉ–XVᵉ siècles)," in *Moyen-Age* 4ᵉ series, 18 (1963), pp. 791–804.

———, "Le commerce en Mer Noire," Rapport, XIII, *Inter. Congress of Historical Sciences*, *Moscow*, 1970.

———, "Venezia e il commercio degli schiavi provenienti dalle coste orientali del Mediterraneo," in *Venezia e il Levante al sec. XV*, Firenze, 1973, pp. 911–29.

F. V. Carter, *Dubrovnik (Ragusa)*, London–New York, 1972.

D. Ayalon, *L'esclavage du Mamelouk*, Jerusalem, 1951.

M. Małowist, *Kaffa, 1453–1475*, Warshaw, 1947.

G. I. Bratianu, *Actes des notaires génois de Péra et de Caffa, 1281–1290*, Bucharest, 1927.

46   ISLAMIC AND JUDEO-CHRISTIAN WORLD

NOTES

1. On slavery in Islam *see* R. Levy, *The Social Structure of Islam*, Cambridge, 1957, pp. 73–78; R. Brunschvig, " 'Abd," in *Encyclopaedia of Islam*² (hereafter *EI*²) I, pp. 24–40; B. Lewis, *Islam*, vol. II, (New York 1974), pp. 236–51; for slavery in the Ottoman Empire *see* M. d'Ohsson, *Tableau Général de l'Empire Othman*, 7 vols., Paris 1788–1824; M. Mevḳūfātī, *Sharh: Multaḳā al-Abhur* (Istanbul 1318 H.), I, pp. 234, 289–301, 314, 342, 358, 154–160, 266–68, 278; for further bibliography *see, Orientalisches Recht*, in *Handbuch der Orientalistik, I. Der Nahe und der Mittlere Osten*, ed. B. Spuler, *Ergänzungsband*, III (Leiden 1964), pp. 294–97. In this article we follow the transliteration system adopted in *EI*².

2. *See* "Ghulām" in *EI*², II, pp. 1079–1091; also H. İnalcık, *The Ottoman Empire*, London & New York, 1973, pp. 76–88.

3. For *Kapı-kulu, see, The Ottoman Empire*, pp. 76–88.

4. *See* "Dewshirme," (Ménage) in *EI*², II, pp. 210–13; P. Wittek, "Devshirme and Sharī'a," in *BSOAS* 17 (1955), pp. 271–8. In his article "Devshirme and Sharī'a" Prof. Wittek has done us the great service of drawing attention to the question of how it was possible that the *devshirme*, a periodical forced levy of children from the Sultan's Christian subjects who were subsequently Islamized, something absolutely contradictory to the Islamic law, should be instituted by the Ottomans. In answer to this question he pointed out that the Shafi'ite school of law excluded from the *dhimma* status those who had embraced any religion of the *Ahl al-Kitāb* after the Koranic revelation, and, on the other hand, that in order to increase their military manpower the Ottomans might also have had recourse to the Islamic principle of *maslaha* which allowed that in case of absolute necessity an established *Sharī'a* rule might be overridden for the good of the Islamic community. But it seems that this canonical point was not, in fact, an issue, since to the Ottomans, *devshirme* did not imply "enslavement" but rather an extension of the *'awārid̄-i diwāniyye*, which were extraordinary services imposed upon the *re'āyā'* in emergency situations. That in this case the word *kul* did not mean slave in the canonical sense is clear from a passage in an Ottoman source explaining why the Muslim Turks were excluded from the *devshirme*. (*See* H. İnalcık, *The Ottoman Empire, The Classic Age*, London and New York, 1973, p. 78). In the Janissary corps *kuls* of *devshirme* origin were distinguished from those of slave status. This point is made clear in a passage from the memoirs of Kanstantin Mihailović (*Memoirs of a Janissary*, trans. B. Stolz and S. Soucek, Ann Arbor, 1975, pp. 158–59). He says, "If the number of them (slaves from foreign lands) does not suffice, then he (the Sultan) takes from the Christians in every village in his land who have boys, having established what is the most every village can give so that the quota will always be full. *And the boys whom he takes in his own land are called cilik* (rather *illik*). Each one of them can leave his property *to whom ever he wants after his death*. And those whom he takes among the enemies are called *pendik* (rather *pendjik*). These latter after their deaths can leave nothing; rather, it goes to the emperor, except that if someone comports himself well and is so deserving that he be freed, he may leave it to whomever he wants."

5. The 'adjemi-oghlan's numbered 7,745 in 1568, 9,406 in 1069 and 4,372 in 1670. *See*, I. H. Uzunçarşılı, *Kapıkulu Ocakları*, Ankara 1943, I,

pp. 5–141; 'Adjemi-oghlan's supplied about 40 per cent of the labor for the construction of the great mosque of Süleyman I in Istanbul between 1550 and 1557 (Ö. L. Barkan, *Süleymaniye cami imareti ve inşaati*, Ankara, 1970, p. 100). According to B. Miller's calculation (*The Palace School of Muhammed the Conqueror*, Cambridge 1941, p. 79) the number of boys levied was three thousand per year in the sixteenth century. Sa'd al-Dīn (*Tādj al-Tawārīkh*, Istanbul, 1279 A. H., I), estimated their total number over two hundred thousand in about two hundred years.

6. See, *The Ottoman Empire*, pp. 77–125; A. H. Lybyer, *The Government of the Ottoman Empire in the Time of Suleiman the Magnificent*, reprint: New York, 1966, pp. 45–110.

7. When a slave is freed both he and his male descendants in perpetuity remain attached to the emancipator and to his or her family by a bond of "clientship" or *walā'*. This bond is inalienable in principle. The property of the emancipated slave or of his descendants in the male line who dies leaving neither priority heirs nor agnates reverts to the patron or patroness or to their agnatic heirs. ("'Abd," *EI²*, p. 31.)

8. Under Süleymān I (1520–1566) İskender Čelebī was reported to own six or seven thousand, and Grand Vizier Rüstem Pasha 1700 slaves (J. von Hammer, *Geschichte des Osmanischen Reiches*, reprint: Graz, 1963, III, pp. 156, 386).

9. By the middle of the sixteenth century the population of Istanbul was 300–400 thousand (*see* "Istanbul," in *EI²*, III, p. 243), *cf. The Ottoman Empire*, p. 83; Towards the end of the fifteenth century in Venice there were three thousand slaves out of a population of one hundred thousand (W. Heyd, *Histoire du Commerce du Levant*, ed. F. Raynaud, Leipzig, 1936, p. 563).

10. Freed slaves were recorded in the Ottoman survey books together with their former masters because of patronage rights (*see*, *Başvekâlet Archives*, Istanbul, series of *Tapu Defterleri*).

11. For the *timâr* system *see*, *The Ottoman Empire*, pp. 107-118.

12. For these obligations *see* the law book published by N. Beldiceanu, *Code des Lois Coutumières de Mehmed II*, Wiesbaden 1967. For the fifteenth century *see*, *Sûret-i Defter-i Sancak-i Arvanid*, ed. H. İnalcık, Ankara, 1954, where the obligations are indicated above each *timâr* entry.

13. Edited by Ö. L. Barkan, in *Belgeler* 3 (1968), pp. 84–472.

14. In the last category we find: Sinān, *sandjak begi* with 7 slaves; Yūnus, *sandjak begi* 11 slaves; Bayram, *sandjak begi* 11 slaves; Mahmūd čawush-bashı 13 slaves; Süleymān Agha, *bostandjı-bashı* 8 slaves; Sinān, ser-bölük 7 slaves; Mūsā, palace saddler 7 slaves. Except the last one all belonged to the higher echelons of the military class.

15. See "Capital Formation in the Ottoman Empire," in *Journal of Economic History* 29 (1969), pp. 142-232.

16. See H. İnalcık, "15 Asır Türkiye İktisadî ve İçtimaî Tarihi Kaynakları," in *Istanbul Üniversitesi, İktisat Fakültesi Mecmuası* 15 (1953–1954), pp. 51–76.

17. "'Abd," p. 30.

18. The register of the cadi of Bursa, No. 1/1, (*Bursa Archaeological Museum*).

19. See Appendix 1 and 2.

20. See "Capital Formation in The Ottoman Empire," p. 118.

21. F. Babinger (ed.), *Hans Dernschwam's Tagebuch*, Munich–Leipzig, 1923, p. 104.

22. "Capital Formation . . . ," pp. 108–18.

23. See note 16.

24. For walā', see note 7. In Islamic law the slave has no patrimony of his own. His master can do as he likes with property in the possession of his slave. The slave can do business only on behalf of his master. However, there is a practice which provides the slave with a real legal competency. It consists in the master's putting the slave in charge of a business and entrusting to him a capital sum where necessary. The slave is then said to be "authorized." He is then quite independent to deal with third parties. The master is not responsible for the debt of his authorized slave. Full payment for the debt of such an authorized slave is deferred until such time as the slave is emancipated. This practice was widely used in the Islamic past, and had a strong impact on the development of commerce ("'Abd," in EI², pp. 28–29).

25. H. İnalcık, "Bursa," in Belleten 24 (1960), p. 91, document 37, and "Capital Formation . . . ," p. 110.

26. See notes 7 and 24; a western observer (C. Le Bruyn, Voyage au Levant, Rouen & Paris, 1728, p. 81) is stunned to find slaves who, after escaping to Europe, returned to their former masters in the Empire.

27. See "Capital Formation . . . ," pp. 101, 111–14, and 136–38; also Ö. L. Barkan, "Kulluklar ve Ortakçı Kullar," in Istanbul Üniversitesi Iktisat Fakültesi Mecmuası 1 (1940), pp. 198–245, and 397–406; idem, "Edirne Askerî Kassâmına Âit Tereke Defterleri, 1545–1659," in Belgeler 3 (1968), especially documents nos. 5, 6, 7, 24, 25, 28, 32, 33, 35, 40, 53, 54, 55, 67, 75, and 79.

28. This type of large farm with servile labor, usually established by members of the ruling class, seemed to be quite a widespread practice in the Middle East before the Ottomans. For Iran see I. P. Petrushevsky, Kashāwarzi wa munāsibāt-i arzī dar Irān-i 'ahd-i Mūghul, trans. from Russian into Persian by K. Kashāwarz, Tehran 1344/1965, pp. 143–53; I. P. Petrushevsky, Cambridge History of Iran, V, Cambridge, 1968, pp. 514, and 522–29; Mukātabāt-i Rashīdī, Letters of Rashīd al-Dīn Faḍl Allāh, ed. M. Shafī', Lahore, 1947, gives interesting details about slaves, 160 in number, imported to Iran via Basra (idem., p. 14), their settlement and reclamation work in four uninhabited villages near Tabriz, settlement of 40 Greek slaves in the village called karye-i Rūmiyān (pp. 52–53); Rashīd al-Dīn's slaves in agricultural works at various places numbered 1,400 men and women (pp. 194–95, and 236), and some of his slaves were placed at the hospital he built near Tabriz to study medical sciences (idem., p. 319); see also for the villages he built along the irrigation canals in Mossul and Malatya areas which were settled by the re'āyā' brought from neighboring provinces (idem., pp. 244–47) which reminds the Ottoman method of rice cultivation by re'āyā' under state control. For the widespread use of servile labor in agriculture during this period see a decree of Gāzān Khan in Geschichte Gāzān–Hān's des Rašid al-Dīn, ed. K. Jahn, London, 1940, p. 306). According to the decree military commanders reclaimed abandoned lands within their fiefs employing their own slaves and animals, and took the produce for themselves. For Anatolia see Osman Turan, "Selçuk Devri Vakfiyeleri," in Belleten 11 (1947), pp. 197–235, and 415–29; 12 (1948), pp. 17–171.

29. See Barkan, "Kulluklar ve Ortakçı Kullar," pp. 198–245.

30. Barkan, "Kulluklar," pp. 405–16; also see T. Gőkbilgin, Edirne ve Paşa Livası, Istanbul, 1952, slaves in the endowments of Karadja Beg (p.

233), of Sarıdja Pasha (p. 249), Turahan Beg (p. 341), Khadım 'Alī Pasha (p. 397), Ibrāhīm Pasha (p. 418), Sinān Pasha (p. 454), Yahyā Pasha (p. 457), also see note 6.

31. Gőkbilgin, op. cit., p. 397; 'Alī Pasha's slaves from Morea; also Barkan, "Kulluklar," facsimile XXX.

32. Document in Gőkbilgin, op. cit., p. 249.

33. Barkan, "Kulluklar..." pp. 29–74. On the status of re'āyā' see H. İnalcık, "The Policy of Mehmed II Towards the Greek Population of Istanbul," in Dumbarton Oaks Papers, 33–34 (1969–1970), pp. 236–49.

34. Forced marriage between slaves was permitted in Islamic law by Abū Hanīfa and Mālik (see "'Abd," p. 27).

35. Barkan, "Kulluklar...," pp. 236–330.

36. "Kulluklar...," p. 413, note 82; also see Ö. L. Barkan, "Tűrkiye'de servaj varmı idi?," in Belleten 20 (1956), pp. 237–46.

37. "Kulluklar...," pp. 436–37. For a similar development in Russia in the fifteenth and sixteenth centuries see R. Hellie, "Recent Soviet Historiography on Medieval and Early Modern Russian Slavery," in The Russian Review 35 (Jan., 1976), p. 26.

38. See "'Abd," p. 26; Muslims declared heretic, rāfidī, by religious authorities can legally be enslaved and sold (see "'Abd," p. 36). Fighting shī'ī schismatic Turkmens and Iranians the Ottoman Sultans obtained sanction by the religious authorities for their enslavement. In 1443 Ottomans sold their Muslim prisoners of war from Karaman in Istanbul (Gazavātnāme-i Sultan Murād Hān, Ankara, 1978, p. 13). Shaykh al-Islām Ibn Kemāl even wrote a treatise to discuss the subject; also see Lutfi Pasha, Tawārīkh-i Āl-i 'Osmān, ed. 'Ālī, Istanbul 1925, p. 455; J. Walsh, "The Historiography of Ottoman-Safavid Relations," in Historians of the Middle East, eds. B. Lewis and P. Holt, London, 1962, p. 205.

39. See "'Abd," p. 30; and Mevkūfātī, I, p. 298. To mention a famous example see Murād II's testament: H. İnalcık, Fatih Devri Üzerinde Tetkikler ve Vesikalar, Ankara 1594, p. 207.

40. For the significance of slave trade as a factor for the rise of the ghāzī principalities in Western Anatolia see my forthcoming article in K. Setton, The Crusades, V. For Greek slaves and slaves from the Balkan countries in the thirteenth and fourteenth centuries see W. Heyd, op. cit., I, pp. 555-56; Vryonis, The Decline of Medieval Hellenism in Asia Minor, (Berkeley, Los Angeles–London, 1971), Index: slave and slavery; B. Krekić, Dubrovnik (Raguse) et le Levant, Paris–The Hague, 1961, pp. 109-111; in the thirteenth century Sivas in central Anatolia was an important slave market, see Ibn Bībī, Al-Awāmir al-'Alāiyya, ed. Adnan Erzi, Ankara, n.d., Index: ghulām; transl. H. W. Duda, Copenhagen, 1959, p. 59; O. Turan, "Selçuķ Devri Vakfiyeleri," in Belleten II (1947), p. 215; and G. I. Bratianu, Actes des notaires Génois de Péra et de Caffa (1281-1290), Bucharest 1927, Index: Sivas. An observer of the first half of the fifteenth century, Piloti (cited by Heyd, I, p. 556) pointed out that Greek and other Christian ships were busy in transporting slaves from Gallipoli (cf. "Gelibolu" in EI², II, pp. 983-87) to Alexandria. See also Ch. Verlinden, "Venezia e il commercio degli Schiavi" in Venezia e il Levante, Venezia 1973. He points out that the Greek slaves appeared in the Levantine markets only from the fourteenth century on, (cf. P. Wittek, Das Fürstentum Mentesche, Amsterdam, 1967, p. 2).

41. B. Krekić, op. cit.; F. W. Carter, Dubrovnik (Ragusa), A Classic City-State, (London–New York, 1972) p. 242. Dubrovnik was the center

50   ISLAMIC AND JUDEO-CHRISTIAN WORLD

for slave traffic from and through the Balkans to Italy from the thirteenth century.

42. In 1489 during the Ottoman–Mamluk war one of the main complaints of the Mamluk Sultan was the arrest by the Ottomans of the Egyptian slave merchants (Ibn Iyas, *Badā'iʿ al-Zuhūr*, Vol. III, ed. M. Mostafa, Kairo, 1963, p. 266).

43. D. Ayalon, "L'esclavage du Mamelouk," (Jerusalem, 1951); for the Mamluks and slavery *see* A. N. Poliak, "Le caractère colonial de l'état mamelouk dans ses rapports avec la Horde d'Or," in *Revue des Études Islamiques* 9 (1935), pp. 231-48; Ch. Verlinden, "La colonie venitienne de Tana, centre de la traite des esclaves au XIVᵉ et au début du XVᵉ siècle," in *Studi in Onore di Gino Luzzatto*, II, Milano, 1950, pp. 1-25; *idem* "Mamelouks et traitants," in *Mélanges E. Perroy*, Paris 1973, pp 734-47; *idem* "Le commerse en Mer Noir," *rapport*, XIII. *Congrès intern. des sciences historiques*, Moscow 1970; E. Skrjinskaja, "Storia della Tana," in *Studi Veneziana* (1968); G. I. Bratianu, *Recherches sur le commerce génois dan la Mer Noire au XIIIᵉ siècle*, Paris 1929; M. Malowist, *Kaffa, Kolonia genuenska na Krymie i problem wschodni w letach 1453-1475*, Warshaw, 1957; M. Balard, *Gênes et l'outre-mer, I: Les actes de Caffa du notaire Lamberto di Sambuceto, 1289-1290*, Paris–the Hague, 1973; E. Skrjinskaja, "Le colonie genovese in Crimea, Feodosia (Caffa)" in *Europa Orientale*, 14 (1934), pp. 113-51; R. H. Bautier, "Les relations économiques des occidentaux avec les pays d'Orient," in *Sociétés et compagnies de commerce en Orient et dans l'Océan Indien*, Paris, 1970, pp. 263-331; M. Małowist, "Les routes du commerce et les marchandises du Levant dans la vie de Pologne au bas moyen âge et au début de l'époque moderne," *ibid.*, pp. 157-75; M. Berindei–G. Veinstein, "Réglements de Süleymān Iᵉʳ concernant le livā' de Kefe," in *Cahiers du Monde russe et soviétique* 16 (1975), pp. 57-104; S. B. Labib, *Handelsgeschichte Ägyptens im Spätmittelalter*, Wiesbaden, 1975, Index: *sklaven*; Piloti estimated that the Sultan of Egypt obtained two thousand slaves yearly at Caffa (Verlinden, *Rapport*, Moscow 1970, p. 11).

44. Ch. Verlinden, *L'esclavage dans l'Europe médievale*, Gent, 1955; I. Origo, "The Domestic Enemy: The Eastern Slaves in Tuscany in the fourteenth and fifteenth Century," in *Speculum* (1955). Perhaps another consequence was the extension of the traffic of black slaves in Europe (R. Lopez, "Market Expansion: The Case of Genoa," in *JEH* 26 (1964).

45. It was always a difficult problem for the Ottomans to man their huge navy. For each galley about 150-200 oarsmen were needed. And Ottoman navy had *12* galleys in 1453, *68* in 1471, *100* in 1520 and about *200* in 1571. A firman dated 1573 (*Başvekâlet Archives, Mühimme defteri*, no. 23, p. 115), reads "each year one hundred galleys is to be equipped and each galley needs one hundred and fifty oarsmen (*Kürekdji*)." Most of the time the government met the need by conscripting wanderers and gypsies or imposing upon the reʿāyā' the obligation to secure a certain number of oarsmen. Oarsmen were also hired for the navy from slave merchants in Istanbul (Rycaut, *Histoire de l'état présent de l'empire Ottoman*, Amsterdam, 1671, p. 493). The galley slaves kept in Galata numbered ten thousand (*Gerlach* and *Barbaro*, around 1590, cited by N. Jorga, *GOR*, III, p. 225). Galley slaves, 1419 in number, supplied about 5 per cent of the labor for the construction of the Süleymaniye Mosque in Istanbul between 1550 and 1557; (Barkan, *Süleymaniye Cami*, pp. 132-35).

Later on the shortage of slaves and oarsmen, along with financial difficulties, was obviously one of the factors in Ottoman naval decline. For Muslim slaves and the French navy see P. Bamford, *Fighting Ships and Prisons, The Mediterranean Galleys of France in the Age of Louis XIV*, (Minneapolis, 1973), pp. 138-72, and the map, p. 145. In his paper to the Conference, *II Mediterraneo nella seconda metà del '500 alla Luce di Lepanto* (published, Florence, 1974) M. Aymard pointed out that Muslims from North Africa and Turkey made up the majority of galley slaves in Italian navies. An able Muslim galley slave cost about 100 gold ducats.

46. *See* J. von Hammer, *GOR*, Index: *Sclaven*; Jorga, *GOR*, III, pp. 36, and 102; Gerlach reported (cited by Jorga, III, p. 267) that the Ottoman frontier commanders in Hungary captured fifteen thousand slaves in 1574. For the exact number of the slaves, the Ottoman registers containing *pendjik*, slave taxation, at the archives should be systematically examined. The figures given by Western sources or Ottoman chronicles (for example, *Silāhdār Tarihi*, ed. A. Refik, Istanbul, 1928, I, p. 300, reported eighty thousand captives from Hungary in 1663) have to be checked by these documents.

47. For regulations of slave markets see "Kānūnnāme," in *EI*[2], IV, pp. 562-66. The amount of slave tax taken at each city can be found among the city taxes in the Tapu Defterleri (series of these survey books in *Başvekâlet Archives*, Istanbul; and *Tapu ve Kadastro Genel Müdürlüğü*, Ankara). For the slave market in Istanbul *see* "Istanbul," *EI*[2], IV, p. 228; also *see* below note 65. In a market regulation of the first decades of the seventeenth century (Topkapı Sarayı Library, Revan no. 1934, pp. 107-111) over one hundred slave merchants, male and female, are registered in Istanbul. For the state regulations concerning slave trade, slave taxation, runaway slaves, freed slaves, Sultan's slaves, etc. *see* Ö. L. Barkan, *Kanunlar, I*, Istanbul, 1943, Index: *ak-esîr, âzâdeler, âzâdlu kâfirler, câriye, ortak, ortakčı, hâssa kullar, kul, kačkun, kenizek, kul-karavaš, oğlan, 'uteka, ümm-i veled, üsera.*

48. *Memoirs of a Janissary*, trans. B. Stolz–S. Soucek, Ann Arbor, 1975, p. 177; *cf.* Jorga, *GOR*, II, pp. 223-24. Turkish epic literature called *ghazavātnāme* (*see* A. S. Levend, *Gazavātnāmeler*, Ankara, 1956) gives a vivid description and background of Ottoman raiders and the organization of raids. 'Āshık Pashazāde describes (ed. Atsız, Istanbul, 1949, p. 180) such a raid in which he participated and tells us that he sold his captives for 950 *akcha* at the frontier city of Üsküb, modern Skoplje. A detailed historical account of a large scale raid (10,000 *akindjis*) in 1479, *see* Ibn Kemal, VII. *Defter*, ed. Ş. Turan, Ankara, 1954, pp. 527-62. Under Süleyman I (1520-1566) there were twelve thousand *akındjıs* active on the Hungarian front (Jorga, *GOR*, III, p. 417). This figure is confirmed by Ottoman documents.

49. *See* Appendix 1; Tulčea on the Lower Danube was the principal market for the slaves from Poland.

50. *Le Voyage d'Outremer*, ed. A. Schefer, (Paris, 1892), p. 124.

51. *Muʿāhadāt Medjmuʿası*, III, 63.

52. *See* note 1; "Since the beginning of the Arab razzias into the land of *Rūm* human booty had come to constitute a very important portion of spoils" (Vryonis, *op. cit.*, p. 174).

53. *See* F. Thiriet, *Réglements des délibérations du sénat de Venise concernant la Romanie*, 3 vols, (Paris–The Hague, 1958-1961), Index:

52   ISLAMIC AND JUDEO-CHRISTIAN WORLD

esclaves and *Crète*; Ch. Verlinden, "La Crète, débouché et plaque tournante de la traite esclaves aux XIVᵉ siecles" in *Etudi in onore di A. Fanfani*, vol. III (Milan, 1962), pp. 593–611.

54. Examined by Ch. Verlinden, "Venezia e il commercio degli schiavi provenienti dalle orientali del Mediterraneo," in *Venezia e il Levante al secolo XV*, (Firenze, 1974), pp. 911-29; *Idem*, "L'esclavage sur la côte dalmate au bas Moyen âge" in *Bulletin de l'Institut Historique belge de Rome* (1970), pp. 57-140; *idem*, "Esclaves du Sudest et de l'Est européen en Espagne orientale à la fin du moyen âge" in *Revue Historique du Sud-est Européen* (1942), pp. 371-406.

55. *See* note 40, 41 and 43; also *see* Verlinden, "Venezia e il commercio," pp. 915-16; P. H. Dopp, (ed.), *l'Egypte au commencement du XVᵉ siècle, d'après le traité d'Emmanuel Piloti de Crète, incipit 1420*, Cairo, 1950.

56. *Başvekâlet archives*, Istanbul, Maliyaden no. 102. The average price of a black slave was then one thousand *akcha* or about 16 gold ducat. I am preparing an edition of this important source.

57. *See* G. E. Rothenberg, *The Austrian Military Border in Croatia, 1522-1747*, Urbana, 1960, pp. 27-87. W. McNeill, *Europe's Steppe Frontier, 1500-1800*, Chicago–London, 1964.

58. *See* "Kırım Hanlığı" in *Islâm Ansiklopedisi*, VI, pp. 752-56.

59. *See* H. İnalcık, "The origin of the Ottoman-Russian Rivalry and the Don-Volga Canal" in *Annales de l'Université d'Ankara*, (1947), pp. 47-110.

60. A. A. Novoselskij, *Struggle of the Muscovite State Against Tatars in the Seventeenth Century*, Moscow, 1948 (in Russian), p. 418.

61. *Siyâhatnâme*, III, Istanbul, 1314 A.H. In order to establish his big farm in Bulgaria, Mihaloghlu Mehmed Beg moved and settled 15 families as slaves from Bosnia during the conquest of this country in 1463 (*see* document in Barkan, "Kulluklar," pp. 1-6, facsimile xxx).

62. Novoselskij, *op. cit.*, p. 434.

63. M. Berindei–G. Veinstein, "Réglements de Süleyman Iᵉʳ concernant le Liva' de Kefe," in *Cahiers du Monde Russe et Soviétique* 15-1 (1975), pp. 57-104.

64. *See* Berindei–Veinstein, Ibid.; The combined tax revenue for three years of the markets of slaves, horses and sheep in Istanbul alone amounted to 360,000 *akcha* or 8000 gold ducats in 1477.

65. *Başvekâlet Archives*, Istanbul, Maliye no. 2283: *Muhasebe-i Wâridat ve Ihrâdjât-i Khâṣṣa-i Kefe, mukâtaʿa-i Esârâ-i Kefe*, from 9 Ramaḍān 986 to 8 Ramaḍān 987.

66. Novoselskij, *op. cit.*, pp. 77, and 86-87.

67. Novoselskij, *op. cit*, pp. 416-38. In conclusion Novoselskij estimates 150,000-200,000 Russian captives during the first half of the seventeenth century. According to Russian reports from the Crimea average price of a Russian slave there varied from 50 to 100 gold pieces or 40 to 80 rubles.

68. Remmâl Khodja, *Tārikh-i Sāhib Giray*, MS: *Bibliothèque Nationale*, Paris, Suppl. Turc 164.

S. *Fischer-Galati*

THE PROTESTANT REFORMATION AND ISLAM

The relationship between the Protestant Reformation and Islam is intimately related to the "Turkish Menace" of the sixteenth century. The establishment of a seemingly powerful and expansionist Muslim Empire in Eastern Europe at a time of profound political and spiritual turmoil in the West rekindled traditional anti-Muslim feelings in Western Christendom, generated new forms of expression and new rationales for condemning Islam, and ultimately forced the leaders of the age of the Reformation to reassess their allegiances to traditional and new values and forms of political and spiritual expression in terms of the new realities imposed, to a significant extent, by Ottoman imperialism.

There are thus a multitude of facets in the relationship varying from region to region, from denomination to denomination, from degree of contact, involvement, or confrontation with Islam by Protestants in the sixteenth century. In this essay we are concerned essentially with two major aspects of the relationship —the theological, with its clear implications for political theory, and the political *per se* reflecting reaction to Turkish military advances and territorial conquests during the years of supreme crisis in Western Christendom which corresponded to the so-called "Golden Age" of the Ottoman Empire, that of Suleiman the Magnificent.

It is fair to say that Protestant theologians, German and non-German, based their views of Islam largely on inherited concepts prevalent in the Middle Ages. Such modifications as were introduced, primarily by Luther and his disciples, were prompted by Protestant appraisals of the religious structure of Latin

Christendom, particularly of the Papacy itself, and focussed on medieval concepts of heresy. Since Islam was patently heretical to all Christians, both before and during the Reformation, and since the Papacy was patently heretical to Luther and other theologians of the Reformation, the equating of the heretical Papacy and Catholic Church with heretical Islam became *de rigueur* for most Protestant reformers if for no reason other than to prove the theological purity of Protestantism.

The most explicit formulator of this inverted syllogism was Martin Luther himself whose logic was more questionable than his faith and whose ideas were more medieval than modern. Luther's perception of Islam in 1517 was similar to that of most students of medieval theology and readers of medieval literature on matters related to Muslims in general and the Turks in particular.[1] Mohammed's religion was heretical because it re-jected the redemptive power of Christ, denied the Trinity, and altered the true Word of God as contained in the Bible. Moreover, Mohammed was anathemized for lechery and for attempting to supplant Christ. These basic views had been expounded ,by the Greek-speaking communities of Syria from as early as the second generation after the Muslim conquest.[2] In Muslim-ruled Spain they were refined in the works of the ninth century Martyr Movement, most notably by St. Elogius and his biographer, Paul Alvarus. Byzantine contributions, such as those of Euthemius Zigabenus, reinforced Western prejudices.[3] Outside of Spain, however, little was known about Islam before the twelfth century when the Crusades made the Westerners aware of the Saracens.[4] Confronted with Islam for the first time, the Latins readily borrowed the stories about Muslims created in Spain and Byzantium and used them to formulate their own versions on the faith and people of Islam. The Cluniac translators under the direction of Peter the Venerable prepared Latin edition of the Koran, of Pseudo-al-Kindi's *Risalah,* and of other Arabic works and adorned them with Peter's own influential commen-taries comprised in the *Summa totius haeresis Saracenorum* and the *Liber contra sectam sive haeresiam Saracenorum.*[5] The titles speak for themselves as sources of objective study and the books became the primary source of knowledge on Islam by Western readers in the High Middle Ages and the Renaissance. The standardized image of Islam as the faith of blood-thirsty, salacious heretics who thanks to the deception of the lusty heresiarch Mohammed had devoted themselves to the service of the Devil was inherited by Luther. Certain refinements, theological and political, were inevitable under the circumstances prevailing in 1517 and during the early years of the Reformation.

It would be rational to expect that the Turkish threat to Eastern Europe and particularly to the domains of the Habsburgs, including Luther's Germany, would have affected the Reformer's views on Islam as such and in relation to the cause of German Protestantism. Upon closer examination, however, there appears to be very little correlation, if any, between Luther's theological and political positions vis-a-vis Islam and the Turks and the political realities resultant from Ottoman imperialism.

Luther's views on Islam and the Turk, important as they were because of their wide adoption by other reformers and Protestants more remote from and ignorant of the Turkish religious and political presence in Europe, were simplistic. Although he was familiar with the Koran and aware of the nature of the Turkish threat to Christendom and to Germany his pronouncements ultimately reflected two specific obsessions —one with Mohammedan heresy and the other with Papal heresy. Despite apparent inconsistencies and contradictions Luther invariably regarded the Turk as the "scourge of God," Mohammed as the "servitor of the Devil," and both Pope and Turk as Antichrist. Luther sought the destruction of the Turk and of the God of the Turks for the sake of serving the cause of the true God, of defeating the Devil, and of destroying Antichrist in his dual incarnation of Pope and Turk.[6] In his *Heerpredigt widder die Türcken*, his most comprehensive statement directed against the Infidel, the Turk assumed the central part in Luther's eschatology. This primarily because of the one-sided interpretation of the Seventh Chapter of Daniel whereby the prophet's vision of "a fourth beast, terrible and dreadful and exceedingly strong" was equated with the Devil's emissary, the Turk.[7] Objections and criticisms levied against Luther's views by contemporary and later critics of his doctrines were essentially concerned with theological detail and priorities. The notion that repentance of sin was a prerequisite for action against the Turk since without repentance war against the Infidel constituted resistance to the will of the God who sent the Turk to punish the unfaithful was unacceptable even to a few of Luther's contemporaries. Similarly, his equating of Pope and Turk and his interpretation of the apocalypse of Daniel also raised many a theologian's eyebrows. Yet, these criticisms focussed on theological detail and did not challenge the essence of Luther's interpretation of the role of the Turk and of his religious mission. For ultimately Luther did provide the blueprint for the predominant views on Turk and Islam held by Protestants in the sixteenth century.

Melanchthon, for instance, frequently expounded theories similar to those of his master including those on the symbolism of Daniel's apocalypse.[8] Men of the English Reformation, such as Theodore Bibliander, parotted Luther and Melanchthon. Bibliander's edition of the Koran contained not less than twenty-nine attacks on Islam based primarily on the writings of the German reformers.[9] Similarly, Turcopapistical polemic reached its height in England by the middle of the sixteenth century achieving its most perfect form in Matthew Sutcliffe's *De Turcopapismo* whose nearly three hundred pages of anti-Turkish and anti-papal invective closely echoed Luther's diatribes and theological expositions on the subject.[10]

The negativism of English Protestant writers is not surprising considering the distance which separated England from the Ottoman Empire. Nor is it surprising to note that in South-Slavic lands ravaged by the Turks reformers preached a theology close to Luther's in that Antichrist was a Janus-like being whose one face was borne by the Pope and the other by the Turk.[11] What is rather astonishing, however, is the relative lack of concern and theological lucidity in the views on Islam and the Turk propounded by Calvin and his followers.[12]

Calvin was apparently as ignorant of the Koran as most of his contemporaries. In fact, it has been asserted that he had never read the sacred book of Islam and was only vaguely familiar with the difference between Turks, Saracens, and Mussulmans. His essential position vis-a-vis Islam was that the true religion, the one conforming to God's word was his, Calvin's and that the false religion was that expressed by Mohammed in the Koran. The French reformer, however, rejected such extreme views as those held by Luther on the meaning of Daniel's apocalypse, declined to associate Pope and Turk, and with the exception of the politically-inspired accusation of Servetus of expounding heretical doctrines favored by the Turks, refused to use the Infidel as a cudgel on his theological and political adversaries.[13] Calvin's concern with Turks and Islam was essentially a function of apprehension over Turkish military imperialism whether directed against Catholic or Protestant rulers and interests.

Several disciples of Calvin reached even more realistic and pragmatic evaluations of Islam and the Turk by enunciating and supporting the position that the Turks were not necessarily inimical to Christianity in view of their tolerant attitude toward Christians inhabiting conquered lands. This position was, as a rule, not predicated on theological arguments since reconciliation with or acceptance of Islam as a tolerable religion was impossible on such grounds in the sixteenth century. It was based, however, on an assessment of the realities of the international situation, or on ignorance of that situation, and in special cases on the necessity for or advantages derived from accommodation with the Turk or even on first-hand experience with the "Tolerant Turk" himself.[14]

It is remarkable that none of Luther's disciples in Germany deviated from Luther's fundamentalist positions. Such deviations, or alternate interpretations, came primarily from disciples of Calvin or from Protestants of other denominations inhabiting lands proximate to the Ottoman Empire or actually politically subordinated to Constantinople. It is true that recognition of the fact that the Turks were religiously tolerant and even benevolent to Christian subjects was first attributable to official emissaries of Catholic sovereigns to the Porte such as Ogier Ghiselin de Busbecq, Antonio Rincon, or Jean de la Forest who were obligated to provide unbiased appraisals of Ottoman conditions to a Charles V or Francis I.[15] Nevertheless, the French Protestant Sebastien Chateillon was willing to state, at an inopportune time for French Protestantism, that "le Turc maintien bien les Chrétiens et les Juifs ses sujets contre la violence qui leur pourroit être faite."[16] The views of Western European Protestants on Turks and Islam, however, were ultimately less significant than those of Protestants in Hungary and Transylvania. Linguistic problems combined with scarcity of sources prevents us from illustrating specific attitudes of Hungarian and Transylvanian

Protestants in the sixteenth century. It seems fair to assume, however, that statements such as those of Gal Huszar that: "Teaching the Testament meets no obstacles in the lands the Turks have conquered. The Turks treat those who preach it humanely," were not atypical.[17] Theological considerations notwithstanding, it is our belief that the lasting significance of the relationship between Protestantism and Islam is a function of political rather than ideological factors and, specifically, of the conflict between Habsburg and Turk.

It is a paradox that the Infidel Turk was, in fact, the probable saviour of Protestantism in Germany and the ultimate guarantor of Protestant interests in Hungary and Transylvania. The validity of the first contention, more contentious than the second of course, has been demonstrated—at least to our satisfaction—in one of my earlier studies on Ottoman imperialism and German Protestantism.[18] Indeed, we agree with Kenneth Setton's summary statement that "Without them (the Turks) Protestantism might conceivably have gone the way of Albigensianism"[19] with the addendum that this view should be extended also to the political presence of Lutheranism in Germany on the basis of the provisions of the Religious Peace of Augsburg of 1555. In brief, it seems fair to argue that the entire course of the Protestant Reformation in Germany would have been different had Charles and Ferdinand of Habsburg assigned priority to German affairs over the consolidating of their family inheritance threatened, *inter alia*, by Ottoman imperialism.

The Turks, together with the French, were the principal opponents of Habsburg hegemony in Europe in the first half of the sixteenth century. As an Eastern power expanding westward, the Ottoman Turks came into conflict with a Western power expanding eastward. The unavoidable clash occurred over Hungary, the coveted state separating the Habsburg and Ottoman empires. The struggle for Hungary continued virtually without intermission since 1526. Its most dramatic manifestations were the sieges of Vienna in 1529 and Güns in 1532. It also took the form of Turkish military action in 1541, 1543, and 1552 and in skirmishes at frequent intervals. More significant than military activity *per se* was its ultimate cause: Ottoman rejection of Habsburg claims to Hungary. As long as this situation existed, as long as the Porte supported such rival claimants as John

Zápolya or John Sigismund or assumed direct control over central Hungary as it did in 1541, the conflict between Habsburg and Turk was bound to continue. While centering on Hungary the conflict between the two powers expanded as the century progressed. As a naval power in the Mediterranean in the early thirties, the Turks challenged Habsburg supremacy in North Africa and west of the Adriatic; as allies of Francis I after 1535 they fomented political instability in Western Europe and made Charles' imperial plans more and more illusory.

The Protestants readily linked the problems presented to the Habsburgs by direct and indirect Ottoman aggression with their struggle for survival, consolidation, and expansion in Germany. Most significantly, they utilized the Habsburg dependence on German assistance for the protection of the Empire and the attainment of Hungarian aims to further their own cause. Almost all major concessions wrested from the Habsburgs since 1526 were connected with Ottoman activities in Eastern and Western Europe, and the all-important Lutheran campaign for legal recognition in Germany exploited the insoluble Habsburg–Ottoman conflict over Hungary. The Recess of Speyer of 1526, the Religious Peace of Nürnberg of 1532, the Compact of Cadan, the Frankfurt Anstand, the Declaration of Regensburg, the Recess of Speyer of 1542, the Treaty of Passau, and the Religious Peace of Augsburg of 1555—all milestones in the Protestant struggle for recognition and the course of the German Reformation—were deeply influenced by the ebb and flow of Ottoman aggression.[20]

To repeat, it is paradoxical that the success of the Reformation in Germany should have been so closely linked with the fortunes of the generally feared and despised Turk. But the Protestant leaders, despite limitations imposed upon them by theological restrictions and German abhorrence of the Infidel which precluded any direct contact with the Turk, relentlessly exploited the opportunities arising from the secular conflict between Habsburg and Ottoman. Their perseverance in pursuing such a policy accurately reflects the nature and importance of the Turkish impact on the Reformation. The Turks diverted the attention of the Habsburg from German affairs and made them dependent on Protestant cooperation for the realization of their secular ambitions in Europe, particularly Hungary. In our view then, the consolidation, expansion and legitimizing of Lutheranism in Germany by 1555 should be attributed to Ottoman imperialism more than to any other single factor.[21]

Whether these contentions bearing on the significance of the Ottoman factor in the survival and consolidation of Protestantism in Germany are generally accepted or not there can be little doubt about the validity of another clearly demonstrable contention that the survival and consolidation of Protestantism in Hungary and Transylvania was to a considerable extent a function of the Ottoman presence in Hungary and of the special position enjoyed by Transylvania in the Ottoman order in East-Central Europe.

As Béla Király has shown, the Turks created the objective conditions for the spread of Protestantism not only in Hungary but also in Transylvania in the sixteenth century.[22] The repressive anti-Protestant enactments of the Hungarian diet in the early 1520's which, in the case of Lutherans provided for their being "rooted out of the country and, wheresoever they be found, they shall be seized without restriction not only by the clergy but also by laymen, and they shall be burned,"[23] is indicative of the prospective fate of Protestantism in pre-Mohács Hungary. For reasons pertaining to internal factors prevailing in Hungary after Mohács, factors directly related to the Turkish presence and interests, Protestantism spread rapidly. In the late twenties already Hungarian students went to Wittenberg where they studied under Luther and Melanchthon. By the middle of the century the Hungarian school system was overwhelmingly Protestant. Protestant intellectuals such as János Sylvester, Mátyás Dévay Biró, István Szegedy Kis, Mihály Sztárai, and others exerted great influence in the country. They were unhindered in the conduct of their activities by forces inimical to Protestantism thanks, in no small measure, to the spirit of religious toleration evidenced by the Turks and their clients and proteges in Hungary.[24] And even if we take with a grain of salt Fessler's assertion that by the time of the death of Maximilian II in 1576 "Only three of the great families of Hungary were still Catholic" the fact is that the defection of the nobility to Protestantism— and primarily to Calvinism—during the middle years of the sixteenth century was a function of political conditions influenced, if not necessarily created, by the Turkish presence.[25]

This is all the more evident in Transylvania where, in the sixteenth century, Protestantism flourished perhaps to a greater degree than anywhere else in Europe. Recapitulating only the most significant legal enactments and activities of Protestant leaders it should be noted that Transylvania was in the forefront of religious tolerance from as early as the middle of the century. The Diet of Torda granted the Lutherans freedom of worship in 1550 and in 1557 the same diet recognized the Lutheran church as an "accepted religion." In 1564 the Diet of Torda recognized the Calvinist church as an "accepted religion" and in 1568 the diet legislated universal and complete freedom of worship. This unusual tolerance allowed the unhindered preaching of such distinguished Protestant theologians as Johannes Honterus, who spread Lutheranism among the Saxons, and of Dávid and Blandrata, who founded the most famous of the Unitarian Churches in Europe at Klausenburg in 1556.[26]

Our ending this review of interrelationships between Protestantism and Islam sometime before the end of the sixteenth century seems justified by the fact that by that time legal recognition had been extended to Protestants in countries and areas affected directly or indirectly by Turkish political actions. Relations between Protestantism and Islam and between Protestants and Turks after legalization transcend the scope of our study and do in fact constitute a chapter in the history of interstatal relationships except for such problems as were created by the spread of Protestantism into the Ottoman Empire itself in the seventeenth and later centuries.[27] Still, the relationships between Protestantism and Islam were most significant in the heroic age of confrontation and consolidation on which we focussed our discussion. It is evident that the political fortunes of the Protestants in Germany, Hungary, and Transylvania were intimately related to Turkish action. The very survival and expansion of Protestantism, in various denominations, may very well have been a function of two interrelated aspects of Ottoman-Islamic imperialism: military action and religious toleration. It is uncertain whether actual fear of Turkish military power was ultimately responsible for the numerous concessions made by the Habsburgs to the German Lutherans. It is also doubtful whether genuine fear of Islam, as a spreading heresy carried by the force of Turkish arms, prevailed in Germany or for that matter in

Hungary, Transylvania, or elsewhere in Eastern and Central Europe during the sixteenth century. The record of Ottoman conquests and religious policies may have been known only by a few men or women of Germany but it was definitely known by the Habsburgs and by many a Hungarian leader. And that record was essentially favorable to the Turks and Islam. Yet the distortion of the character of the Turkish and Mohammedan threat to European Christendom was an essential part of the rationale for political and theological action by Catholics and Protestants alike in Germany and, albeit to a lesser degree, in Hungary as well. The cogency of Luther's theological argumentation particularly with regard to the Papacy would have been even less coherent, and certainly less persuasive, without the equating of Turk and Pope. The exhortations for financial and military assistance for the realization of the imperial designs of the Habsburgs would also have been less persuasive without reference to the Infidel. And it was precisely this negativism, theological and political, which facilitated the attainment of the aims of the antagonists in Germany in the long years which elapsed from the nailing of the Ninety-five Theses to the Religious Peace of Augsburg.

Anti-Turkish propaganda was less evident in Hungary and Transylvania reflecting awareness of the interrelationship of favorable Turkish policies and the status of Protestantism. Adoption of theological arguments enunciated by Luther and his disciples were *de rigueur* among Lutherans but, apparently, were toned down or used *in camera* only by beneficiaries of direct or indirect Turkish largesse. And, to our knowledge, theological tracts and pronouncements by Hungarian Calvinists or Transylvanian Unitarians were hardly concerned with anti-Islamic polemics.

It may very well be asked what was the actual doctrinal and political significance of German, Hungarian, and Transylvanian Protestantism in the history of Eastern Europe and of Ottoman–European relations in the sixteenth century. Tentatively, we would tend to conclude that theologically the significance was of secondary importance. It was also of secondary importance politically being, as it was, a function of the ultimate confrontation between Hasburg and Turk.

NOTES

1. The most comprehensive general statement on this problem is by K. M. Setton, "Lutheranism and the Turkish Peril," *Balkan Studies*, 3 (1962), pp. 113–168 with ample bibliographical references.

2. N. Daniel, *Islam and the West: The Making of an Image*, Edinburgh, 1960, pp. 5–6.

3. M. T. d'Alverny and G. Vajda, "Marc du Tolede, Traducteur d'ibn Tumart," *Al-Andalūs*, 16 (1951), p. 118. *See also* R. W. Southern, *Western Views of Islam in the Middle Ages*, Cambridge, 1962, pp. 22–24.

4. D. C. Munro, "Western Attitudes Toward Islam During the Crusades," *Speculum* 6 (1931), p. 329.

5. For a detailed discussion of the works of the Cluniac school and the Latin texts of Peter's two books *see* James Kritzeck, *Peter the Venerable*, Princeton, 1964.

6. Setton, *Lutheranism*, pp. 148 ff.

7. *Idem.*, pp. 152–56.

8. *Idem.*, pp. 154–55.

9. Th. Bibliander, *Machumetis Saracenorum Principis, Eiusque Successorem Vitae, Doctrina, Ac Ipse Alcoran*, Zurich, 1550.

10. M. Sutcliffe, *De Turcopapismo*, London, 1599.

11. Setton, *Lutheranism*, p. 167.

12. The best account is by J. Pannier, "Calvin et les Turcs," *Revue Historique*, 180 (1937), pp. 268–286.

13. *Idem.*, pp. 282–85.

14. *See* particularly P. Coles, *The Ottoman Impact on Europe*, New York, 1968, pp. 145–58.

15. S. Fischer-Galati, "Judeo-Christian Aspects of *Pax Ottomanica*," B. K. Király, ed., *Tolerance and Movements of Religious Dissent in Eastern Europe*, Boulder–New York, 1975, pp. 189 ff.

16. For these and comparable views *see* C. D. Rouillard, *The Turk in French History, Thought, and Literature, 1520–1660*, Paris, 1938, pp. 397–98 and 412–13.

17. B. K. Király, "The Sublime Porte, Vienna, Transylvania and the Dissemination of Protestant Reformation in Royal Hungary," Király, ed., *Tolerance*, p. 202.

18. S. A. Fischer-Galati, *Ottoman Imperialism and German Protestantism, 1521–1555*, Cambridge, 1959.

19. Setton, *Lutheranism*, p. 133.

20. Fischer-Galati, *Ottoman Imperialism* is devoted to this specific set of problems.

21. *Idem.*, pp. 111–17.

22. Király, *The Sublime Porte*, pp. 199 ff. *See also* C. M. Körtepeter, *Ottoman Imperialism During the Reformation: Europe and the Caucasus,* New York, 1972, pp. 123–30.

23. Király, *The Sublime Porte*, p. 202.

24. *Idem.*, pp. 202–204.

25. Fessler's views and other interesting materials are contained in R. W. Seton-Watson, *A History of the Roumanians*, Cambridge, 1934, pp. 107 ff.

26. Király, *The Sublime Porte*, pp. 204-205; Körtepeter, *Ottoman Im-*

perialism, pp. 125–27; Seton-Watson, *History of the Roumanians*, pp. 107–109.
27. Important issues relative to Turkish actions have been raised in H. Inalcık, "Ottoman Methods of Conquest," *Studia Islamica* 2, pp. 103–29.

D. A. Rustow

WESTERN NATIONALISM AND THE OTTOMAN EMPIRE

In the late fifteenth and early sixteenth centuries, there was a large-scale exodus of Sephardic Jews from Spain and Portugal to Istanbul and other cities of the Ottoman Empire. In the Iberian peninsula, now fully conquered by Christian arms, Jews (as well as Muslims) had a choice of forced conversion, persecution by the inquisition often resulting in death at the stake—or emigration. In the Ottoman Empire they were cordially received and encouraged to preserve and develop their religious-communal organization, as did Orthodox Greeks, Armenian Gregorians, and other non-Muslim subjects of the Sultan. Sultan Süleyman is said to have commented on the perversity of the king of Spain who deprived himself deliberately of the services of some of his most industrious subjects and let him, his archrival the Sultan, reap the benefits—and this for no better reason than the Spanish king's religious fanaticism.

In 1878, Prince Otto von Bismarck, who shared the habit of most of his European contemporaries of thinking of the Ottomans as "Turks" and as Asiatic, Muslim, and backward, was surprised to find that the Ottoman delegation to the Congress of Berlin was headed by Karatodori Pasha, an orthodox Greek, and Mehmed Ali Pasha, a native of the city of Magdeburg, not far from Bismarck's own estate of Schönhausen. Nor were Karatodori and Mehmed Ali untypical. The Ottoman foreign service had its origin in the traditional office of the Chief Translator (Tercüman or Dragoman) which handled the Sultan's correspondence with European rulers and was staffed mostly by Greek families associated with the Patriarchate at Phanar, the main Greek quarter of Istanbul. And Mehmed Ali Pasha was one of the small but steady and prominent group of individual immigrants who escaped various personal misfortunes in their European home countries by journeying to Istanbul, espousing Islam, and taking the Sultan's service. The best known of these individual converts was Ibrahim Müteferrika, a Hungarian Christian, who in 1727 established the first Turkish printing press in Istanbul. Müteferrika's problem seems to have been that he was a Unitarian in Catholic Hungary. Mehmed Ali's problem was not religious but genealogical—he was born as the illegitimate son of a German washerwoman and a French soldier of Napoleon's army of occupation.

Five years before the Congress of Berlin, the Ottoman authorities of Istanbul banned a patriotic play, called *The Fatherland or Silistria,* that celebrated the selfsacrifice of a young officer in the defense of a Romanian frontier fortress against the Tsar's armies, and condemned its author, Namık Kemal, to three years of banishment.

Half a century later, in the summer of 1919, the last Ottoman parliament appointed a committee of investigation to look into the circumstances of the Ottoman Empire's fatal entry into the First World War. One of the committee's more vocal members was Raghib Nashashibi, head of one of the leading Arab families of Jerusalem. The Ottoman cabinet of 1914, whose policies the committee was investigating, had been headed by Said Halim Pasha, member of a younger branch of the Egyptian (and Albanian-descended) Khedivial dynasty.

On May 1 of 1920, the newly convened Grand National Assembly at Ankara faced a tense moment as its Commissioner of Health made an eloquent bid for more generous appropriations for public health. "If there is no health left, if there are no Turks left, we cannot undertake anything else with these Turks." the commissioner explained. "To preserve Turks we must first of all preserve health." This elicited an angry intervention from an Anatolian deputy of Circassian origin, who emphasized that Circassians, Chechens, Kurds, Lazes, and other ethnic groups were equally entitled to measures of public health. "Let us not speak of Turks," the deputy implored his colleagues, "let us speak of Muslims, or let us even speak of Ottomans; that is enough." The incident was closed with an earnest plea from the presiding officer, Mustafa Kemal Pasha, the later Atatürk, who stated for the record: "The concerns of this high assembly, and the members who compose it, are not only Turks, not only Circassians, not only Kurds, not only Lazes. They are the Muslim elements comprising all of these, a sincere community . . ."

The five episodes which I have selected all illustrate a basic historic truth still insufficiently appreciated by Western observers. The realm of the Ottoman sultans was not a "Turkish" empire; the members of its ruling class did not think of themselves as "Turks"; and its demographic, economic, and administrative centers of gravity were in Europe and not in Asia.

From the fifteenth to the nineteenth centuries, the Ottoman Empire was the largest realm of the European Mediterranean region. Its capital, Istanbul, ranked with London and Paris as Europe's most populous city. In the sixteenth century it stretched from Algiers to Baku and from Budapest to Aden. Along with ancient Rome, with China, Russia, and the United States, it ranks as one of the largest and most durable contiguous states in human history. It was a multiethnic and multireligious state held together by the continuity of its ruling dynasty, the House of Osman (or, in Arabic, 'Uthman, of which "Ottoman" is an Italian corruption). Its administrative-military ruling class was drawn overwhelmingly from Christian converts to Islam from Southeastern Europe, native Muslims of the Balkans and Istanbul, and Muslims from the Caucasus. Only in the Islamic religious establishment were natives of Anatolia and the Arab Fertile Crescent predominant. Although the official language of the Empire was called "Turkish," it was a thorough mixture of Turkish, Arabic, and Persian elements both in its vocabulary and its grammar. As an ethnic designation, the term "Turk," until the beginning of the present century, was never used for the imperial ruling class but rather reserved, as a term of condescension, for the illiterate peasantry of Anatolia. Even the political dissidents of the late Ottoman period who came to power after the 1908 revolution, and who earlier in their European exile became known to their hosts as "jeunes Turcs," referred to themselves first as the "New Ottomans" and later as the "Ottoman Society of Union and Progress." The official name of the Empire, until its demise in 1922, was "The High Ottoman Devlet" with the word devlet meaning first dynasty and later state. Even the Assembly of Ankara did not call itself the "Grand National Assembly of Turkey" until 1921, more than a year after the public health debate recounted above, and the discussion at that time indicated some hesitancy in choosing between the name Turkey in the form *Türkiya,* an adaptation of the Italian *Turchia,* or in the Ottomanized-Arabized form *Türkiye* that eventually won out.

II

Nationalism came to the Ottoman Empire as a cultural import from Europe and a byproduct of Western military and imperialist pressures. It spread first among Balkan Christians, and here the official dates of secession and independence may be taken as rough landmarks for the conversion of key elements in the local political elites: Greece 1830; Romania 1856, Serbia 1878, Bulgaria 1908. Nationalism spread only later to the Christian Armenians, whose scattered pattern of settlement among Turks and Kurds in rural Eastern Anatolia and in towns and cities throughout present-day Turkey gave less hope of effective secession. And it was not until the second decade of this century that nationalism became the political creed of political elites among the major Muslim ethnic groups of the Empire—Albanians, Arabs, Kurds, and last of all Turks. The emotional and political support that these nationalist movements received from the Ottoman Empire's foreign antagonists is well illustrated by the careers of Lord Byron and of T. E. Lawrence.

But if European imperialism had furnished an important stimulus to nationalism on the Balkans and in the Middle East, the response of the Ottoman ruling class provided a further impetus. For example, a major item of the reform program of the Ottoman revolution of 1908 was the expansion of public schooling and the tightening of administration throughout the empire. When high schools were to be established in the Albanian region, the local population assumed that the language of instruction would be Albanian, the Istanbul authorities that it would be Turkish. The result was the rapid flaring up of a political conflict that culminated in the secession of Albania in 1912. In the Arab provinces, the sending out of a governor from Istanbul to the Hijaz became a major factor in prompting the "Arab Revolt" in 1915–1916 of the hereditary local potentate, Sharif Husayn of Mecca.

The harshness with which Ottoman authorities time and again reacted to stirrings of disloyalty against the Empire made a major contribution to solidifying national identifications and exacerbating communal tensions—the massacre of the adult population of Chios in 1832, the wholesale deportation of Armenians from Eastern Anatolia in 1915 and 1916, the public hanging of Arab nationalist conspirators in Beirut in the latter year.

The political careers of such figures as Karatodori Pasha, Said Halim Pasha, and Raghib Nashashibi, to which I referred initially, illustrate, however, that the conversion to nationalism among such groups as Greeks and Arabs was far from instantaneous or complete. Indeed, with the exception of the Arab parts of the Empire (where Syrian-Lebanese Christians made a major contribution to the emergence of national sentiment) the more readily obvious alternative to Ottoman imperial loyalty was a sense of religious rather than national identity.

Two further historic episodes may serve to emphasize this point. A British journalist who at the turn of the century served on the international control commission for Macedonia reports arriving in a small town and inquiring of the local elders as to the nationality of the townspeople. A few years ago, was the answer to the bewildered visitor, we used to be Greeks, but now we are Bulgarians. On further investigation it turned out that the Greek orthodox church, pressed by financial stringency, had recently cancelled its appropriation for the local parish priest, and the exarchate of Sofia, alert to its political opportunity, had replaced him.

The second and better known episode concerns the large scale population exchange between Greece and Turkey agreed upon in the Treaty of Lausanne of 1923. The effective criterion for the exchange turned out to be not the language but the religious affiliation of the population, so that a sizable Turkish speaking Greek orthodox group was transferred to Greece and several Greek speaking Muslim groups to Turkey.

The same religious basis of nationality is evident to this day in Turkey. The Ottoman Empire, particularly in its later centuries of retreat, and its successor the Turkish Republic, have frequently served as a haven for Muslim refugees—and these are, with very minor reservations, accepted as Turks regardless whether their original language was Turkish (*e.g.* Crimeans and Azeris) or not (*e.g.* Bosniaks, Votyaks, Bashkirs, Circassians, Muslim Georgians, or more recently Muslims from Sinkiang). On the other hand, no member of any Greek, Armenian, or Jewish family that may have been resident in Istanbul for centuries will identify himself—or be identified by others—as a "Turk"; although he will typically hasten to add in answer to a stranger's question: "Of course, I am a Turkish citizen."

III

It was the established policy of the Ottoman Empire to leave rural populations to their religious observances, their language, and their other local customs. In the towns and cities linguistic and religious diversity were reinforced by the economic facts of an ethnic division of labor. In its legal institutions, the Empire left the regulation of marriage and inheritance to the religious-legal authorities of each denomination, or *millet*. This was a natural consequence of the Ottomans' conception of the legal-moral as well as religious character of Islam: if the Koran and the Sunnah, as interpreted by the *'ulama*, settled such matters for Muslims, it was only appropriate that priests and rabbis should have corresponding jurisdiction in their respective communities. This implied that the Greek and Armenian Patriarchs and the Grand Rabbi were established officials of the Ottoman state—of a lesser rank, to be sure, than the corresponding Muslim dignitaries, but established nonetheless. It followed further that not only family law but any other legal disputes among members of a single denomination were settled by the authorities of the respective *millet*—and the well-known capitulations, formalized in the sixteenth century, were merely an extension of that pervasive principle of Ottoman legal theory to Europeans resident in Istanbul and other port cities. On the other hand, Muslim authorities were competent to judge disputes among members of different *millets*.

It may here be objected that Greeks, Armenians, and other non-Muslims were obviously second- or third-class subjects, since they could not hold office outside their particular *millet*s in the general government of the Empire. The example of the Dragoman's office, virtually monopolized by Greeks, shows that the factual premise of such a judgment is only partly valid. The conclusion, however, is altogether erroneous, because the broad masses of the Muslim population—rural Turks and Arabs, nomadic Arabs and Kurds—were just as firmly excluded from access to the general government—a direct implication of the theory and practice that made the administrative-military establishment an extension of the sultan's personal "slave household."

The sultans thus had compelling reasons for considering any form of nationalism or patriotism, even "Ottoman" or "Turkish" patriotism, such as Namık Kemal's, a subversive threat. Yet under the continuing pressure of European imperialism, secessionist nationalism proved infectious, and whatever countermeasures the Sultans' government devised were likely to spread rather than contain the infection. Proclamations of civic equality, such as the Rescript of Gülhane (1839) risked antagonizing not only conservative Muslims but also the hierarchies of the non-Muslim *millets*; nor could they be consistently implemented. For example, the principle of universal military service introduced in the 1840s, was violated in practice by setting a substantial exemption fee for Muslims and a nominal one for non-Muslims. What earlier had been tolerant religious-ethnic separatism among subjects now turned into religious-ethnic discrimination among newly-proclaimed citizens. And draconian measures of repression, as noted before, merely solidified secessionist sentiment.

In sum, intimate coexistence of Muslims, Christians, and Jews, of Turks, Greeks, Arabs, Albanians, Serbs, Romanians, Bulgarians, Armenians, Kurds, Circassians, and many others, was the single most characteristic feature of the Ottoman Empire throughout most of its existence. But what had been a major source of strength in the days of imperial expansion became a fatal source of weakness in the days of imperial decline.

IV

Why, we may ask in conclusion, is the tolerant, multiethnic, multireligious character of the Ottoman Empire so little appreciated not only by the general public but even among historians who specialize in other than Ottoman subjects?

One answer is that much of our historiography continues to be written from a parochial Western European perspective. From that viewpoint, the Ottoman Empire from the thirteenth to the

seventeenth century appears as an undifferentiated outside mass—
in such events as the "fall" of Constantinople in 1453, or the
breaking of the siege of Vienna in 1683. Only from the late
eighteenth century onward—with such events as Bonaparte's
arrival in Egypt in 1798 or British and Russian support for the
Greek uprising of the 1820s and 30s—does this Europe-centered
historiography begin to take note of internal conditions in the
Ottoman Empire. Only at this point do Ottomans make their
appearance on the historical stage—as the "Sick Man of Europe."
The distortion becomes even more pronounced where historiography adopts not a continental European but a nationalist
viewpoint. Ernest Renan once observed that a nation is defined
as much by what it chooses to forget as what it remembers.
Specifically, in the words of Bernard Lewis, Western scholars
have often "been influenced by the national historiographical
legends of the liberated former subject peoples of the [Ottoman]
Empire in Europe and Asia. These have tended to blame all the
defects and shortcomings of their societies on the misrule of
their fallen Imperial masters, and have generalized the admitted
failings of Ottoman government in its last phases into an indict-
ment of Ottoman civilization as a whole."[1] I might add that
even Turkish nationalists, who as residual legatees of the Ottoman Empire might have been expected to know better, often
found it convenient to join this chorus of obloquy—a distortion
only recently being remedied through the dedicated scholarship
of Halil İnalcık, Ömer Lutfi Barkan, and others.

A second answer is that the episodes of ruthless repression—of
Greeks on Chios in 1832, of Armenians in the Eastern *vilâyet*s
in 1916, of Arab nationalists in Syria during the First World
War—are more recent and hence more vivid in historical memory
than the centuries of relatively peaceful coexistence that pre-
ceded them. But it is appropriate to remember that if ethnic
suppression rather than tolerance had been the practice during
the first five hundred years of Ottoman rule, no genocidal conflicts could have occurred in the final century of the Empire's
decline. And here the contrast between European-Christian and
Ottoman-Muslim practices is particularly striking. No instances
of antisemitism or of mass persecution of Muslims are recorded

---

1. B. Lewis, *The Emergence of Modern Turkey*, London 1968, p. 22.

in Spain or Portugal in the nineteenth and twentieth centuries; the inquisition had taken care of all that long before.

European and American historians of the late nineteenth and early twentieth centuries used to deal with the Ottoman Empire mainly under the rubric of the "Eastern Question." But in the 1920s, Arnold Toynbee dramatically broke with that tradition by entitling his book "The Western Question in Greece and Turkey." The nationality conflicts that have endangered world peace from Sarajevo in 1914 to the Golan Heights in our own day are the essence of that Western question in what used to be the Ottoman Empire.

III. THE SLAVIC WORLD AND ISLAM

A. W. *Fisher*

SOCIAL AND LEGAL ASPECTS OF RUSSIAN–MUSLIM RELATIONS IN THE NINETEENTH CENTURY: THE CASE OF THE CRIMEAN TATARS

The Russian annexation of the Crimean peninsula, whose population at the time was predominantly Turkic and Muslim, opened a chapter in the history of the Tatars that is characterized by a number of important paradoxes. They derived in large part from the fact that the Russians did not consider this annexation "the conquest of a foreign land," but as a "reunification," a "reestablishing of Russian rights to its own land." During the nineteenth century, most Russians believed that:

> "The Crimea was in no way a colony because the Crimean land was from ancient times Russian land. . . . The economic development of the Crimea was accomplished by Russians, the towns were built by Russian workers, the fields were tilled in the great majority by Russian peasants."[1]

At the same time the Tatars experienced one of the most heavy-handed policies of Russification anywhere in the Empire. Yet it must be said that in the 1920s, the Tatars were among those Soviet nationalities who most successfully developed and maintained a system of National Communism which emphasized Tatar cultural and political identity. This paper will suggest some explanations for this paradox in Russian administrative, social, and cultural policies towards the Crimean Tatars.

Tatar society had been organized before 1783 in the conventional Muslim fashion. Tatar *mirzas* controlled more land and wealth than any other group. On their lands Muslim peasants maintained personal freedom limited only by financial responsibilities to the landowners. Within the Khanate, the Muslim clergy was responsible for the administration of justice and the system of education. The *mirzas* had been accustomed to a high level of political participation through their assemblies (*kurultays*) and offices within the Khan's administration. The Tatar urban classes were important, too, as artisans and merchants. Yet these shared their position with large Christian minorities, almost all of whom lived in the Crimean cities.

The disorders beginning in 1768 left the traditional social bonds of Crimean society broken. The Christians were removed at the instigation of Catherine during the civil wars before 1783; agricultural production had ceased, bringing Tatar peasants to a state of complete impoverishment; the economic foundations of *mirza* power suffered from the same cause. Only the Muslim clergy escaped relatively undisturbed.[2]

Russian administrative policy in the Crimea may be summed up briefly. The Tsars simply incorporated the Crimea into the structure of the Empire, and did not consider it a *corpus separatum*. The keynote of this policy was a disinterest in the Crimea as a "special region," different from the rest of the southern frontier. Tavricheskaia oblast' in 1784, then Tavricheskaia guberniia after 1802, included areas not historically part of any Crimean Tatar entity, and served political and economic purposes distinct from their Tatar inhabitants.[3] The peninsula lost its particular identity with the annexation; its Tatar population was diluted through territorial reorganization.

Just as in Catherine's other acquisitions in the south, so in the Crimea, administrators, colonists, businessmen, and noble farmers were allowed almost unrestricted access into what were often empty lands. New ports were built and beach resorts and sanitoria constructed to attract Slavic colonization. Although some efforts were made to bring Tatars into the administrative system, the obvious distrust between old enemies remained and most of the Tatar elite did not take part in local Crimean government after 1783. This was a result of benign indifference toward the Tatars, and more than any other factor, led to a rapid Russification of the peninsula.

Although the administration viewed the Crimea as a valuable

economic resource and an exotic place to live, it surprisingly had difficulty in persuading landowners and peasants to move there. By 1802, of a total population of 185,000, there were only 4500 foreign settlers and 8700 *pomeshchik* peasants on the peninsula.[4]

After 1820, the government was more successful. On the southern coast village and town settlement intensified and by 1854 there were more than 70,000 Russians in the Crimea and only 150,000 Tatars.[5]

Russian social policies in the Crimea were more complicated. At first, under Catherine, the government simply announced that the *mirza*s were the Crimean equivalent of the Russian *dvorianstvo* and granted to the Tatar nobility the privileges acquired by their Russian counterparts in 1775 and 1785. But by 1800 complications had surfaced in the application of these principles. It was soon discovered that Tatar categories of nobility did not correspond to those of the *dvorianstvo*. The years of war and invasion had so disorganized relationships between *mirza*s and land that the Russian governors could not decide which Tatars were nobles and which lands belonged to them. The *mirza*s also found it difficult to adapt to the new *dvoriane* organization and could not always perform according to the rules and regulations governing that class. They did not know Russian (which was used in all *dvorianstvo* proceedings). They felt uncomfortable sitting beside their former enemies (a feeling which was reciprocated). Consequently, they resisted attempts to fit them into the new molds.

The government had to create in 1802 a commission of *mirza*s and bureaucrats to attack these problems, to make some clear definition of Tatar nobility, and to apply the laws of *dvorianstvo* among the Tatars. The commission discovered that much Tatar land had already been seized and transferred to *pomeshchik* ownership, leaving many legitimate *mirza*s without land. Other lands had been vacated by emigrating Tatars who were replaced by Tatar collaborators, many not of traditional *mirza* rank.[6] After four years, the commission finally recommended that most of the Tatar nobility be assigned the title of *dvoriane*. But no attempt was made to restore lands seized from *mirza*s since 1783, and those with no land were excluded.[7]

Yet in spite of these recommendations, problems for the

Tatar nobility persisted. In the face of Slavic colonization and land seizure, Russian official distrust, and their loss of wealth since 1783, their power and prestige steadily eroded. Although Russian laws give the impression that the rights and privileges granted to the *mirzas* after 1784 were preserved and reaffirmed throughout the century, the fact that one edict after another called for the "introduction of *dvoriane* rights" for them indicates that they had not received or were unable to retain these rights. For example, an 1835 edict permitted (as if for the first time) Tatar *mirzas* to take part in *dvorianstvo* elections— this some fifty years after they were first admitted to that rank. And growing pressure on Tatar landholding was applied by an ever increasing Slavic population much better able to cope with the bureaucratic system.[8]

Despite these difficulties, some of the Tatar nobles did adapt to Russian principles and served the state in both civil and military capacities. By the end of the eighteenth century, there had been three Tatar Collegiate Councillors and five Collegiate Assessors. In 1784 Potemkin had created three Tatar regiments commanded by members of the late Shahin Girey's army which took part in the next Russo–Turkish war in the battle for Ochakov. Tatar units served also in the wars with Napoleon and against the Ottomans in 1828.[9]

The critical military test for the Tatars came during the Crimean War, fought on their land against allies of their religious and ethnic brothers. Although the local governor ordered the local civilian population transported from the coast and resettled inland for security reasons, Tatar leaders did not put up any significant opposition. In fact, the *Kadı* of Simferopol' ordered local *mirzas* to provide supplies for the Russian military forces. Tatar regiments served against the French and British. Partly in recognition for their wartime service, Alexander II created a special cavalry convoy regiment in 1863, composed of these Tatar *dvoriane*, for his personal service.[10]

Yet the Crimean War proved to be the "final straw" for the great bulk of Tatar *mirzas* who had been unable to adapt to Russian service requirements. Alexander II had received faulty information that the Tatars had collaborated *en masse* with the Allies. This, influenced by his hope of using the Crimea for large-scale agricultural expansion, made the presence of the Tatars a nuisance. When Alexander announced that "it is not appropriate to oppose the overt or covert exodus of the Tatars . . ., (and that) this voluntary emigration should be considered a beneficial action calculated to free the territory from this unwanted population," the "voluntary emigration" turned into panic and flight. By the summer of 1860, as many as 100,000 Tatars had left. Added to the earlier emigrations after 1783, this exodus left the former Tatar "ruling class" in ruins.[11]

The Crimea's population dropped to 193,000 in 1860. This development did not bode well for a future increase in agricultural and economic production, and the government decided belatedly to stop the Tatar emigration. By mid-summer of 1860, no more passports were issued to Tatars and threats were made that any Tatars who left could never return. Yet the damage had been done. A government investigator recommended at the end of the year that the government "rid itself of the idea that the Tatars were enemies of the state, a notion which had helped trigger the emigration." Yet the remaining Tatars had grown apprehensive about future government policy.[12]

Unlike the rural areas and small villages, the Crimean cities had been turned over to Russian and other non-Tatar peoples in the nineteenth century. Except for Bahçesaray and Karasu Bazaar, the rest of the urban centers became virtual Slavic and Greek/Armenian islands in a Tatar sea. It is not difficult to see why this happened. Kefe and Gözleve, which were important under Tatar rule for the economic role which they played in the southern trade, lost their function as the Russians built new port cities. The expansion of Sevastopol', Balaklava, Kherson and Odessa served to replace the old Tatar ports in importance. The new cities were built and populated by urban groups introduced by the government for military and economic reasons. The few remaining Tatar urban classes moved away.[13]

For Tatar culture, this development had serious repercussions. Before 1783, the Crimean towns had served the dual purpose of gathering and communications centers for the *mirza* stratum, and as the seats of Tatar consciousness. In the nineteenth century, without the catalytic effect of a Tatar urban life, the upper class found it increasingly difficult to maintain a separate culture. Only towards the end of the century did a new Tatar urban class emerge in the old Tatar cities of Bahçesaray and Karasu Bazaar, bringing with it the reestablishment of a national culture, quite different in form and content from what it had been before 1783.

The Russians had problems with the Tatar peasants too. Before the annexation individual Tatar peasants had been legally free. Catherine determined that Imperial interests would best be served if their free status would be preserved, yet found that she had to incorporate them into the Russian class of "state peasants" to do it. This created difficulties for Russian *pomeshchik*s granted titles to the peasants' lands. One local governor noted in 1823 that the *pomeshchik*, "receiving land with free Tatars on it, did not have the right to consider it his property. He could neither drive the Tatars away nor lay upon them the duties that he wished."[14]

This policy provided a motive for both *pomeshchik*s and bureaucrats to "persuade" Tatar peasants to leave for the interior where they would lose their legal status, and at the same time free up some land for serfdom. Yet the Tatars proved resistant and found that many of the local governors could be counted upon to protect them from illegal *pomeshchik* pressure. Alexander I's land commission found itself in the position of defending free Tatar peasants against claims by *pomeshchik*s for their inclusion into serfdom.[15]

When many peasants were removed from the coast during the Crimean War, *pomeshchik*s took advantage of the opportunity it afforded. They expended great effort to prevent the Tatars' return. Imposing higher taxes and duties on returning Tatars, seizing village water supplies, they forced many peasants to remain inland, or as a last resort, to emigrate to the Ottoman Empire. By this time, the government's policy of protecting the peasants had eroded, and the growing weakness of the Tatar *mirza*s and the strength of the immigrants made the peasants' exposure severe.[16]

In summary, the social policies of the government during the first two-thirds of the nineteenth century compounded the ruin and uprooting of the traditional Tatar social structure taking place prior to 1783. The *mirza* class was decimated through emigration and Slavic displacement; the economic basis of their position had crumbled. That portion of Tatar nobles which had become *dvoriane* were essentially Russified, thereby satisfying official requirements for "loyalty." Thus Alexander II could at the same time both encourage deportation and emigration and also establish "loyal" Tatar military units for his own service. The Tatar urban class had diminished in size and importance, being isolated in the two central Tatar towns, both outside the mainstream of Crimean society. The peasants, after an auspicious start, suffered a collapse of major proportions as a result of the government's policies during the Crimean War. It became clear that if a Crimean Tatar national identity or movement were to appear, it would have to emerge from a new configuration of Tatar society.

Russian cultural policy may be divided into two parts: towards the Muslim cultural heritage and then to strictly religious matters. Briefly, the Russians manifested utter disrespect for the Muslim Tatar culture. Since they did not really consider the Crimea a Tatar province, most Russians saw those monuments of Tatar culture which survived the annexation to be reminders of a backward and uncivilized past. Most governors and bureaucrats made no effort to preserve any architectural remainders of the Khanate period. Foreign visitors to the Crimea were horrified by the acts of destruction which they observed in all parts of the Crimea except for Bahçesaray. The cities, once the centers of Tatar cultural life, were now an exclusive preserve of the non-Muslims. Thus there was no practical reason to preserve useless buildings.

The first acting governor of the Crimea, Kakhovskii, ordered the destruction of many of the most priceless treasures of Tatar and Italian architecture. Later in the century, the traveller Haxthausen remarked that Kakhovskii had destroyed "the finest monuments of antiquity, amongst others a beautiful tower built by the Genoese, which had served as the minaret of the chief mosque in Kefe." Even Professor Druzhinina characterized "Kakhovskii as no better than his Mongol and Tatar predecessors."[17]

On the other hand, the Tsarist government paid extraordinarily careful attention to religious matters. Pursuant to Catherine's "enlightened" policy towards Islam throughout the Empire, the new regime introduced no religious persecution. Despite the fact that they were living under a colonial regime, the Muslim

dignitaries became a part of the regime itself. Regulated by the
government, receiving much of their income from the Russians,
they were supportive of the Tsarist system. From the annexation
manifesto which stated that "all Muslim clergy, existing in the
time of Khan Şahin Girey, were to remain in their positions,
and to retain their former authority," the government consistently
pursued a policy of allowing much initiative to the Crimean
clergy.[18]

Catherine had separated religious from civil matters, and
had permitted religious governance to operate on different
principles from those of social and political life. She had
established a "Muslim Committee" of Muslim dignitaries to
supervise religious matters, and instructed Russian bureaucrats
to keep their distance from strictly Muslim religious matters.
It was not until 1831 that comprehensive legislation was enacted
which put the Crimean Muslim establishment into a form re-
sembling other imperial institutions, yet even this edict differed in
important respects from similar laws regulating Islam elsewhere in the Empire.[19] Although much happened in the Tatar
Muslim community in the ensuing seventy-five years, the edict
survived with only minor revisions until 1914. After repeating the
philosophy underlying Catherine's decisions separating religious
from civil matters, it recognized the competency of the Crimean
Muslim Committee. It defined and enumerated all the positions
within the Crimean clergy, including the Mufti, his chief advisor,
the *kadıasker*, and the *imams*, *mullas*, and other mosque servitors
in each parish. Finally, it listed the *muderris* and *hocas* in the
local schools.

The top officials were to be selected in "elections" supervised
by the Department of Spiritual Affairs in Simferopol', and participated in by the upper level of the Muslim clergy, the Marshal
of the *guberniia* nobility, and the Muslim elders throughout
the Crimea. The Muslim Committee on which these officials
sat had within its jurisdiction all mosques, their schools and
tekkes, as well as all *vakıf* land.

This was an unusual document because it provided for the
maintenance of local particularism to a degree not pursued
elsewhere in the Empire. Its closest parallel was the 1822
Code of the Steppe, but the situation in the Crimea was not
comparable to that in central and eastern Siberia. Its main

effect on the upper clergy was to tie it more closely to the interests of the Throne, to recruit, in effect, the "clergy" as the major instrument of Tsarist control over the Tatars, and to create a gap between the clergy and the Tatar *mirzas*. The latter, it must be remembered, are experiencing a policy of Russification on the one hand, and exclusion from local politics on the other.

By allowing the Muslim clergy a monopoly over Tatar education, the government encouraged cultural traditionalism. Since Tsarism had effectively wrecked the secular structure of Tatar society, this policy ensured that the Tatars had no *social* defense against Westernism. The Russians insisted that only a sense of traditional religious identity remain intact. When in the great reform period the regime installed among the Tatars, as elsewhere, a *zemstvo* system and western schools, the predictable result was the emergence of an intelligentsia free of the old social structures, but still consciously Tatar.

After early failures, the government after 1860 competed strenuously with the Muslim schools for the loyalty of Tatar youth. It took measures to increase the enrollment of children of lower ranking Tatars in Russian schools whose number greatly increased after 1877 with the aid of the local *zemstvos*.[20] These schools and other local organs of the Crimean *zemstvos* were to be the source for a new Tatar intelligentsia. Here the Tatars became in time represented in positions ranging from schools staffs to sanitation workers. It is no surprise that the next generation of the Tatar elite would lavish great praise on the *zemstvo* movement.[21]

But the new intelligentsia was not from the start revolutionary in outlook. (Here lies the difference between the Tatar development and that in Poland, where the Russians encouraged the survival, until 1863, of the old social structure.) The first generation of the Tatar intelligentsia featured İsmail Bey Gaspıralı (Gasprinskii). Emerging from an impoverished Tatar *dvorianstvo* family, he began his education in the traditional village *medrese*. With the encouragement of a friend in the city merchant guild, Gaspıralı went on to first St. Petersburg, then Paris, to learn Russian and French, returning five years later to the Crimea in 1866.[22]

His origin from the class which had suffered most during

the century, his training in traditional Islamic subjects, followed by his exposure to what must have appeared as a somewhat fantastic society in Russia and France, led him to introduce among the Tatars the first internal challenges to their inherited traditions. Convinced that his own society was in danger of complete internal collapse because its traditions were too weak to resist political and social assaults from Russian pressure, he believed that only two options faced the Crimean Tatars, indeed the whole of the Russian Islamic community. The first was complete assimilation *via* Russification; the second, a renewal of Islamic and Tatar society through an acceptance of western (Russian) forms enclosing an Islamic and Tatar content.

Ironically, he felt that assimilation would be the inevitable result of permitting the Muslim clergy a continued monopoly over Tatar education. For their extreme conservatism and outmoded curriculum could not prepare the Tatars to resist Russification. Only an adoption of Russian educational and cultural methods could form a class of Tatars which would be able to retain the best of their own traditions. This put Gaspıralı in the awkward position of advocating the study of Russian, and the introduction of western (Russian) natural and social sciences into the curricula of Tatar schools. Only students who had mastered such skills would be equipped to resist Russian encroachment upon their Islamic society.

These views placed Gaspıralı in the company of such reactionary Russian officials and educators as the Curator of the Odessa School District who presented in 1879 a memorandum to Count Tolstoi which claimed that the government had been lax in its dealings with the Empire's Muslims, that these latter must be required to learn Russian. Gaspıralı of course realized the risks that such a policy incurred, a risk for the Muslims aptly reflected in Tolstoi's response that "the official aim of education for all natives must indisputably be their Russification and their merging with the Russian people."[23]

In 1881, Gaspıralı published his first important book, *Russkoe musulmanstvo*, in which he called for the total and immediate modernization of Russian Islam. He believed that Russia "would be one of the greatest Muslim states in the world," that Russia was the heir to the former Tatar possessions, and that sooner or later Russians and Tatars would enjoy the same rights. He was convinced that the government would sooner or later abandon its idea of Russification. He wrote:

"I believe ... that the Russian Muslims will be more civilized than any other Muslim nation. We are a steady nation, give us the possibility to learn. You, great brothers, give us knowledge. The sciences should be admitted to the Tatars' schools. ... Russians and Muslims will come to an understanding in this way."[24]

Two years later, Gaspıralı introduced his journal, *Tercüman Perevodchik*, on April 10, 1883. In its editorial, Gaspıralı wrote that:

Exactly one hundred years ago, on April 8, 1783, the small Khanate, worn out by disorder and bloodshed, was made a part of the greatest empire in the world and received peace under the patronage of a mighty power and the protection of just laws. ...

Celebrating this day together with all the other peoples (of the Russian Empire) the Crimean Muslims cannot fail to recall all of those good deeds by which they have already profited for one hundred years."[25]

In *Tercüman*, Gaspıralı called for a revival of Russia's Muslims through education. In his own school in Bahçesaray, he began a "new method" of education, in which traditional Islamic subjects such as the study of the Koran and the fundamentals of Islamic law remained in the curriculum in Arabic; but added to this base he introduced history, geography and mathematics in Russian and Tatar.[26] Gaspıralı was always careful to direct his followers away from political opposition to the Russian government. Convinced that an openly hostile attitude to the imperial regime would be quickly crushed, he argued that there was no contradiction between support for Tsarism and a striving for Muslim Tatar reform and national identity. Any struggle against Russia would be impossible and Islam would actually benefit from a cooperation with Russia. This view he most clearly expressed in his essay entitled *Russkoe vostochnoe soglashenie*, in 1896, in which he wrote that "Muslims and Russians can plow, sow, raise cattle, trade and make their livings together, or side by side."[27]

With the old Tatar elite gone and the clergy in the hands of the Tsarist government, Gaspıralı had to produce a new audience for these views. This he found among the Tatar youth, attending or recently graduated from Crimean Russian schools or his own "new method" *medrese*. Not all would accept his answers, yet all found it necessary to address themselves to the problems he voiced.

There were three chronologically different groups of Tatar intelligentsia which emerged as a result of Gaspıralı's efforts. Not surprisingly, the first was closely tied to the master himself, and like him, was not revolutionary. It accepted his ideas and joined him in pressing for cooperation between Muslim and Russian. Within the Crimea this group succeeded by 1905 in establishing over 350 "national schools," in which the languages of instruction were both Russian and the Turkic of *Tercüman*. These intellectuals were closely associated with the leadership of the Russian pan-Turkic and pan-Muslim movements which had taken advantage of the 1905-1906 disruptions to press for improvement for Russia's Muslim communities. This group supported Gaspıralı's desire to work within the Russian system, to participate in the new political institutions alongside of Russian liberals. Even the reactionary electoral laws issued for the Second Duma did not dissuade Gaspıralı from retaining his hopes for a change of heart by the regime when times became calmer. The law stated that "The State Duma, created to strengthen the Russian state, must be Russian also in its spirit."[28]

This attitude persuaded a growing number of Crimean intellectuals that Gaspıralı's dreams were unrealistic. And the Crimean clergy was putting more pressure on the government to remove even Gaspıralı's relatively harmless group from circulation.[29] This second generation of the new Crimean intelligentsia was more revolutionary in both form and content than Gaspıralı's and reacted against what it considered Gaspıralı's political inaction. They charged that he was a bureaucratic and monarchist reactionary and a "scholastic writer" totally behind the times.[30]

Led by Abdürreşit Mehdi, the new group called themselves

Young Tatars. Concerned with neither pan-Islamic nor pan-Turkic ideas, their attention was directed towards the problems of the Tatars living in the Crimea. Their political aim included an active struggle for the "national, social and political liberation of the Crimean Tatar people," which would involve an "active struggle against the statist autocratic system of Tsarist Russia."[31]

Mehdi, though, had not removed himself so far from support of the Russian system to reject his election as a delegate to the Second Duma, in spite of the harsh electoral law. In his only speech before the Duma delegates, he declared that:

> "Our misery proves that our riches are in the pockets of others, the treasury, the financial interests. . . . All (our) lands have in the past belonged to the Tatar people; all have now passed into the hands of others."[32]

The Crimean delegation to the Duma, and many Crimean Tatar members of the All-Russian Muslim movements in the next decade were more self-consciously nationalistic than Turks and Tatars from other groups, who to the end continued to speak in terms of pan-Islam or pan-Turkism. Some historians have suggested that the preference of the Volga Tatars at these meetings for cultural rather than territorial autonomy was a function of their not having an easily defined territory of their own. Yet the Crimean Tatars were in the Crimea a distinct minority by this time too, and it seems that the differences in approach were rather a function of the distinctly different social and cultural policies of the Tsarist regime in both areas during the century.

Finally, a third group of intellectuals emerged after 1907. In the midst of the Young Turk movement, it included most of the Crimean Tatar exiles in Istanbul. Led by Noman Çelebi Cihan, later to be an important Tatar leader during the revolution, this group called *Vatan* (Fatherland), worked toward the goal of an independent Crimean Tatar state. Its members engaged in continuous conspiratorial activity in the Crimea and by the beginning of 1917 had succeeded in forming secret nationalist cells in almost all Crimean towns.[33]

By the beginning of World War I, the Crimean Tatar community bore almost no relation to that which had existed in 1783. With the large number of Tatar schools pursuing a curriculum modernized under the direction of Gaspirali, a new generation of Tatar leaders was coming of age. Participation in Imperial political life in the Dumas and a close association with other Muslim groups in the Empire, had given the Crimean Tatars a broader horizon on which to view their own predicament. Yet their community was not a united one. The fact that those Tatar leaders most closely associated with the Tatar traditions, the Muslim clergy, were tied to the interests and policies of the Russian regime, forced the new intellectuals to search in other directions for their new identity. And in this search, many fell victim to the quicksand of western influences, in the process rejecting many of the elements of their past that were necessary for the national identity.

This does not mean that the Crimean Tatars were unsuccessful between 1917 and 1928 in creating the foundations for a national existence. Thanks to the peculiarities of Tsarist policy in the first half of the nineteenth century, which did the work of destroying the Tatar "old Regime," Tatar society and its intelligentsia in 1921 were more advanced in the national sense than many other groups in old Russia.

But there was a degree of shallowness in Tatar political life during and after the Revolutions of 1917 that was the direct result of the contradictions which a century of Russian policy in the Crimea had produced. The difficult questions which Tatar leaders had to answer in 1917–1921 were not unlike those which Professor Von Grünebaum identified as the stumbling blocks for Arab nationalists in the twentieth century:

"Not the perfecting of potential or heritage was the objective of the admission of Western influence, but the removal of what was felt to be an inferiority. . . . The question was not what to adopt, whence to select, but rather, what to retain, or perhaps even, was there in the traditional culture anything worth retaining?"[34]

NOTES

1. P. A. Madinskii, *Ocherki po istorii kryma*, Simferopol', 1951, I, p. 168. He speaks of the view held after the Tatar deportation in 1944, but the statement could have been written in the nineteenth century.
2. See A. Fisher, *The Russian Annexation of the Crimea, 1772–1783,*

Cambridge, 1970, for a detailed examination of these years of disorder.

3. *Polnoe Sobranie Zakonov* (hereafter PSZ), first series, XXII, no. 15,920; XXIV, no. 17,634; XXVII, no. 20,449; E. I. Druzhinina, *Iuzhnaia ukrania v 1800–1825 gg.*, Moscow, 1970, p. 174.

4. P. Sumarokov, *Dosugi krymskago sud'i ili vtoroe puteshestvie v Tavridu*, St. Petersburg, 1803, I, p. 158; S. D. Shiraev, "Pomeshchichi'ia kolonizatsiia i russkie usad'by v Krymu v kontse XVIII i per. pol. XIX veka," *Krym* 2 iv (1927), pp. 169–186.

5. J. Schnitzler, *Description de la Crimée, surtout au point de vue de ses Lignes de Communication*, Paris, 1855, p. 67.

6. F. Lashkov, "Sbornik dokumentov po istorii Krymsko-tatarskago zemlevladeniia," *Izvestiia tavricheskoi uchennoi arkhivnoi kommissi* (here after *ITUAK*) 26 (1897), pp. 28–29, and 90–102; *PSZ* first series, XXVII, nos. 20,270 and 20,276; XVIII, no. 21,275; XXIX, nos. 22,002, and 22,203; XXX, no. 23,325, and XXI, no. 24,349.

7. F. Lashkov, "Arkhivnyia danniia o beilikakh v Krymskom Khanstve," *Arkheologicheskii S'ezd: Trudy* 6 iv (1889), pp. 96–110; F. Lashkov, "Sbornik...," pp. 24–154.

8. *PSZ* second series, X, no. 8,676; other similar edicts are in XIV, no. 12,419; and XV, no. 13,304.

9. I. Muftiizade, "Ocherk voennoi sluzhby krymskikh tatar s 1783 po 1889 god," *ITUAK* 30 (1899), pp. 1–7; *PSZ* second series, XII, no. 10,862; A. Markevich, "Tavricheskaia guberniia vo vremia krymskoi voiny," *ITUAK* 37 (1905), pp. 6–8.

10. *PSZ* second series, VIII, no. 5,994; Muftiizade, pp. 17–18.

11. F. Lashkov, "K voprosu...," p. 160; *PSZ* first series, XXIII, no. 17,265; M. Pinson, "Russian Policy and the Emigration of the Crimean Tatars to the Ottoman Empire," *Güney-Doğu Avrupa Araştırmaları Dergisi* 1 (1972), pp. 37-38, and 45-47; Ch. Lemercier-Quelquejay, "The Tatars of the Crimea: a Retrospective Summary," *Central Asian Review* 16 i (1968), p. 19.

12. *PSZ* second series, XXXV, no. 36,297; XXXVI, nos. 35,063 and 35,126; XXXVII, nos. 37,859 and 38,307; Pinson, p. 55.

13. H. D. Seymour, *Russia on the Black Sea and the Sea of Azof*, London, 1855, p. 247.

14. Druzhinina, *Iuzhnaia...*, p. 236.

15. Druzhinina, *Iuzhnaia...*, pp. 69–75.

16. Pinson, pp. 40–41; *PSZ* second series, XXXI, no. 30,152.

17. Baron von Haxthausen, *The Russian Empire*, London, 1856, II, p. 99; E. I. Druzhinina, *Severnoe prichernomor'e v 1775–1800 gg.*, Moscow, 1949, p. 139.

18. *PSZ* first series, XXII, no. 15,708; I. F. Aleksandrov, "O musulmanskom dukhovenstve i upravlenii dukhovnymi delami musul'man v Krymu," *ITUAK* 51 (1914), pp. 211–12.

19. *PSZ* second series, VI, no. 5,033.

20. A. Markevich, "Nachal'naia stranitsa istorii Simferopol'skoi gimnazii," *ITUAK* 50 (1913), pp. 236–240; *PSZ* second series, V, no. 4,167; XXXIV, nos. 34,147 and 34,647; B. Veselovskii, *Istoriia zemstva za sorok let*, St. Petersburg, 1909, I, pp. 718, and 723.

21. C. Seidahmet, *La Crimée: Passé-Present, revendications des Tatars*, Lausanne, 1921, p. 54; *Sbornik po shkol'noi statistike Tavricheskoi gubernii* vyp. 2 (1903).

22. C. Seidahmet, *Gaspıralı Ismail Bey*, Istanbul, 1934. The best treat-

ment of his ideas is found in E. Lazzerini, "Ismail Bey Gasprinskii and Muslim Modernism in Russia, 1878–1914," (Ph.D. dissertation, Univ. of Washington, 1973), and his article *"Gadidism* at the Turn of the Twentieth Century: A View from Within," *Cahiers du monde russe et soviétique* April–June, 1975, pp. 245–277.

23. I. Kreindler, "Educational Policies Toward the Eastern Nationalities in Tsarist Russia: a Study of Il'minskii's System," (Ph.D. dissertation, Columbia Univ., 1969), pp. 84–85.

24. Z. V. Togan, *Bügünkü Türkili,* Istanbul, 1947, p. 551.

25. Cited in Lazzerini, "Ismail Bey Gasprinskii...," p. 17.

26. S. Zenkovsky, *Pan-Turkism and Islam in Russia,* Cambridge, Mass., 1960, p. 35.

27. A. Benningsen & Ch. Lemercier-Quelquejay, *La presse et le mouvement national chez les musulmans de russie avant 1920,* Paris, 1964, pp. 40–41; Gaspıralı found a friend in V. D. Smirnov, a Russian historian of the Crimean Tatars, who shared Gaspıralı's desires for Tatar–Russian cooperation. See V. Gordlevskii, "Wasilij Dmitrjiewitsch Smirnov, 1846–1922," *Mitteilungen zur osmanischen Geschichte* 2 (1926) pp. 325–33; see also A. Bennigsen & Ch. Lemercier-Quelquejay, *Islam in the Soviet Union,* New York, 1967, p. 41.

28. M. Szeftel, "The Reform of the Electoral Law to the State Duma on June 3, 1907," *Liber Memoralis Georges de Lagarde,* London, 1968, p. 331.

29. A. Krichinskii, *Ocherki russkoi politiki na okrainiakh,* ch. I, "K istorii religioznikh pritesnenii krymskikh tatar," Baku, 1919, contains numerous police records with Tatar Muslim clergy reporting about Gaspıralı's activities.

30. Bennigsen, *La presse...,* pp. 138–39; E. Kırımal, *Der nationale Kampf der Krimtürken,* Emsdetten, 1952, pp. 17–18.

31. Kırımal, *Der nationale...,* pp. 19–20.

32. Bennigsen, *La presse...,* p. 141.

33. Krichinskii, pp. 234–35; Kırımal, *Der nationale...,* pp. 24–25.

34. G. E. Von Grünebaum, "Problems of Muslim Nationalism," in R. Frye, *Islam and the West,* Gravenhage, 1957, p. 25.

J. Pelenski

STATE AND SOCIETY IN MUSCOVITE RUSSIA
AND THE MONGOL-TURKIC SYSTEM
IN THE SIXTEENTH CENTURY

A comparison between the relationships of the state and society in Muscovite Russia and in the countries of the Mongol-Turkic system* has not yet been made, nor has any scholar attempted to determine whether there was any influence of one upon the other during the sixteenth century. General comparisons between Muscovy and the Golden Horde and some evaluations of the Mongol-Tatar impact on Muscovy had been undertaken by, among others, N. Karamzin, M. Kostomarov, and, more recently by V. Gordlevskii, B. Spuler and G. Vernadsky, but their analysis did not extend beyond the first decade of the sixteenth century, i.e., the time of the final disintegration of the Golden Horde. With these notable exceptions, historians of Eastern Europe have tended to typologize the forms of government and the socio-political systems of Muscovy and the countries of the Mongol-Turkic system, and then to look to the West for similarities and differences. Most recently some historians have attempted to develop broader frameworks into which the Muscovite system could be integrated in order to detect synchronic structural elements in the states and societies of both Eastern and Western Europe. One can discern three distinct phases in the development of scholarly views and theories which dealt with the definition of Muscovite socio-political system and the comparison of this system with other, primarily European states, during the period in question.

The first major phase in the development of these scholarly interests was dominated by the historians of the critical, positivist, philological and juridical orientation, as well as of the social-institutional school, at the end of the nineteenth and in the early part of the twentieth century. After reevaluating the sources and rejecting many of the unfounded assumptions of traditional national historiography, they tried to define the form of government and the socio-political system of Muscovite Russia.

Of the theories pertaining to Old Muscovy, the most influential were those put forth by M. A. Diakonov, N. P. Pavlov-Sil'vanskii and A. E. Presniakov. Diakonov maintained that the form of "theocratic absolutism" advocated by Iosif Volotskii combined with the notion of unlimited autocracy formulated in the official Muscovite pronouncements became the basis for the new concept of Muscovite ruler's authority and characterized best the political system of Old Muscovy.[1] The only limitation of the Muscovite ruler's authority was traditional religious morality (*i.e.*, the Orthodox faith).[2]

Pavlov-Sil'vanskii came to another conclusion about the nature of the Muscovite political system. He characterized the Russian socio-economic system from the end of the twelfth century to the fifteen-sixties as "feudal,"[3] and regarded the last third of the fifteenth and the major part of the sixteenth century as the period of the formation of Russian estate monarchy.[4] Pavlov-Sil'vanskii's book received the immediate recognition it deserved. The views of V. Latkin, who wrote an earlier book on the institutional foundations of a hypothetical Russian estate monarchy, attracted little attention.[5]

Presniakov advanced the thesis that, following the incorporation of a variety of Great Russian ethnic territories, and in particular after the annexation of Novgorod and the Tver Grand Principality in the fourteen-seventies and -eighties, Muscovite Russia was transformed into a unitary national state, the political system of which represented a patrimonial autocracy (*votchinnoe samoderzhavie*).[6] The Russian state retained a patrimonial character until the latter part of the sixteenth century, or, according to some authors, until the end of the seventeenth century, or even the end of the *ancien régime*.

The second major phase coincided chronologically with the nineteen-fifties when the concept of a centralized national monarchy resting upon strong military foundations and a rapidly developing bureaucracy became very popular. This particular system was considered as the most progressive among the existing socio-political systems of the late Middle Ages and the early modern period, and Muscovite Russia was regarded as having come very close to the ideal model, even when compared with Western monarchical states.[7]

Finally, in the past decade, historians have placed less emphasis on the alleged superiority of the centralized, bureaucratic, and absolutistic monarchy and have attempted to establish institutional as well as constitutional, parallels between Russia and the countries of Central and Western Europe. The theory that, from the late fifteenth century, Muscovite Russia, while retaining most of the typical features of a centralized national state, was moving in the direction of a representative and even limited estate monarchy, and indeed has become one by the mid-sixteenth century is a striking example of this trend.[8]

It appears that most historians of Muscovite Russia have traditionally displayed a strong "Western" preference in their efforts to compare the Muscovite system with those of other countries, a tendency based on the assumption that, by the middle or the later part of the fifteenth century, alternative models had simply ceased to exist. Following rather uncritically the interpretations of Muscovite chroniclers and publicists, they have adopted the view that, after the fall of Constantinople in 1453 and the end of the Mongol-Tatar supremacy in the late fifteenth century, Muscovy had extricated herself from the traditional Byzantine and Mongol-Turkic dependence and influences and embarked upon a new and more dynamic course of socio-political development, similar to that of Western Europe. The evident neglect of Byzantine and Mongol-Turkic influences on the history of Muscovite Russia is probably the result of attempts to discover dynamic political transformation in Muscovy, despite the solid evidence for residual statism, stagnation, and even retardation. The latter revealed themselves in the continuous reception of traditional theoretical concepts and ideological justifications of rule from the cultural milieu of the bygone Byzantine Empire[9] and the belated acceptance and almost mechanical adaptation of institutional and societal models, as well as economic and political arrangements, from the Mongol-Turkic socio-political system (especially its Kazanian variant)[10] which was also departing from the historical scene.

The recent revival of the views of Latkin and Pavlov-Sil'vanskii on the institutional parallels between Muscovy and the

Western countries and especially the classification of the Muscovite political system as a representative and limited monarchy is indicative of the prevalence of "Western" preferences and also reflects the limitations of certain comparativist endeavors in contemporary studies of Muscovy. The view that reforms and institutional innovations in Muscovite Russia had resulted by the middle of the sixteenth century in her transformation into a new type of state on the Western model is not necessarily valid. It can be argued just as convincingly that Muscovite institutional changes and bureaucratic reforms from above were patterned on the Mongol-Turkic model and that they were instrumental in the evolution of the Muscovite system into a monarchical despotism based upon the service system of the *dvorianstvo* in Ivan IV's reign. It was precisely the establishment of this despotic form of government in the later part of the sixteenth century that prevented the formation of genuine estates and of a limited constitutional monarchy in Muscovite Russia.

Arguments in favor of the existence of a representative and limited estate monarchy in Muscovy have been based on the evaluation of the socio-political structure and the role of the *boiarskaia duma* (the Advisory Council of Boiars) and the *zemskii sobor* (the Assembly of the Land). It has been maintained that the *boiarskaia duma* was an institution that represented the aristocracy and shared power and political decision-making with the ruler, that it actually participated in the exercise of administration with the Grand Prince and, later, the Tsar and that more significantly, it limited his legislative authority.[11]

No conclusive answer can be given on the social composition of the *boiarskaia duma* until a thorough study is undertaken regarding the influx into the *duma* of elements of non-princely origin.[12] Evidence that power and decision-making were shared by the Grand Prince or Tsar with the *boiarskaia duma* is derived from a few references in the chronicles to discussions of important state matters, *e.g.*, the divorce of Grand Prince Vasilii III from his first wife, Solomoniia and the preparation of his political testament.[13] These references may, however, simply mean that a distinction was made between "holding council" (receiving advice) and making decisions. The view that the *boiarskaia duma* placed legislative limitations on monarchical authority is based on phrases in the Preamble to the Law Code of 1497 and the Preamble and Article 98 of the Law Code of 1550,[14] but these provide insufficient evidence for upholding the assertions of the "neoconstitutionalists." In the Preambles of the Law Codes, not only the *boiars* but also the "children" and the "brothers" of the rulers are mentioned: if we follow a "neo-constitutionalist" interpretation, this would suggest that members of a ruler's family could limit his legislative authority, which of course was not the case. These references more probably reflected a traditional patrimonial practice. Finally, the reference to the *boiars* in Article 98 has to be regarded as a curiosity; in fact, Ivan IV more often than not disregarded the *boiars* when he enacted new legislation, and the wording of Article 98 was not invoked as a precedent in the history of Russian law. The conclusion that can be drawn is quite simple: the *boiarskaia duma* was an advisory council, the members of which, in addition to giving advice, performed a variety of undefined and often ambiguous administrative functions.

Of greater importance for our discussion is the assessment of the institutional character and the functional role of the *zemskii sobor*.[15] During the sixteenth century, seven safely attested *sobors* were held (1549, 1550, 1566, 1575, 1580, 1584, 1598);[16] concrete data on the socio-political composition of their members are available for the *sobors* of 1566 and 1598, but the latter is of less importance to the present consideration. The *sobor* of 1566 was summoned to deal with problems arising from the Livonian War. Its membership was as follows:[17]

Sobor of 1566

Participants	in numbers	in %
Osviashchennyi sobor (ecclesiastical hierarchy)	32	8.5
Boiarskaia duma	30	8.0
Dvoriane (predominantly service nobility)	204	54.7
Prikaznye liudi (bureaucrats)	33	8.8
Torgovye liudi (merchants)	75	20.0
Total	374	100.0

Since the *zemskii sobor* has been compared to such Western institutions as the *Etats généraux, Landtag, Cortes,* parliament, and *sejm,* and its participants to the representatives of the estates, the first question that arises is whether one can justifiably speak of the existence of "estates" in sixteenth- and even seventeenth-century Russia.[18] The evidence is scanty. With the possible exception of the ecclesiastical "estate," all other Russian secular societal groups, members of which participated in the *sobors,* particularly in the sixteenth century, can hardly be classified as "estates" in the Western or East Central European sense of the term.

First of all, they lacked that developed political and corporate organization so essential for the transformation of a relatively amorphous social group into an estate. Second, they had no concept of a contractual relationship with the ruler, either as a group or as individuals, and they failed to develop either noteworthy ideological justifications for their own significance or a legal substantiation of their status in the fabric of Muscovite society and in the structure of governmental hierarchy. Third, they did not act as a corporate group when called upon to take part in the proceedings of the *sobors.* Finally, the overwhelming majority of the participants was not elected by its peers to act as their representatives: the *sobors* were summoned by the ruler to provide support in matters of crucial importance to the state. However, they had no prerogatives with regard to decision-making and no control over taxation.

What then was their model? Partly, it was the indigenous tradition of church councils, such as those of 1503, 1504, 1547, 1549, and the *Stoglav* of 1551. An even more influential model was the Mongol-Turkic *qurultai* (*khurultai, khuriltai*) (which had evolved from a family or tribal council into a more defined and structured "Assembly of the Land"), especially its Kazanian version.[19] The Kazanian *qurultai* is mentioned fourteen times in Russian sources: the first reference is dated 1496, the last, 1551. Interestingly enough, the terms used in Muscovite sources for the Kazanian *qurultai* and the Russian *sobor* are strikingly similar: *vsia zemlia kazanskaia, vse liudi kazanskoi zemli* were used for the former; and *vsia zemlia, vse liudi* for the latter. The function of the Kazanian *qurultai* and of its traditional Mongol-Turkic model was to deal with major problems of state.

The social composition of the Kazanian *qurultai* can be reconstructed from the sources. The *qurultai* of 1551, for example, was attended by high ranking ecclesiasts, the great *karaçi* (a Tatar council which bore some resemblance to the *boiarskaia duma*), princes and *mirzas*, and the *oglans*, (*i.e.*, landed aristocracy and military elite). Evidence exists that the social basis of the *qurultai* was broadened to include *tarkhans* and *kazaks* as well. Thus, it is quite apparent that in structure the Kazanian *qurultai* closely corresponded to the Muscovite *sobor*. There is also little justification to view the *qurultai* and the *sobor* as representative bodies of the estates or parliaments. Both the *qurultai* and the *sobor* can be more justly regarded as servitorial and administrative assemblies, which were called occasionally by the Kazanian khans and Muscovite rulers to provide formal appearances of the socio-political support "of all the land" for their actions and policies.

The striking similarities between the institutions of the Muscovite *pomest'e* and the Kazanian *soyūrghāl* and between the socio-political and military obligations of the Muscovite *dvoriane* (*pomeshchiki*) and the Kazanian *tarkhans* (and to some degree also *mirzas* and *oglans*) serve as further examples of the reception of the Kazanian institutional models and societal arrangements in Muscovite Russia. In Muscovy the *pomest'e* represented conditional landownership contingent upon administrative and, especially, military service for the ruler. The term *pomest'e* appears in the sources (Muscovite chronicles) for the first time under the entry for the year 1484.[20] The earliest legal definition of the status of *pomestnik* or *pomeshchik,* albeit pertaining only to land litigation, was made in the Law Code of 1497.[21] However, the development of the *pomest'e* into a specific type of conditional landownership contingent upon military service took place gradually during the first half of the sixteenth century, and was institutionalized by the military service reform of 1555–1556,[22] a decade before the *sobor* of 1566. At the end of the sixteenth century, the distinction between *pomest'e* and *votchina* (*patrimony*)[23] became less pronounced, and the *Sobornoe Ulozhenie* of 1649 was responsible for the further disappearance of legal differences between those two institutions, namely the *votchina* and the *pomest'e*. The Decree of

March 23, 1714, formalized the final fusion of the two forms of landownership and institutionalized their hereditary status.

The earliest historical parallel to the Muscovite *pomest'e* system was the Byzantine *pronoia*, a temporary, revokable grant of state-owned land, usually awarded for life in exchange for the obligation of military service by the landholder and by the peasants tilling his land.[24] The origins of the *pronoia* institution can be dated back to the reign of Alexius I Comnenus (d. 1118) and the term itself can be documented by 1162. The *pronoia* became hereditary possession by the middle of the fourteenth century. Another Byzantine institution, the *topion* should also be mentioned because, according to some authors, it was used to designate military service grants.[25] *Topion* is derived from the word *topos* ("place," "locality," "piece of land"), meaning in Russian *mesto*. The Russian economic and socio-political term *pomest'e* was formed from the Russian translation of *topos*. Although the terminological borrowing is obvious, establishing a direct institutional adaptation from Byzantium is more tenuous, partly because the *pronoia* underwent changes over time, but more importantly because Byzantium had already been conquered by the Ottoman Empire by the time the *pomest'e* was introduced in Muscovy. Furthermore, Muscovy tended more frequently to borrow its governmental practices and military models from those of the Mongol-Turkic system than from Byzantium.

It can be argued that the model for the Russian *pomest'e* service system, at least as it was defined by the military service reform of 1555–1556, was the Kazanian *soyūrghāl*.[26] Sh. F. Mukhamed'iarov, on the basis of the evidence found in the *yarlık* (charter) of Khan Sahip Girey (1523), has advanced a convincing hypothesis for the existence of "a conditional military-feudal landownership in the form of *soyūrghāl*" in the Kazan Khanate.[27] The term in Mongol meant "grant," or "bestowal" (*Lehen*),[28] and it was generally used to denote privileges, hereditary land grants and bestowal of offices in the Mongol, as well as Turkic, socio-political system beginning with the age of Chingiz Khan. The term *soyūrghāl* in the period between the fifteenth and the seventeenth centuries included both grants awarded to the military, as well as to members of other social strata, and grants involving large territories. In Kazanian society during the later part of the fifteenth and sixteenth centuries the *soyūrghāl* was understood to mean land grants contingent on military service to the ruler. However, these lands were regarded as hereditary and as exempt from taxation. Since the Muscovite military service system based upon *pomest'e* received its final form in the mid-1550s, *i.e.*, more than three decades following the granting of the *yarlık* of Sahip Girey of 1523, which attested to an already existing system of *soyūrghāl*, it can be concluded that Muscovy had ample time and opportunity to borrow this institution from the Kazan Khanate.

The *tarkhans*[29] were the principal social group which served in, and benefitted from, the institution of the Kazanian *soyūrghāl* and which can be regarded as the closest societal prototype of the *dvoriane* (*pomeshchiki*). The original meanings of *tarkhan* in Mongol-Turkic social vocabulary were "smith," "master," or "craftsman," but it could also designate a freedman. Already by the time of Chingiz Khan, *tarkhans* were exempt from taxes and various economic services; they later became a privileged estate or class. In the Kazanian society, the *tarkhans* constituted a privileged, landowning, and conditionally hereditary nobility which was exempted from taxes and most other obligations. The great majority of the Muscovite *dvoriane* with their relatively clearly defined obligations for which they received conditional socio-economic rewards were the obvious equivalents of the Kazanian *tarkhans*. Their participation in the *sobor* did not make them an estate, nor did it make the *sobor* a parliament.

The Muscovite service system received its tentative legal definition and rudimentary institutional structure during the reforms of the 1550s. It considerably strengthened the autocratic political regime. This system, which had survived in Russia for over two hundred years, had undergone some external organizational changes, but no substantial socio-political ones. It distinguished to a considerable extent Muscovite socio-political and institutional arrangements from those in East Central and Western Europe, and it represented the Muscovite version of the "Eastern" service model developed in Byzantium and in the Mongol-Turkic state system that had been transmitted to Muscovy by way of the Kazan Khanate with whom Muscovy had had an intimate relationship for over a century. This Muscovite service system also helped to prevent the formation of estates or other representative institutions and institutional barriers that could limit the authority of the ruler. Its implementation along with other reforms of the 1550s paved the way for the political and institutional legitimation of the despotic regime of Ivan IV in the period of the *oprichnina*.[30] It could not be resisted partly because of the new police forces which the ruler had at his disposal and partly because of the lack of limiting safeguards on the power of the ruler. Viewed against the background of institutional adjustments and bureaucratic reforms, the *oprichnina* can be regarded as a culmination rather than as a traumatic break with the past.

Finally a few comparative comments on the relationship of state authority as personified by the ruler, and the society: In the Mongol-Turkic system, the sovereignty of the state and the political authority were vested in the office of the khan; he was according to Mongol-Turkic political theory an unlimited ruler. When the Mongol-Tatars established their supremacy over the lands of Old Rus' which were then incorporated into the Horde's imperial framework by the twelve-sixties, the Russian sources began to translate—or substitute—the title of "khan" by "tsar," a Slavicized version of "Caesar," "Kaiser," "emperor"; by analogy, "khanate" became the equivalent of "tsardom," "empire."[31] This usage and, more important, the political perception that the khan's authority was that of a monarch with the status of an emperor were perpetuated into the late fifteenth and sixteenth centuries, when Muscovite ideologists and political protagonists of the Grand Prince's authority began to refer to him, at first in publicistic writings, as "tsar" and, simultaneously to try to obtain formal recognition of this title from East Central European and Western powers.[32] The final assumption of the lofty title of "tsar" by the Russian ruler and his imperial coronation came in 1547,[33] an act meant to signify the transformation of the Muscovite grand princely territorial state into an empire. It was not a coincidence that this move was made in the last phase of the Kazanian wars and on the eve of the conquest of the Kazan Khanate (1552).

The immediate political and ideological consequences of the Kazan conquest were twofold: Externally they can be seen in Ivan IV's assumption of the title of "Tsar of Kazan" and, somewhat later, of "Tsar of Astrakhan," additions to the title of the

Russian ruler which reflected a change in the character of the Muscovite state. Until 1552, it had primarily existed as a Great Russian state. By acquiring these new titles, Ivan IV acknowledged his succession to the thrones of the successor states of the Golden Horde and thus, by implication to the Golden Horde herself. Subsequently Russia ceased to be regarded as a single homogeneous country and began to be viewed as an empire (state of states) composed of a diversity of tsardoms, lands, and cities.

The annexation of the two Tatar khanates and the subsequent assumption of the titles of "Tsar of Kazan" and "Tsar of Astrakhan" by the Russian ruler were used by the Muscovite government to enhance its ruler's monarchical status and exalt his position vis-à-vis other sovereigns. They were utilized in the diplomatic struggles for the recognition of the tsar's title by other powers, especially the Polish-Lithuanian state. In like manner, Ivan IV exploited the conquests of the Tatar khanates as an argument in favor of his request to the Greek Patriarch to confirm his new title (1557). The Patriarch granted the request in 1561, but he used a different set of justifications, some of them based on Muscovite ideological claims resting in turn on Vladimir Monomakh's alleged acquisition of the imperial regalia from Constantinople. It deserves to be noted that leading Muscovite publicists of the seventeenth century, for example, Prince Ivan Katyrev-Rostovskii and Grigorii Kotoshikhin associated the foundation of the Muscovite Tsardom with the conquests of Kazan and Astrakhan.[34]

Internally, and this is more important for our considerations, the reception of the Mongol-Turkic concepts of a ruler's power and authority over his subjects had profound and lasting implications for Russia's political and societal development. While speaking about the concepts of state power and authority, one should keep in mind that the Muscovite reception was characterized by the dichotomy (duality) of Byzantine and Mongol-Turkic influences. Whereas the Byzantine model and imagery were used for ideological justifications and theoretical substantiations the Mongol-Turkic example was followed in practical matters (although also, in some crucial instances, with regard to the definition of the ruler's authority). The notions of supreme sovereignty and unlimited authority were expressed in Russian sources by the term *volnyi* ("free"), a paradoxical definition for the contemporary reader. It was applied to the Kazan Tatar Khan Mamut in the mid-fifteenth century by no other than the first autonomous Metropolitan of Moscow, Iona.[35] Following the assumption of the title of Tsar by Ivan IV, the term was used frequently by Muscovite bureaucrats and publicists.

The concept of a Muscovite "free" (*i.e.*, unlimited) imperial autocracy had very concrete implications for the relationship between state authority and those segments of the society that participated in the political affairs of the country (peasants and plebeians were in general excluded from partaking in political affairs). The relationship between ruler (and state), on the one hand, and the pseudo-aristocracy and service nobility, on the other, was characterized by extraordinary respect, obedience, and subordination of the latter to the former. The term used to denote members of elite groups in Muscovy can serve well to illustrate this relationship. In official Muscovite terminology, the highest official, or the servitor, was called, and referred to himself, as *kholop*, meaning "slave," at worst, and "servant," at best, at a time when in neighboring Poland-Lithuania, for example, his Polish, Lithuanian or Ruthenian-Ukrainian counterpart was conceived of as *obywatel*, meaning "citizen" in the modern sense of the word.[36] If a member of the elite group was only a *kholop*, it is all too easy to surmise the status of the average member of society. The theoretical foundations being what they were, the Muscovite ruler could rely on extraordinary authority to a degree known in only a few other continental states. He could easily dispose of his internal enemies, and his bureaucracy was never held in check by any effective countervailing socio-political force.

Thus by studying the late medieval and early modern Muscovite notions and perceptions of the relationship between authority and societal elite groups, not to speak of the individual, at least some understanding of the longevity and extraordinary durability of Russian authoritarianism may be obtained. It is precisely this acceptance of state authority as the ultimate source of power, wisdom, and morality by the great majority of inhabitants of ethnic Russia that has decisively shaped the Russian political system, not only in the *ancien régime* but right up to the present day.

NOTES

* The term Mongol-Turkic system refers to the socio-political organization and the state form or forms which were developed in the nomadic (and later mixed nomadic-sedentary) Mongol-(Tatar) Empire of the Golden Horde which existed in Eastern Europe roughly from the mid-thirteenth to the beginning of the sixteenth century. The socio-political organization and the state forms in question were perpetuated in modified form by the successor states of the Golden Horde, that is the Khanates of Kazan, Astrakhan, Siberia, and Crimea, from the mid-fifteenth through the sixteenth century and, in the case of Crimea, until her annexation by the Russian Empire in the seventeen-eighties.

1. M. Diakonov, *Vlast' moskovskikh gosudarei* (*Ocherki iz istorii politicheskikh idei drevnei Rusi do kontsa XVI veka*) (St. Petersburg, 1889), especially Chapters IV and V; *see* also his *Ocherki obshchestvennogo stroia drevnei Rusi* (Moscow-Leningrad, 1926⁴), pp. 314–48.

2. V. Val'denberg, *Drevnerusskiia ucheniia o predelakh tsarskoi vlasti* (*Ocherki russkoi politicheskoi literatury ot Vladimira Sviatogo do kontsa XVII veka*) (Petrograd, 1916), pp. 351–52.

3. N. P. Pavlov-Sil'vanskii, *Feodal'nye otnosheniia v udel'noi Rusi* (St. Petersburg, 1901); *Feodalizm v drevnei Rusi* (Moscow-Petrograd, 1923²); *Feodalizm v udel'noi Rusi* (*Sochineniia*, vol. III) (1916).

4. Pavlov-Sil'vanskii, *Feodalizm v drevnei Rusi*, p. 155.

5. V. Latkin, *Zemskie sobory drevnei Rusi, ikh istoriia i organizatsiia sravnitel'no s zapadno-evropeiskimi predstavitel'nymi uchrezhdeniiami* (St. Petersburg, 1885).

6. A. E. Presniakov, *Obrazovanie velikorusskago gosudarstva* (*Ocherki po istorii XIII–XV stoletii*) (Petrograd, 1918), pp. 457–58.

7. The most forceful presentation of this view is to be found in *Ocherki istorii SSSR* (*Period feodalizma IX–XV vv.*) (Moscow, 1953), Part II, pp. 144–66; *Ocherki istorii SSSR* (*Period feodalizma konets XV v.–nachalo XVII v.*) (Moscow, 1955), pp. 101–47; 321–49. The following are the major scholarly works in which this thesis has been substantiated: L. V. Cherepnin, *Obrazovanie russkogo tsentralizovannogo gosudarstva v XIV–XV vekakh* (Moscow, 1960); Ia. S. Lur'e, *Ideologicheskaia bor'ba v russkoi publitsistike kontsa XV–nachala XVI veka* (Moscow-Leningrad, 1960); I. I. Smirnov, *Ocherki politicheskoi istorii russkogo gosudarstva 30–50kh godov XVI veka* (Moscow–Leningrad, 1958), and A. A. Zimin, *Reformy Ivana Groznogo* (Moscow, 1960).

8. For the origins of this reassessment, *see* S. V. Iushkov, "K voprosu o soslovno-predstavitel'noi monarkhii v Rossii," *Sovetskoe gosudarstvo i pravo*, No. 10, 38–51. However, more substantive statements on the problem of *soslovno-predstavitel'naia monarkhiia* appeared in print beginning in 1964: G. B. Gal'perin, *Forma pravleniia russkogo tsentralizovannogo gosudarstva XV–XVI vv.* (Leningrad, 1964), and also his *Genezis i razvitie soslovnoi monarkhii v Rossii* (*XV–XVI vv.*), Avtoreferat na soiskanie uchenoi stepeni doktora istoricheskikh nauk (Leningrad, 1968); N. E. Nosov, *Stanovlenie soslovno-predstavitel'nykh uchrezhdenii v Rossii; Izyskaniia o zemskoi reforme Ivana Groznogo* (Leningrad, 1969). The problem of the existence of a Russian representative estate monarchy during the period in question received renewed attention in the recent debates about the nature of Russian absolutism. In particular, *see* L. V. Cherepnin, "Zemskie sobory i

utverzhdenie absoliutizma v Rossii," *Absoliutizm v Rossii* (*XVII–XVIII vv.*) (*Sbornik statei k semidesiatiletiiu so dnja rozhdeniia i sorokapiatiletiiu nauchnoi i pedagogicheskoi deiatel'nosti B. B. Kafengauza*) (Moscow, 1964), pp. 92–106, and his "K voprosu o skladyvanii absoliutisticheskoi monarkhii v Rossii XVI–XVIII vv.," *Dokumenty sovetsko-ital'ianskoi konferentsii istorikov 8–10 aprelia 1968 g. Absoliutizm v Zapadnoi Evrope i Rossii. Russko-ital'ianskie sviazi vo vtoroi polovine XIX veka* (Moscow, 1970); A. Ia. Avrekh, "Russkii absoliutizm i ego rol' v utverzhdenii kapitalizma v Rossii," *Istoriia SSR*, 1968, II, pp. 82–104; M. P. Pavlova-Sil'vanskaia, "K voprosu ob osobennostiakh absoliutizma v Rossii," *Istoriia SSR*, 1968, IV, pp. 71–85; *cf.*, also A. A. Zimin, "V. I. Lenin o 'moskovskom tsarstve' i cherty feodal'noi razdroblennosti v politicheskom stroe Rossii XVI veka," *Aktual'nye problemy istorii Rossii epokhi feodalizma* (*Sbornik statei*), (Moscow, 1970) pp. 292–93. For a convenient summary of the debate on Russian absolutism, *cf.* H. J. Torke, "Die neuere Sowjethistoriographie zum Problem des russischen Absolutismus," *Forschungen zur osteuropäischen Geschichte* (cited hereafter as *FOG*), 20. (1973), pp. 113–33.

9. So far as the Byzantine theoretical influences on the Muscovite state ideology are concerned, the seminal study of the subject by I. Ševčenko has put to rest the lingering assumption that Iosif Volotskii may have been a Muscovite Machiavelli and that, beginning in the late fifteenth and especially in the sixteenth century, Muscovite political thought has reached new and original heights ("A Neglected Byzantine Source of Muscovite Political Ideology," *Harvard Slavic Studies*, 2 (1954) pp. 141-180; for additional use of Byzantine materials in Muscovite political documents, *see idem*, "Muscovy's Conquest of Kazan: Two Views Reconciled," *Slavic Review* (cited hereafter as *SR*) 26, IV. (1967), pp. 542–43, n. 1; and his study entitled "Agapetus East and West: Fate of a Byzantine 'Mirror of Princes,'" to be published in J. Pelenski (ed.), *State and Society in Europe from the Fifteenth to the Eighteenth Century* (*Proceedings of the First Conference of Polish and American Historians*, Nieborów, Poland, May 27-29, 1974) (Warsaw, 1978). While acknowledging Ševcenko's contribution to the identification of Agapetus as a major source of Muscovite political ideology, a number of scholars still adhere to the notion of its relative originality in the late fifteenth and sixteenth centuries. For some recent examples of this attitude *see* W. Philipp, "Die gedankliche Begründung der Moskauer Autokratie," *FOG*, 15 (1970), pp. 59-118; A. A. Zimin, *Rossiia na poroge novogo vremeni* (Moscow, 1972), especially Chapter VII, "Zemnii Bog"; E. Donnert, *Russland an der Schwelle der Neuzeit* (*Der Moskauer Staat in 16. Jahrhundert*) (Berlin, 1972), pp. 132-47.

10. For the most recent discussion of Muscovy's annexation of the Kazan Khanate and in particular the relationship of ideology and the politics of conquest, as well as the literature on the subject, *see* J. Pelenski, *Russia and Kazan: Conquest and Imperial Ideology* (*1438-1560s*) (The Hague–Paris, 1974).

11. For a comprehensive statement of this view and the literature on the subject, *cf.* Gal'perin *Forma pravleniia . . .*, pp. 39-55. A. Wyczański, apparently by following this view, made an unwarranted comparison of the *boiarskaia duma* with the Polish *sejm* (*Polska w Europie XVI wieku* (Warsaw, 1973), pp. 156-57).

12. For some data on the problem, *see* V. O. Kliuchevskii, *Boiarskaia duma drevnei Rusi* (Petrograd, 1919⁵), pp. 216-27; A. A. Zimin, "Sostav

Boiarskoi dumy v XV - XVI vv.," *Arkheograficheskii Ezhegodnik za 1957g.* (cited hereafter as *AE*) 1958.

13. The relevant phrases are: "... i nachat dumati so svoimy boiary o svoei velikoi kniagine Solomonii chto neplodna est' ..." and "I nacha zhe kniaz' veliki dumati s temi zhe boiary i prikazivati o svoem synu velikim kniaze Ivane, i o velikoi kniagine Elene, i o svoemu synu kniazy Iuri Vasilevichi, i o svoei dukhovnoi gramote," *Polnoe sobranie russkikh letopisei* (cited hereafter as *PSRL*), VI [1853], pp. 29, 270.

14. The phrase in the Law Code of 1497 reads as follows: "... ulozhil kniaz' velikii Ivan Vasil'evich vseia Rusi s detmi svoimi i s bojari o sude..." (B. D. Grekov (ed.), *Sudebniki XV–XVI vekov* (Moscow–Leningrad, 1952) p. 29); the relevant phrase in the Law Code of 1550 states: "... tsar' i velikii kniaz' s svoieiu brat'eiu i boiary sei sudebnik ulozhil" (*idem.*, p. 141); Article 98 reads as follows: "A kotorye budut dela novye, a v sem sudebnike ne napisani, i kak te dela s gosudareva dokladu i so vsekh boiar prigovoru vershaetsia, i te dela v sem sudebniki pripisyvati" (*idem.*, p. 176). For the literature on the various interpretations of Article 98, cf. B. A. Romanov's Commentary (*Sudebniki XV–XVI vekov*, pp. 334-37). A convenient English translation of the *Sudebniki* has been provided by H. W. Dewey (ed. and tr.), *Muscovite Judicial Texts, 1488-1556* (*Michigan Slavic Materials*, No. 7) (Ann Arbor, 1966).

15. The literature on the *zemskie sobory* is quite extensive. For the sixteenth century, the following selected studies ought to be mentioned: Latkin, *Zemskie sobory drevnei Rusi*; V. O. Kliuchevskii, "Sostav predstavitel'stva na zemskikh soborakh drevnei Rusi," *Sochineniia* (8 vols.; Moscow, 1956-1959), VIII, pp. 5-112; S. A. Avaliani, *Zemskie sobory, Literaturnaia istoriia zemskikh soborov* (Odessa, 1916²); M. N. Tikhomirov, "Soslovno-predstavitel'nye uchrezhdeniia (zemskie sobory) v Rossii XVI veka," in *Rossiiskoe gosudarstvo XV-XVI vekov* (Moscow, 1973), pp. 42-69; V. I. Koretskii, "Zemskii sobor 1575 g. i postavlenie Simeona Bekbulatovicha velikim kniazem vseia Rusi," *Istoricheskii arkhiv* 1959, II; Zemskii sobor 1575 g. i chastichnoe vozrozhdenie oprichniny," *Voprosy istorii* (cited hereafter as *VI*), 1967, V; "Materialy po istorii Zemskogo sobora 1575 g. i o postavlenii Simeona Bekbulatovicha 'velikim kniazem vsea Rusi'," *AE za 1969* (1971); G. Stökl, "Der Moskauer Zemskij Sobor," *Jahrbücher für Geschichte Osteuropas* (cited hereafter as *JfGOE*), 8, II (1960), pp. 149-70; "Die Moskauer Landesversammlung-Forschungsproblem und politisches Leitbild," in K. E. Born (ed.), *Historische Forschungen und Probleme* (*Festschrift für Peter Rassow*) (Wiesbaden, 1961), pp. 66-87; A. A. Zimin, "Zemskii sobor 1566 g.," *Istoricheskie Zapiski* (cited hereafter as *IZ*), 71 (1962), pp. 196-236; S. O. Shmidt, "Stanovlenie 'zemskikh soborov,'" in *Stanovlenie rossiiskogo samoderzhavstva* (Issledovanie sotsial'nopolitcheskoi istorii vremeni Ivana Groznogo) (Moscow, 1973), pp. 120-261.

16. Shmidt maintains that several additional *sobory* had taken place in the late 1540s, mid-1550s, one in 1560, and still another in 1564-1565. The last *sobor*, according to Shmidt, inaugurated the *oprichnina* (*Stanovlenie rossiiskogo samoderzhavstva*, pp. 120-261). Serious reservations have been entertained as to this extraordinary increase in the number of the *sobors* held in the sixteenth century (*cf.* N. I. Pavlenko, "K istorii zemskikh soborov XVI v.," *VI*, 1968, V, pp. 82-105).

17. The *prigovornaia gramota* of the 1566 *sobor* dates from July 2,

108   ISLAMIC AND JUDEO-CHRISTIAN WORLD

1566, and its text has been published in *Sobranie gosudarstvennykh gramot i dogovorov*, I (1813), No. 192, pp. 545-56. For the calculation of numbers and percentages, *see* Zimin, *IZ*, 71 (1962), p. 201. Zimin's categorization and his figures do not differ significantly from those offered by Kliuchevskii (*Sochineniia*, VIII, p. 26).

18. The concept was applied to the Russian conditions in a comprehensive but vague manner by V. O. Kliuchevskii in a course he offered at Moscow University in 1886 (*Istoriia soslovii v Rossii* [Petrograd, 1918³]). Its applicability in the seventeenth century has been recently analyzed by G. Stökl, "Gab es im Moskauer Staat Stände?" *JfGOE* 11, III (1963), 321-42; *cf.*, also J. Keep, "The Muscovite Elite and the Approach to Pluralism," *The Slavonic and East European Review* XLVIII, 3 (1970), pp. 201-31. For comparativist aspects of this problem, *see* D. Gerhard, "Regionalismus und ständisches Wesen als ein Grundthema europäischer Geschichte," in *Wege der Forschung*, II. *Herrschaft und Staat in Mittelalter* (Darmstadt, 1956), pp. 332-64; also D. Gerhard (ed.), *Ständische Vertretungen in Europa im 17. und 18. Jahrhundert* (*Veröffentlichungen des Max-Planck-Institut*, XXVII) (Göttingen, 1969).

19. M. Khudiakov was the first to raise the possibility of the influence of *qurultai* on the *zemskii sobor* (*Ocherki po istorii Kazanskogo khanstva* (Kazan, 1923)), p. 231. However, his comparison was restricted to the *qurultai* of 1551 and the *Stoglav* of 1551, which were not the best examples. His response to his own inquiry was somewhat enigmatic ("Vopros etot dolzhen byt' razreshen avoritetnymi spetsialistami" (*idem.*, p. 231)). Khudiakov's analysis of the Kazanian *qurultai* is a good introduction to the problem (*idem.*, pp. 184-88).

The Mongol-Turkic *qurultai* dealt with important matters such as the election or deposal of a khan, questions of war and peace, trade and crucial policy decisions. The *qurultai* was attended by heads of clans, prominent personalities, vassals, and service aristocracy or nobility (B. Ia. Vladimirtsov, *Obshchestvennyi stroi mongolov* (*mongol'skii kochevoi feodalizm* (Leningrad, 1934), pp. 79, 99 and n.6, 115).

20. *PSRL*. XXV (1949), p. 330; *PSRL*. XXVII (1962), p. 286.

21. *Sudebniki XV-XVI vekov*, p. 28.

22. A synopsis of the Decree concerning the obligation of service is to be found in the Continuations of the *Letopisets nachala tsarstva* ... (*PSRL*, XIII, Part I (1904/1965), pp. 268-69).

23. For a discussion of the meaning of the term *votchina* in the old Russian sources and the literature on the subject, *see* Pelenski, *Russia and Kazan* ..., pp. 76-78, n. 1.

24. For the classical work on the subject of *pronoia*, *see* G. Ostrogorski, *Pronija, Prilog istoriji feudalizma u Vizantiji i u južnoslovenskim zemljama* (Srpska Akademija Nauka, Posebna izdanija, knjiga CLXXVI, Vizantološki Institut, knjiga I (Beograd, 1951), especially pp. 22-23. *Cf.* also a review of this work by I. Ševčenko, "An Important Contribution to the Social History of Late Byzantium," *The Annals of the Ukrainian Academy of Arts and Sciences in the U. S.*, 2, IV (VI) (Winter, 1952), pp. 448-59.

25. G. Vernadsky, "On Some Parallel Trends in Russian and Turkish History," *Transactions of the Connecticut Academy of Arts and Sciences* (cited hereafter as *Transactions* ...) 36 (July, 1945), p. 34.

26. For a discussion of the meaning of the term *soyūrghāl* and the literature on the subject, *see* Pelenski, *Russia and Kazan* ..., p. 57, n.

112. Vernadsky mistakenly assumed that the Turkish *timar* was the closest parallel to the *pomest'e* (*Transactions* . . . , pp. 33-34). It ought to be pointed out that it was the Golden Horde and her successor states and not the Ottoman Empire that provided governmental and social models for Muscovite Russia.

27. Sh. F. Mukhamed'iarov, "Tarkhannyi iarlyk kazanskogo khana Sakhib-Gireia 1523 g.," *Novoe o proshlom nashei strany* (Pamiati akademika M. N. Tikhomirova) (Moscow, 1967), p. 106.

28. Vladimirtsov, *Obshchestvennyi stroi mongolov*, p. 115, n. 2.

29. For a discussion of the meaning of the term *tarkhan*, and the literature on the subject, *see* Pelenski, *Russia and Kazan* . . ., pp. 56-57, n. 109.

30. For the most recent reevaluations, and the literature on the subject, *see* A. A. Zimin, *Oprichnina Ivana Groznogo* (Moscow, 1964); R. G. Skrynnikov, *Nachalo oprichniny* (Leningrad, 1966), and *Oprichnyi terror* (Leningrad, 1969).

31. A. N. Nasonov, *Mongoly i Rus'* (*Istoriia tatarskoi politiki na Rusi*) (Moscow–Leningrad, 1940/1969²), p. 30 n. 2.

32. Muscovite diplomacy scored its first, albeit temporary, success by receiving the acknowledgment of the title "tsar," or the Western "caesar" ("Kaiser"), for its ruler from the real emperor, Maximilian I, in the anti-Polish offensive alliance treaty concluded by Muscovy and the Empire in 1514. The best critical edition of the text of this treaty, its German translation, and the commentary were provided by G. Stökl, in L. Santifaller (ed.), *1100 Jahre österreichische und europäische Geschichte* (Vienna, 1949), pp. 53-56. For the historical background of the treaty and additional documents, *cf.* J. Fiedler, "Die Allianz zwischen Kaiser Maximilian I und Vasilij Ivanovič, Grossfürsten von Russland, von dem Jahre 1514," *Sitzungsberichte der Kaiserlichen Akademie der Wissenschaften, Philosophisch-Historische Classe*, 43, II (1863), 183-289, especially pp. 196, 197-99 and n. 1.

33. For the most recent account of the coronation and the relevant literature, *cf.*, D. B. Miller, "The Coronation of Ivan IV of Moscow," *JfGOE*, 15, IV (1967), pp. 559-74.

34. For a more extensive discussion of the external consequences of the Kazan conquest, *see* Pelenski, *Russia and Kazan* . . ., pp. 299-301.

35. *Akty istoricheskie, sobrannye i izdannye Arkheograficheskoiu Kommissieiu*, I (1841), Nos. 67, 266, pp. 119-20, 497.

36. For a more extensive discussion of these problems, *see* my study entitled "Muscovite Russia and Poland-Lithuania, 1450-1600: State and Society—Some Comparisons in Socio-political Developments" to be published in J. Pelenski (ed.), *State and Society in Europe from the Fifteenth to the Eighteenth Century* (*Proceedings of the First Conference of Polish and American Historians*, Nieborów, Poland, May 27-29, 1974) (Warsaw, 1978).

IV. DANUBIAN EUROPE AND THE OTTOMAN EMPIRE

SERBIANS AND RUMANIANS IN
OTTOMAN SOUTHEASTERN HUNGARY: *DETTA*

As I already pointed out in two of my previous articles dealing with certain aspects of the Rumanian question ("The Rumanians of *Districtus Volahalis Tverd*," *AO* 6 (1974); and "The Rumanians of the *Districti Volahales Monostor* and *Sugya*," *AO* 8 (1976), the rich and minutious anthroponymic material contained in the sixteenth-century Ottoman domesday book *Mufassal 579*— dealing with the area of Southeastern Hungary and presently under our treatment—furnishes clear and irrefutable evidence that the fifteenth-century Hungarian *districti volahales*, though not de jure but certainly de facto, lived on as close-knit entities in the Ottoman setup even after 1536. A detailed explanation of why and how the medieval Hungarian administrative units survived under Ottoman rule is given in my article "Ottoman Toponymic Data and the Medieval Boundaries in Southeastern Hungary," *L'acculturation turque dans l'Orient et la Méditerranée*, Paris, 1977. And in a fourth article centering around the same problem, the question of why the Hungarian Valakhian districts had only a de facto and not a de jure continuation in their Ottoman equivalents is being dealt with in detail ("The *Jus valachicum* or *Eflâk kanunu* in *Transirmium*," *The Fiftieth Anniversary of the Turkish Republic*, New York, 1973–1977).

In decyphering the material serving as basis to the first two of the above-mentioned articles, *i.e.*, the articles treating the anthroponyms listed in the Ottoman *nahiyes Ferdiya, Şuydya,* and *Monoştor* (=*districti Volahales Tverd, Sugya,* and *Monostor*), I started with the assumption that, since that part of the *Mufassal 579* referred to a territory predominantly Valakhian in the fifteenth century, the personal names listed in it must be an Otto-

114   ISLAMIC AND JUDEO-CHRISTIAN WORLD

man reflection of Rumanian anthroponyms. A rewarding assumption indeed; my readings were easily born out and corroborated by the listings of Valakhian names given in the classic and yet unparalleled, but unfortunately much neglected work of K. Kadlec: *Valaši a valašské právo v zemích slovanských a uherských, S úvodem podávajícím přehled theorii o vzniku rumunského národa*, Prague, 1916. The anthroponyms found in Kadlec' listings on the one side, and in the listings given on the three *nahiyes* in the *Mufassal 579* on the other, show striking similarities: they are to a large extent South-Slavic name formations peculiar to *Eflâk*, that is, Valakhian areas, and only to a lesser extent direct Rumanian name formations; indeed, even Hungarian and Kipchak Turkic elements are not uncommon among them. A more detailed explanation of this colorful and characteristic spectrum of anthroponyms is offered in the first of the above-mentioned four articles, the one on *Tverd*.

The whole matter gains added interest if one considers that, while on the one side relevant Rumanian literature shows an obvious tendency to underplay the importance of the Valakhian question, especially when it refers to territories south of the Sava–Danube line (=medieval *Transirmium*),[1] on the other side the relevant South-Slavic literature tries to equate the same question with Serbian pastoralism,[2] and tends to look at the Valakhs south of the Sava–Danube line not so much as ethnic but rather as social groupings. Yet, it is in these clusters of Valakhian people that the true ethnic roots of the Rumanian people of today are mostly to be sought. Accordingly, the clarification of the matter is of considerable historical value and meaning.

Notwithstanding the colorful spectrum of Valakhian anthroponyms found in the listings of both Kadlec and the *Mufassal 579*, it is my contention—and to prove it is the subject of this article—that even when living together in the same settlement, the Serbians and Valakhians of earlier periods clustered in clearly distinct, separate linguistic-ethnic units, entities in their own right not to be mixed or confused with each other. The rich material offered by the *Mufassal 579*, coincidentally originating from 1579—a date close enough to 1536, the year when Valakhian privileges were brought to an end in Danubian-European territories under direct Ottoman rule,[3] so as to lend its contents considerable relevancy—gives irrefutable evidence to the correctness of this contention. The closeness of the two dates is of paramount importance since, as is shown in the fourth of my articles mentioned above, the article on the *Jus valachicum*, the cancellation of the Valakhian privileges usually, indeed, one might say as a rule, brought in its wake an easily recognizable slavicization and often ottomanization of the Valakhians living in territories under direct Ottoman rule, and above all in *Transirmium*, while in Transylvania, Valakhia, or Moldavia, that is in territories that were never under direct Ottoman rule, similar large-scale changes do not seem to have taken place.

From the profusion of settlements listed in the *Mufassal 579* in the relevant area I selected *Dite / Lovıran* (Hungarian: *Detta*) as one of the most informative ones on the *Eflâk, i.e.*, on the Valakhian question. At the time of the composition of the domesday book, *Dite* was a flourishing settlement with *derbent* privileges, privileges very similar to those granted in earlier times to the Valakhs. They consisted mainly of exemption from certain taxes in return for which the inhabitants of the settlement so privileged were committed to render public, *i.e.*, *derbent* services required in their immediate area. Among their obligations we find stage and postal services as well as the policing, in the form of auxiliary military units, of fords, bridges, passes, and other crossing points in their area. In other words, a closer look at the *derbent* villages clearly establishes them as the backbone of the Ottoman transportation system. If one were to plot on a map all *derbent* villages listed in a domesday book and connect the major thoroughfares they represent, one would be drawing a rough outline of the basic road system of that given area. And if one were to do the same with a row of domesday books of different areas, one would be able to establish by and large the whole "highway" system connecting the various parts of the Empire.

Located on the *Tımışvar* (*Temesvár*)–*Şemlit' / Vırşaç* (*Ér-Somlyó / Versec*)–*Haram* (*Harám / Uj-Palánka*) military route, at the crossing point over the *Berzava* River (*see* maps enclosed), in 1579 *Dite*, as already mentioned, was a flourishing *derbent* settlement with 2,380 inhabitants to the settlement proper. It formed a cluster with two nearby settlements: *Sredna-Dente / Vıratı-Gay* (*Denta*) and *Dolna-Dente* (*Kun-Dent*), totaling a population of 3,120 inhabitants in which *Sredna-Dente* figures with 58, and *Dolna-Dente* with 90 taxpayers, equaling 290 and 450 inhabitants respectively.

Very revealing in its setup, the *Mufassal* 579 lists the population of *Dite* in three well-separated groups:

1) Muslim district (*cemaat-i Müslümanan*): 37 taxpayers, *i.e.*, 185 persons;

2) Serbian district (*mahalle-i Sırf*): 269 taxpayers, *i.e.*, 1,345 persons;

3) Valakhian district (*mahalle-i Eflâk*): 170 taxpayers, *i.e.*, 850 persons.

No such division can be seen, however, in the case of the two other settlements of the cluster, which were settlements without *derbent* privileges. There our scribe simply listed the taxpayers without any classifications or qualifying remark.

In the *Çakova* Sub-county (*Çakova nahiyesi*) of the *Mufassal* 579 we find the following pertinent entries:

a) On pp. 121ᵃ–126ᵃ, after the city of *Ohobod*[4] and before *Mali-Selişte*:[5]

[123ᵇ]

94. Varoş-i Dite, nam-i diğer Lovıran.[6] Derbent. Vilâyet-i mezbure tahriri ferman olunmazdan mukaddem varoş-i mezbur derbent olup ayende ve revendenin karargâhı olduğundan gayrı Tımışvar'dan Haram iskelesine gider yol üzerinde vâkı olmağla üçer koçı tutup ve dokuz reis ulak beygirlerin beslemeğe mültezim olup ellerinde olan emr-i sabık üzere ve mezkûrlar derbent âdeti üzere kayıt olmasın rica eyledikleri hâlâ defter-i cedid-i hakani pâye-i serir-i âleme arz olundukta derbent âdeti vazı olunması ferman olunmağın mademki mültezim oldukları üçer adam ve üçer koçı tutup ve dokuz reis ulak beygirlerin besleyip ve her haneden yirmi beşer akçe ispence ve ikişer kile buğday ve ikişer kile arpa ve öşr-i şıra ve resm-i fıçı ve resm-i arus [ve resm-i] asiyapların eda eylediklerinden sonra resm-i hime ve giyah ve resm-i bid'at ve öşr-i kevare ve kendir ve kelem ve keten ve sair

[124ᵃ]

hurdavattan ve kale yapmaktan ve çerehor vermekten ve beyler ve ümena ve subaşılar hizmetinden ve bilcümle vech-i meşruh üzere tekâlif-i örfiyeden muaf ve müsellem olmak üzere defter-i cedid-i hakaniye derbent kayıt olundu.

Cemaat-i Müslümanan-i varoş-i mezbure.

SERBIANS AND RUMANIANS 117

Cami-i şerif-i Derviş Çelebi.

Abdülaziz—al-ḫaṭib, Hacı Piri—al-mu'addin, Bayram Abdullah, Ridvan—al-cundī, Demirci Memi, Murat Çavuş, Ramazan Abdullah, Hüseyin Abdullah, Abdi Mahmut, Mehmet Hüseyin m., Abdülaziz Nasuh c., Hüseyin Mustafa, Ali Abdullah, Ekber Abdullah, Sipah Mustafa, Muhyiddin Hoca, Mustafa—al-cundī, Hamza Abdullah, Şaban Mehmet, Mehmet Yeniçeri Abdullah, Mustafa Abdullah, Derviş—al-zaʿīm, Mustafa Çavuş m., Kurt—alnā'ib Abdullah, Ömer Hoca, Ahmet Abdullah, Arslan Abdullah, Hasan Abdullah, Memi Abdullah, Dede Çavuş, İbrahım Ağa, Berber İdris, Malkoç—al-rayīs, Turmış Reis, Yiğit Memi, Yusuf Abdullah, Resul Abdullah, Divane Ahmet.

Cemen: 38
Mahalle-i evvel: Sırf.

Pribe Pribiç c., Pavun veledeş m., Dimitre veledeş m., Lığıtka veledeş m., Radul Patkovıt' c., Peşa veledeş m., Radona biradereş m., Pavun Aleksa c., Jıvko veledeş m., Yovan biradereş m., Radona Radosalıt' c., Gruban veledeş m., Yovan Yakşıt' c., D'ura veledeş m., Yovan Boğdan c., Radıvoy veledeş m., Boğoy Radonıt' c., Mıhal veledeş m., Petre biradereş m., Vukaşın Petrovıt' c., Sımşa veledeş m., Vu[çı]hine biradereş m., Radul Dimitrovıt' c., Mıloş Yurısıt' c., Lubıc biradereş m., D'urat' Koyıt' c., Peroyıça veledeş m., Yaka biradereş m., Mirçeta Oliver m., Jıvko biraderzade m., Pavun Petre c., Petre biradereş m., Yovan Marınıt' m., Luka biradereş m., Çıraç Radul c., Sımşa biradereş m., Yovan biradereş m., D'ura Hlopovıt' c., Manolo Nıkolıt' c., Vukman biradereş m., Radona Duşıça c., Velimir veledeş m., İliye Nıkolıt' c., Tomaş biradereş m., Nıko Radıç c., Radul veledeş m., Vuçıt' biradereş m., İçvetko Mıloş c., Istoyan veledes m., Pradan Nıkolıt' c., Istoyan biradereş m., Radosav Veçerin c., Radıvoy İstepan c., Jıvko Radosav c., Radıça biradereş m., Istanısav Duşlaç c.,
Manoylo Mılaşın

[124ᵇ]
Manoylo Mılaşın c., Paval veledeş m., Vukovoy Radosav c., Rayak Boğdan c., Radosav veledeş m., Vukovoy Radovan c., Vuçıhine biradereş m., Istoyan Nıkolıt' c., Pavun Istoyan c., Vukışa Yovan c., Mılışa biradereş m., Mıladın Radul c., Adam veledeş m.,

D'okışa Vukmır c., Sımşa Radıovy c., Yaka Radosav c., İçvetko biraadereş m., İçvetko Vukotıt' c., Lazar Vuk c., Petar biraadereş m., Nedelko Nıkolıt c., İçvetko veledeş m., Pantalıye veledeş m., Petre Yovan c., Vuk veledeş m., Petar Bun c., Nıkola veledeş m., Petar Plafşa c., Yovan veledeş m., Matey Marko c., Petre biraadereş m., Yovıça Rayçetit' c., Radosav veledeş m., İçvetko biraadereş m., Vasıl Vuçıhine c., D'urat' biraadereş m., Radıça Marınkovıt' c., Komlen—kuyumcu c., Vukosav biraadereş m., Dımıtar—kojuhar c., Petar veledeş m., Simeun biraadereş m., Nıko Dimitrovıt' c., Vuk Prerad c., Yanko Mıokovıt' c., Stoya veledeş m., Voyıça Istanısav c., Voyıça Vukmır c., Radohine veledeş m., Radosav Nıkola c., Radıvoy Mıloş c., Dimitre—terzi c., Peyak veledeş m., Manoylo Dobretit' c., Istoyan veledeş m., Radohine—gırınçar c., Petar veledeş m., Dımıtar Lukıt' c., Yakup biraadereş m., Kosta—kasap c., Pantalıye veledeş m., Luka— kasap c., Istoyan—terzi c., Yoja Nıkolıt' c., Vuk Militen c., Ferençe Yakup c., Anatolı Latın c., Nıkşa Radenkovıt' c., İstepan—Kovaç c., Mıladın Yovıcıt' c., Istoyan Vuk c., Novak Istoyıt' c., Vucıhine Radovan c., Radul veledeş m., Istoyan biraadereş m., Radıvoy Prerad c., Nıkola veledeş m., Istoyan—gırınçar c., Matey veledeş c., Radan Vuça c., Vıtomır veledeş m., Beloş Petre c., Lupşa veledeş m., Vukışa Barnıcıt' c., Lubana Durıç c., Mıhal veledeş m., Matey Markovıt' c., Dimitre veledeş m., Istanoye Istoyan c., Dimitre Tomaş c., Nıko Dırman c., D'urat' veledeş m., Dıragomır Borçul c., Toma veledeş m., Lovul Dırman c., Nikola biraadereş m., İstepan Vuçınıt' c., Radıvoy Vuk c., Mıhaylo veledeş m., Nıko biraadereş m., Tafun Brayayaç c., Peşa Radıvoy c., Rakıta Radovan c., Damokuş veledeş m., Avram Yovan c., Yoka veledeş m., Bun Yaka c., Yovan veledeş m., Mıladın veledeş m., Peşa— terzi c., Yovan veledeş m., Yovan Mılkovıt' c., Subota biraadereş m., Marınıko Todor c., Dımıtar Botıt' c., Damyan veledeş m., İsteye veledeş m., Peyak Vukodırag c., Radıca Radıvoy c.,

[125ª]

Radulın Nıkolıt' c., Dan Marko c., Adam veledeş m., Beloş Baçıla c., Nıkola veledeş m., Lazar veledeş m., Por Mıkloş c., Durıç veledeş m., Boyın veledeş m., Petar Bran c., Oprışa veledeş m., Durka İstefan c., Paşkota veledeş m., Por Ferençe c., Lupul veledeş m., Yanoş biraadereş m., Dobrın Mıhal c., Yanoş veledeş m., Mıkloş veledeş c., Barta Mıkloş c., Petre veledeş m.,

Dan Dobra c., Vlad veledeş m., Toma Dan c., Petre veledeş m.,
Peyak biradereş m., Manoylo Yakşıt' c., Radan Dabıjıv c., Vuçıhine
Vuko[dı]rag c., Mılovan Istarhına c., Marko veledeş m., Radul
Pribit' c., Nedelko veledeş m., İstepan Istoyan c., Petar Todor
c., Toma veledeş m., Yaka Istoyan c., İçvetko Radonıt' c., Istanoye
Pribit' c., İstefan Pandoy c., Mıhal veledeş m., Yovan veledeş
m., Korneş Bakoy c., Petar biradereş m., Rumun Istoyka c.,
Balaban veledeş m., Kosta Yankul c., Kraçıl veledeş m., Yovan
biradereş m., Beloş İliye c., Yanoş veledeş m., Simeun Mıhal c.,
Durka biradereş m., Petre Markovıt' c., Mıhal veledeş m., Yovan
Kaçağan c., Petre veledeş m., Mıloş Tomaş c., Matıyaş biradereş m., İstefan biradereş m., Istoyan Radosav c., İliye Nıkolıt'
c., Jıvko veledeş m., İçvetoy Istefan c., Vukodarıg[!] veledeş m.,
Voyın Petrak c., Vuçıhine—terzi c., Vuk Istepan c., Mıhal An-
drıyaş c., Por Yanoş c., Petar Radıvoy c., Bun İçvetoy c., Vukovoy Karaçon c., Luba Vukosav c., Jıvko Nıkolıt c., Yaka Yovan
c., Steçul Kaçkan c., Doman Vuk c., Dımıtar Duşıça c., Radovan—
gırınçar c., Yankul—satıcı c., Rakıta Yovan c., Beloş Yovan c.,
Vuk Volkan c., D'urat' Vukas c., Rayko Doyıt' c., Radosav
biradereş m., Dıragoylo biradereş m., Darko Nıkolıt' c., Petre
veledeş m., Yaka Day c., Yovan Mıloş—müsellem ba berat.
Hane: 155.
3. Mahalle-i Eflâk.
Tıvança Yanoş c., Opre veledeş m., Tıvança Yovan c., Opre
Kapre c., İstefan Pribit' c., Dumitre Bradanel c., Prodan Ferençe
c., Petre biradereş m., Ruska Yanoş c., Petre biradereş m., Farkaş
Yovan c., Opre veledeş m., Yovan Vluko c., Mıhal veledeş m.,
Dumitre Opre

[125ᵇ]
Dumitre Opre c., Rumun Petre c., Bun veledeş m., Delje Yanoş
c., Petre veledeş m., Vuk biradereş m., Boğdan Vana-vinçe c.,
Dumitre biradereş m., Oprışa Şandor c., Mıkloş veledeş m.,
Mıkloş Gruba c., Istançul veledeş m., Faur Opre c., Drağıça
Dançul c., Petar veledeş m., Bud Baçul c., Tomaş biradereş m.,
Moj Ferençe c., İstefan veledeş m., Mıkşa Monul c., Tiheşe
İstefan c., Dumitre biradereş m., Mıla Dumitre c., Petre veledeş
m., İstefan biradereş m., Munta Pavel c., Yanoş veledeş m.,
Lazar Yanoş c., Dorbe veledeş m., Oprışa Yanoş c., Durıç vele-
deş m., D'urat' Radoya c., Toma Petrovıt' c., Bun İstefan c.,

Petar veledeş m., Nıku veledeş m., Bayça Yanoş c., Petre veledeş m., Mıklaşa Luba c., Stoya veledeş m., Dançul Duşlaç c., Haydu Ferençe c., Petre veledeş m., Bozdur Hanka c., Floreş veledeş m., Nağoy Rumun c., İstanıslav veledeş m., Petre İşpan c., Gavrılo Yanoş c., Petre veledeş m., Tatıl Mıkşa c., İsto[y]ka Mıhal c., Lazar Petre c., Toma veledeş m., Antal Yanoş c., Orban veledeş m., Mıla Laçko c., Balın veledeş m., Paşkota Hranetit' c., Petre veledeş m., Favur Moyşa c., Petre veledeş m., Opre biradereş m., İştirbey Yanoş c., Baçula veledeş m., Dança Petre c., Lupul veledeş m., Yakşa İstefan c., Petar veledeş m., Bun Petar c., Vıran Yovan c., Luka veledeş m., İçvetko veledeş m., Petar veledeş m., Karaçon Diyeniş c., Petar veledeş m., Petar Lazar c., Toma veledeş m., Mıkloş Lazar c., Doba İstefan c., Durıç veledeş m., Mıla Balın c., Mıla veledeş m., Mıhal biradereş m., Bardonya Balın c., İstefan veledeş m., Doba Yovan c., Yanoş veledeş m., İmre Çerugar c., Stoya veledeş m., İstefan Voyanar c., Kurta İstefan c., D'urd' Favur c., Ursul veledeş m., Mıhal Toma c., Petar Petroska c., Lupul biradereş m., Kaçkan İstefan c., Petre veledeş m., Nagıra Dumitre c., Toma biradereş m., Mıkşa biradereş c., Kaçkan Orban c., Yançul veledeş m., Haydu Mıhal c., Mıkşa veledeş m., Koşutar İstefan c., Dobre veledeş, m., Munta Vançul c., Dumitre veledeş m., Rumun Bolovan c., Ivan Drağul c., Yanoş veledeş m., Kaçkan Bun c., Petre veledeş m., Rakoşı Vinçe c., Çerugar Petre c., Yanoş veledeş m., Çerugar Durka c.,

[126ª]

Yanoş veledeş m., Filip Dan c., Vıdoşa veledeş m., Arıça İstefan c., Durka veledeş m., Olkuran İstefan c., Beçkereki Yanoş c., Petar biradereş m., Martın Istoyan c., Ferençe veledeş m., Opre biradereş m., Petre biradereş m., Mureşka Rumun c., Yanoş Lazar c., Petre veledeş m., Dumitre biradereş m., Bratul Mıkloş c., Pırıbşa Balın c., Morar Tomaş c., Ferençe biradereş m., İstefan Drağan c., Petre veledeş m., Mıkul biradereş m., Mıkula Drağoya c., İstefan Govran c., Dumitre İstever c., Yanoş veledeş m., Moldovanı Dan c., Iştırban Yanoş c., Petre veledeş m., Raden biradereş m., Sion Araça c., Sion Barçe c., Sion Reloça m., Sion Borkulça m., Sion Vanışa m., Sion Alaçe m.
    Hane: 89.
    Mezraa-i Vadat.[7] Varoş-i mezbure halkı ziraat ederler.

SERBIANS AND RUMANIANS 121

Mezraa-i Leskofça,⁸ nezd-i varoş-i mezbure. Varoş-i mezbure halkı ziraat ederler.

Hasıl maa mezari-i mezbur[!]: 51147.

Kapı, 244 fı 25: 6100.

Kendum, keyl 488: 5368.

Mahlût, keyl 488: 3928.

Şıra, pinte 50: 300.

Asiyap, maa dibek, bap 17, resim: 850.

Resm-i arus, maa resm-i fıçı: 960.

Mahsul-i bac-i pazar, ve ıhzar, ve ıhtısap, ve beyt-ül-mal, ve yava, ve kaçkın, ve baha-i şemi-i esel, ve bâd-i hava, ve ... fı sene: 34541.

Varoş-i mezburenin panayırlarına gelen boş arabadan dörder penz, ve yüklü arabadan sekizer penz, ve vilâyet-i Erdel'den gelen tuz arabasından birer kıta tuz, ve satılık galleden ve alaşadan satandan dörder alandan dörder penz, ve hanazırdan dahi dörder penz, ve koyundan birer penz kadim-ül-eyyamdan alınagelmeğin geri vech-i meşruh üzere alınmak defter-i cedid-i hakaniye kayıt olundu.

b) On pp. 96ᵃ–97ᵃ, after Banluğa⁹ and before Udvar:¹⁰

[96ᵇ]

33. Kariye-i Sredna-Dente, nam-i diğer Vıratı-Gay.¹¹ Tâbi-i m.

Vukodırag D'ord'evit' c., Koml'en veledeş m., Jıvko Vuyıçıt' c., Radon'a Duşıça c., Dıragoye Pavun c., Bela biradereş m., İliye Raşkovit' c., Istanko veledeş m., Vukayıl Popovıt' c., Bela veledeş m., Bela Vukodırag c., Mıhal veledeş m., Mıladın Radovan c., Putnık Vukomır c., İçvetko veledeş m., Vukomır Radonıt' c., Avram veledeş m., Istanısav Duşıça c., Mılovaç veledeş m., Mıloş Duşıça c., Damyan Duşıça c., Rayko veledeş m., Pavun veledeş m., Rayak Boğdan c., Filip veledeş m., Vuk biradereş m., İliye Ivladko c., Nıkola Radonıt' c., Yovan veledeş m., Istoyan Radonıt' c., Peşa Petrovıt' c., Filip biradereş m., Dıragoylo Radovan c., Istoyan Bojıt' c., Petar veledeş m., Novak Vukovıt' c., Yovan Vuk c., İçvetko veledeş m., Voyın Duşıça c., Vuk veledeş m., Boğoy Veçerit' c., Lukaç biradereş m., Momçıl İçvetko c., Zone veledeş m., Radan Radenovıt' Dıranış c., İliye biradereş m., Radovan Radosalıt' c., Nıkola veledeş m., D'urat' veledeş m., Raya Mukıçevit' c., Martınko veledeş m., İstefan veledeş m., Vuk D'urıt' c., Peyak veledeş m., Jıvko Padosaç c., Lazar veledeş m.,

Vuyıça Şirit' c., Rado Duşıça.
Hane: 32.
Hasıl: 6825
Kapı: 32 fı hamsīn: 1600.
Kendum, keyl 280: 3080.
Mahlût, keyl 60: 360.
Resm-i kendir ve kelem: 50.
Resm-i kevare: 150.
Resmi-bid'at: 380.
Resm-i arus: 60.
Resm-i fıçı: 90.
Resm-i hime, giyah: 800.
Asiyap, bap 2, resim: 100.

[97ª]
Bâd-i hava: 155.
c) On pp. 112ª–112ᵇ, after *Dobrıç*[12] and before *İgentö*:[13]

[112ª]
71. Kariye-i Dolna Dente[14]. Tâbi-i m.
Raden Radıvoy—kenez ba berat, Mıloş veledeş m., Milen veledeş m., Jıvko veledeş m., Novak Radıvoy c., Doba veledeş m., Rayak veledeş m., Yaka Vukıt' c., Jıvko Raçık c., Nıkola veledeş m., D'ura veledeş m., Radan Radıvoy c., Vuk biradereş c., Putnık veledeş m., Radıç Hırn'ak c., Vuk veledeş m., Vuk Botıt'—müsellem ba berat, Komlen veledeş m., Filip veledeş m., Bun Vuçko c., Raleta İçvetko c., D'urd' veledeş m., Pavun Pavle c., Radıç Belavesit' c., Radosav veledeş m., Dıragoylo Hırn'ak c., Lukaç veledeş m., Radıvoy Radıç c., Yaka veledeş m., Rayak Radıç c., Damyan veledeş m., Kuzma veledeş m., Ogn'an Vukoy c., Damyan biradereş m., Marko Novak c., Vuk Istoyan

[112ᵇ]
Vuk Istoyan c., Lukaç veledeş m., Istanışa Ivan c., Mılaşın Duşıça c., Rahoye veledeş m., Radan İstefan c., Novak veledeş m., Petar Pavlovıt' c., Todor veledeş m., Radov Vukas c., Yovan veledeş m., İçvetko—kalud'er c., Lazar veledeş m., Dıragoylo Vukman c., Mıhal veledeş m., Petre biradereş m., Rayko İstepan c., Kırasan veledeş m., Predrag veledeş m., Dıragıt' Vukovıt' c., Radıç, veledeş m., Radıvoy Vuk c., Gruba veledeş m., Vukaşın İlit' c.,

Radovan—kalud'er c., Avram veledeş m., Radov Radoş c., D'ura veledeş m., Manoylo Vukaşın c., Vılk veledeş m., Martın veledeş m., Vukoy biradereş m., Yovan Rayak c., Marko biradereş m., Radak Yovan c., Dıranov veledeş m., İçvetko Panıt' c., Peyak veledeş m., Vukoy Radıç c., Yaka veledeş m., D'ura biradereş m., Filip Radkovıt' c., Jıvko veledeş m., Vuyıça Duşıça c., Yovan veledeş m., Radovan Radıvoy c., Avram veledeş m., Bojıt'ko veledeş m., Mılak Petrovıt' c., Jıvko veledeş m., İstepan Belit' c., Dıragoy Jıvko c., İliye Duşiça c., Yovan Radonıt'—müsellem ba berat, Vuk Yovan—müsellem ba berat.

Hane: 41.
Hasıl: 8932.
Kapı: 31 fı hamsīn: 2050.
Kendum, keyl 300: 3300.
Mahlût, keyl 250: 1500.
Resm-i kendir: 120.
Resm-i kevare: 50.
Resm-i bid'at: 525.
Resm-i arus: 90.
Ösr-i piyar: 82.
Resm-i fıçı: 60.
Resm-i hime ve giyah: 1025.
Bâd-i hava: 250.

123^{b2}
124^{a2}
124^{a1}
124^{b2}
124^{b1}
125^{a2}
125^{a1}
125^{b2}
125^{b1}
126^{a1}
97^{a1}
96^{b2}
112^{b1}
112^{a2}

If one compares the above deciphered listings of the *Mufassal* 579 with the name listings given by Kadlec, it becomes immediately evident that many of the anthroponyms given in the *mahalle-i*

Eflâk of *Dite* of the domesday book also appear among the anthroponyms of the various listings given by Kadlec.[15] Such names are: *Alaçe, Baçula, Balın, Barçe, Bardonya, Bayça, Boğdan, Bolovan, Bratul, Bud, Bun, Dan, Dança, Dançul, Doba, Dobre, Dorbe, Drağan, Drağoya, Dumitre, Durka, D'urd', Farkaş, Gruba, Hanka, Hranetit', Istançul, Istanıslav, Istoyan, Istoyka, Ivan, İstefan, İstever, Karaçon, Lazar, Luba, Lupul, Martın Mıhal, Mıkul, Mıla, Moyşa, Nagoy, Opre, Oprışa, Petar, Petre, Pırıbşa, Pribit', Prodan, Raden, Radoya, Rumun, Stoya, Şandor, Tatıl, Vana-vinçe, Vanışa, Vinçe.*

Although one has to be cautious with anthroponomyc statistics, it is interesting to note that—though some of them do not appear on the Kadlec listings—there are names in the *mahalle-i Eflâk* of *Dite* which are clearly Rumanian in their character and which are completely lacking from the *mahalle-i Sırf.* Such names are: *Alaçe, Bardonya, Bolovan, Bud, Dança, Dançul, Dumitre, Faur, Favur, Gavrılo, Hanka, Istançul, İstever, Mıkşa, Nıku, Tatıl.*

Some of the names listed in the *mahalle-i Eflâk* of *Dite* but not given on the Kadlec listings are strongly South-Slavic in their formation. Still, since they are listed as such in the register, we can rightfully consider them as *Eflâk* anthroponyms. (Even more so since, except *Koşutar,* they all occur among the anthroponyms of the three *Eflâk nahiyes,* that its, of *Ferdiya, Monoştor,* and *Şuydıya,* too.) And they are: *Çerugar, Duşlaç, D'urat', İçvetko,* and *Koşutar.*

As mentioned above (pp. 113-14), beside the South-Slavic name formations Kipchak Turkic and Hungarian elements are not too uncommon among the *Eflâk* anthroponyms either. Among the Turkic elements we find names like *Bozdur, Kaçkan, Tıvança,* etc. in *Dite; Balaban, Bayça, Karyul, Kuş,* etc. in the *nahiye of Ferdiya;* and *Bayan, Bayça, Beşe, Şısman, Toğan, Uz,* etc. in the *nahiyes* of *Monoştor* and *Şuydıya.* The Hungarian elements are even more numerous. In *Dite* we find *Antal, Beçkereki, Ferençe, Haydu, Işpan, Imre, Laçko, Mıkloş, Orban, Rakoşı, Yanoş,* etc. In the *nahiye* of *Ferdiya* we have *Bajo, Dıkan, Ferençe, Laçko, Laslo, Mıkloş, Yanoş,* etc. And in the *nahiyes Monoştor* and *Şuydıya* we see *Andraş, Antal, Barta, Çuka, Dıkan, Endre, Ferençe, Iştvan, Imre, Joltan, Laçko, Laslo, Löçe, Lörinç, Sabo, Şebeşt'en, Şığa, Yanoş, Yoşa,* etc.

All in all, the deciphered and identified material of the *Mufassal* 579 clearly indicates that in the case of the sixteenth-century *mahalle-i Eflâk* of *Dite* we have to reckon with an ethnic group which, at least in the make up of its anthroponyms, is very similar to those described by Kadlec in the thirteenth-fourteenth centuries.

If, in addition, we consider that the three sixteenth-century Ottoman *nahiyes* of *Ferdiya, Monoştor,* and *Şuydıya* were a de facto continuation of the three *districti Volahales* of medieval Southeastern Hungary, it becomes evident that, at least till the later part of the sixteenth century, the denomination *Eflâk* used by the Ottoman drafters of the domesday books referred to linguistic-ethnic clusters and not to mere social groupings, as so often assumed.

The most important criterion in the question undoubtedly is the fact that in certain cases, as can be seen for instance in the case of *Dite,* the Ottomans clearly differentiated between the Serbians (*Sırf*) and the Rumanians (*Eflâk*) living in separate parts of the same settlement. From the anthroponyms listed in them it is evident that the drafter's differentiation between the two, or more exactly three sections of *Dite* is a reflection of a given situation rather than that of an artificial administrative division. This is borne out further by the fact that anthroponyms of the same origin appear in different forms in the different parts of the settlement. Just to give an example: while in the Serbian sector we have the forms *Dimitre* or *Dımıtar,* the same name will consistently appear as *Dumitre* in the listing on the Rumanian sector. On the other hand, certain names, such as *Olivir* for instance, are specific to and occur only among the Serbian population. In general, South-Slavic patronymics are almost entirely lacking among the inhabitants of the Rumanian sector.

In conclusion, as is evident from the foregoing, the Ottomans, for centuries, used the term *Eflâk* to designate conglomerations that can easily be established as ethnic units in their own right. And they did so not only in Danubian Europe, but also in Anatolia.[16]

NOTES

1. A welcome exception are the studies of N. Beldiceanu and I. Beldiceanu-Steinherr. N. Beldiceanu's most recent article on the Valakhs of Bosnia ("Les Valaques de Bosnie à la fin du XVe siècle et leur institutions," *Turcica* 7 (1975)) gives a detailed bibliography of studies relating to the Valakh / *Eflâk* question.

2. Most recently, for instance in the French summary of D. Bojanić-Lukač, "Vlasi u severnoj Srbiji i njihovi prvi kanuni", *Istorijski časopis* 18 (1971) the word *vlasi* is given as *Serbes-Valaques* (p. 269).

3. H. İnalcık, "Adaletnameler," *Türk Tarih Belgeleri Dergisi* 2 iii-iv (1967), pp. 63-67.

4. Modern: *Obád*, NE of *Csák* (Ótelek und Széphely 23 XXIV; S. Borovszky, *Temes vármegye*, Budapest, n.d., pp. 83-84; ancient: *Jobbágy* (B. Milleker, *Délmagyarország középkori földrajza*, Temesvár, 1915, p. 196). –Csánki's identifications (D. Csánki, *Magyarország történelmi földrajza a Hunyadiak korában*, Budapest, 1894, ii, p. 54, *s.v.*: *Ohát*, and p. 43, *s.v.*: *Jobbágy*) not acceptable.

5. Unidentified.

6. Modern: *Detta*, NW of *Denta* (Denta 24 XXIV; Borovszky, *Temes vármegye*, p. 39); ancient: *Déd / Kis-Déd / Deta* (Milleker, *op. cit.*, pp. 79-80; Csánki, *op. cit.*, ii, p. 100; Kriegs-Charte des Temeswarer Banath, plate 103; Borovszky, *idem.*, p. 39).

7. Unidentified; not to be identified with *Vadad*=*Versecvát*, E of Zichyfalva (Werschetz und Alibunár 25 XXIV; Milleker, *op. cit.*, p. 140), which is listed in the *Mufassal* 579 (p. 154^{a-b}) as *Vatına* among the villages of *Semlit' nahiyesi*.

8. Unidentified.

9. Modern: *Bánlak*, W of *Detta* (Detta 24 XXIV; S. Borovszky, *Torontál vármegye*, Budapest, 1911, pp. 21-22); ancient: *Banlok* (Kriegs-Charte des Temeswarer Banath, plate 103), *Panlogh*, *Bánlok* (Borovszky, *idem*, p. 21).

10. Modern: *Idvor*, *Gradac*, SW of *Dócz* (Detta 24 XXIV; Borovszky, *Torontál vármegye*, pp. 43, and 50); ancient *Újudvar* (Csánki, *op. cit.*, ii, p. 69; Borovszky, *idem*, p. 43).

11. Modern: *Denta*, SE of *Detta* (Denta 24 XXIV; Borovszky, *Temes vármegye*, p. 36; Csánki, *op.cit.*, ii, p. 100); ancient: *Dent / Dente/ Denta* (Kriegs-Charte des Temeswarer Banath, plate 103; Milleker, *op.cit.*, pp. 80-81. Csánki, *op.cit.*, ii, p. 100; Borovszky, *idem*, p. 36).

12. Modern: *Kevedobra / Dobricza*, NW of *Ferdinándfalva* (Werschetz und Alibunár 25 XXIV; Borovszky, *Torontál vármegye*, p. 61; Csánki, *op.cit.*, ii, p. 118); *Dobravicza* (Csánki, *op.cit.*, ii, pp. 34, and 118; Milleker, *op.cit.*, p. 24; Borovszky, *idem*, p. 61).

13. Modern: *Egentova*, E of *Kisnezsény* (Nagybecskerek 24 XXIII; Milleker, *op.cit.*, p. 29); ancient: *Igentő* (Csánki, *op.cit.*, ii, p. 118; Milleker, *op. cit.*, p. 128; Borovszky, *Tonontál vármegye*, p. 32).

14. Ancient: *Kun-Dent*, S of *Denta* (Milleker, *op.cit.*, p. 81; *Mufassal* 579, p. 112^a; T. Halasi-Kun, "Unidentified Medieval Settlements in Southern Hungary: dolna-, sredna-, and gorna-", *AO* 2, pp. 156, 159, 177, and 179.

15. The combined list of the anthroponyms appearing in the three *Eflâk nahiyes* (*Ferdiya*, *Monoştor*, *Şuydıya*) and the *mahalle-i Eflâk* of

Dite of the register as well as on the Kadlec listings is as follows:
*Alaçe, Alça, Andrıya, Baçula, Balın, Balya, Ban, Baranko, Barçe, Bardonya,
Barla, Bayça, Beloş, Bera, Berçe, Bıka, Bilik, Boğdan, Bojıça, Boleşa,
Bolın, Bolovan, Boyça, Bratul, Brayşa, Bud, Buda, Budışa, Budıt', Bula,
Bun, Damıyan, Dan, Dança, Dançul, Dayşa, Dayul, Deyçe, Deyko,
Dımıtar, Dırağan, Dimitre, Doba, Dobre, Dorbe, Drağan, Drağoman,
Drağoya, Dumitre, Dura, Durka, D'ıla, D'ura, D'urd', D'uren, D'urka, Far-
kaş, Gaşpar, Goşpar, Gruba, Hangul, Hanka, Hiraç, Hranetit', Iskola, Istan,
Istanıča, Istançul, Istane, Istanıslav, Istanko, Istankovıt', Istankul, Istoyan,
Istoyka, Ivan, Ivanka, Iliye, Istefan, Istepan, Istever, Karaçon, Karyul, Kosto,
Kuzma, Lajko, Laşko, Lazar, Luba, Luben, Lukaç Lupşa, Lupul, Manul,
Marko, Markul, Martın, Martıne, Matey, Mıhal, Mıkanda, Mıkla, Mıkul, Mıla,
Mıladın, Mılos, Mılotıt', Mırja, Mitre, Moyşa, Nağoy, Nıkola, Opre, Oprışa,
Panta, Pençe, Petar, Petre, Pırıbça, Pıribşa, Pırodan, Pırovan, Pirbil,
Pop, Prıbısa, Pribit, Prodan, Rad, Raden, Radoya, Radul, Radulıça, Rayan,
Ristiye, Roğa, Roman, Rumun, Simeven, Sinye, Stoya, Şandor, Şandra,
Şışman, Tatıl, Tatul, Todor, Vana-vinçe, Vanışa, Vanna, Vinçe, Vlad,
Volıça, Yakup, Yankul, Yanya.*

16. Beldiceanu, "Les Valaques de Bosnie," *Turcica* 7 (1975), pp 122-23
note 4.

123b2

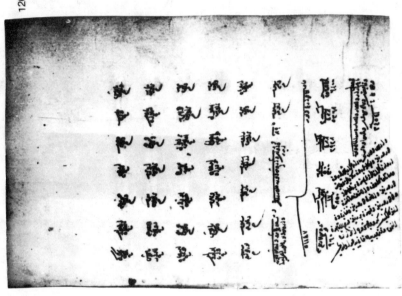

112b1

212

[illegible]

112a2

[illegible]

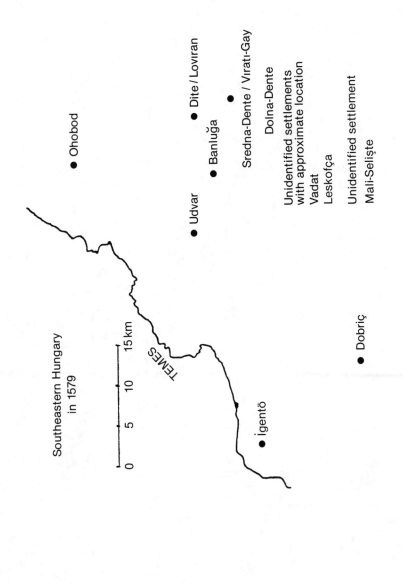

Southeastern Hungary
in 1579

0   5   10   15 km

TEMES

• igentö

• Dobriç

• Ohobod

• Udvar

• Dite / Loviran

• Banluǧa

• Sredna-Dente / Virati-Gay

Dolna-Dente

Unidentified settlements
with approximate location
Vadat
Leskofça

Unidentified settlement
Mali-Selişte

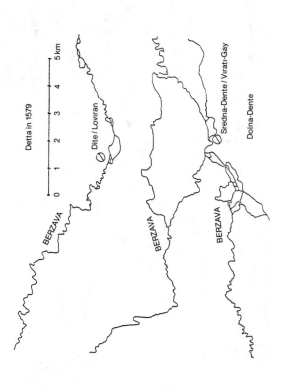

Detta in 1579

0 1 2 3 4 5 km

BERZAVA

Dite / Loviran

BERZAVA

BERZAVA

Sredna-Dente / Virati-Gay

Dolna-Dente

B. K. Király–P. Pastor

THE SUBLIME PORTE AND FERENC II RÁKÓCZI'S
HUNGARY

AN EPISODE IN ISLAMIC CHRISTIAN RELATIONS

The Hungarian War of Independence of 1703–1711 coincided
and had connections with both the War of Spanish Succession
and the Great Northern War. During the latter two conflicts,
which actively engaged all the European great powers, Ferenc
II Rákóczi's government made various attempts to enter into
cooperation with France, the Ottoman Empire, Prussia, Poland,
Sweden and Russia. Rákóczi's aim was to extricate Hungary from
its isolation and make the War of Independence an integral part
of high European policy.[1] Among all Rákóczi's initiatives the most
lasting and mutually beneficial was Hungary's cooperation with
Louis XIV's France. The Hungarians also expended great energy
in trying to involve the Ottoman Empire in an alliance or at
least in clandestine cooperation against the Habsburg dynasty.
These efforts came to naught just as did Rákóczi's design for a
Nordic alliance with Sweden, Prussia and Poland.[2] The last
project for cooperation between Hungary and Russia came too
late to be effectual, although it was desired by both Rákóczi
and Peter the Great.

Two key factors dominated Rákóczi's foreign policies: the
conflict of Hungary's constitutionalism and desire for autonomy
with the Habsburgs' despotic tendencies, and Transylvania's
traditional role as guarantor of Hungary's liberties. Both factors
were affected by Hungary's unhappy fate as the metal between
the anvil of Germandom and the hammer of the Ottoman Empire, to use the metaphor popular among contemporary Hungarians.

There had been clashes between Habsburg despotism and

Hungary's constitutional liberties ever since the dynasty had acquired St. Stephen's crown in perpetuity.[3] Oscar Jászi described the Hungarian concept of Habsburg intentions in the following terms: "The Hungarian tradition attributes to [Cardinal Count Leopold] Kollonics the ill-famed dictum: 'I will make Hungary first a prisoner, then a beggar, and finally a Catholic.' This maxim may be apocryphal but it expresses without doubt the state of mind, the hatred and profound exasperation with which the great masses of the Hungarian population regarded the triumphant predominance of the Habsburgs."[4] But there were limits on Habsburg predominance. Hungary was a very large country with poor communications, both of which hampered military operations. With heavy commitments in Italy and Western Europe, the military forces the dynasty had available to keep Hungary in check were always sparse and often inadequate. Another problem until the end of the seventeenth century was the Ottoman menace. Besides, the Hungarians themselves were always ready to take up arms in defense of their constitutional liberties. The combined effect of these factors was a repeated cycle in Habsburg–Hungarian relations: constitutional reign—absolutist efforts—tension—political and/or armed conflict—deadlock—compromise—and back to constitutional reign again. King Rudolf's (1567–1608) absolutist policies, for instance, were brought to an end by the Hungarians' armed resistance under Prince István Bocskay and the compromise of 1606, the Treaty of Vienna, the first *Ausgleich* between the dynasty and the Hungarian estates. The first phase of absolutist rule under Leopold I (1657–1705) led to the Wesselényi Fronde (1666–1671) and Imre Thököly's rebellion and the eventual Sopron compromise of 1681. The period of extraconstitutional rule from the last diet under Maria Theresa to the death of Josef II (1765–1790) was to conclude with the accord of 1790. The neoabsolutist regime that followed the revolution of 1848–1849 gave rise to the most famous compromise of all, the *Augsleich* of 1867. The feature common to all these accords was compromise in the proper sense of the word. Each of them acknowledged the validity of the crown's fairly extensive privileges and the later ones recognized the Habsburgs' hereditary rights (in 1606 and 1681 the throne was still elective). And each time the dynasty in turn bowed to the privileges of the estates.[5] The Rákóczi War of Independence flared up in reaction against the second period of absolutism under Leopold I and it, too, ended in a compromise, the Treaty of Szatmár of 1711.[6]

The second string to Rákóczi's foreign-policy bow was his insistence that Transylvania should remain a separate political entity independent of Vienna as a surety against Habsburg violation of the constitutional liberties of the kingdom of Hungary. This had been the part played by Transylvania between the late sixteenth and late seventeenth centuries. Before 1541 Transylvania had been an integral part of the unitary state of Hungary. In that year, however, Sultan Suleiman the Magnificent had issued a firman that bestowed it on János Zsigmond Zápolya (Szapolyai), the son of the late János I, the last native king of Hungary. The separate existence of Transylvania was geographically possible because, with the Ottoman capture of Buda in 1541, the Habsburgs lost year-round communications with the area. The only roads connecting the Habsburg lands with Transylvania then passed through northern Hungary (Northern Highlands) and were impassable in winter. Transylvania, which officially became a principality in 1588, existed as a separate state under the suzerainty of the Sublime Porte. The Sheyh ül-Islâm told Gábor Bethlen, prince of Transylvania (1613–1629): "We shall never let Transylvania be united with Hungary. Transylvania is Sultan Suleiman's invention and is the property of the Mighty Sultan. . . . We don't give anyone else what belongs to us."[7] Thus under Ottoman protection the power of the flourishing principality was beyond the effective reach of Habsburg military forces, while parts of German Austria and the Czech provinces as well as the remainder of the kingdom of Hungary lay within the radius of military action by Transylvania.[8] After Buda was liberated in 1686, however, Vienna's military access to Transylvania was restored and the principality was soon subdued. The Diploma Leopoldinum of 1961 submitted Transylvania to Vienna's direct administration, effectively reversing the role the principality had played. For a century it had guaranteed Hungary's constitutional liberties by acting as a counterbalance to Habsburg military power. Now it became the guarantor of Habsburg despotism in Hungary by its use as a military base in the Hungarian rear. Ferenc II Rákóczi wanted to redress the balance by restoring Transylvania as a strong, independent state under international guarantee that could again offset Habsburg military power and ensure Hungary's constitutional rights.

The main aim of Rákóczi's foreign policy was to elevate the Hungarian cause out of isolation and make it an issue in the European balance of power. To this end he tried to establish common cause with the France of Louis XIV, the archenemy of the Habsburg dynasty. He approached Louis XIV in 1700 with the offer of an alliance but was betrayed and arrested; only his escape from prison saved his life.[9] Rákóczi fled into exile in Poland and from there continued corresponding with Paris urging cooperation. All his overtures were in vain, for the likelihood of a Hungarian insurrection seemed too remote and problematical to warrant Louis' aid. Without a foreign ally, Rákóczi himself was reluctant to start an uprising. Then the peasants of northern Hungary themselves rose up and successfully battled the Habsburg forces in their area. At their invitation Rákóczi assumed leadership of the revolt. In very short order a considerable proportion of the nation had joined the anti-Habsburg revolt.[10] The spectacular success of the insurgents (kurucok) changed the French government's mind. From the summer of 1703 Louis XIV began paying Rákóczi monthly subsidies and sent engineering and artillery officers to train his troops. In 1704 French envoys were officially accredited to Rákóczi's court. The growing Franco–Hungarian cooperation and the continuing military successes raised hopes that the French and Bavarian forces marching from the west and Rákóczi's insurgent army attacking from the east would be able to meet in Vienna and there dictate peace terms to the Habsburgs. These hopes were dashed dramatically in 1704 by the Battle of Blenheim (Höchstädt) in which the forces of the Duke of Marlborough and Prince Eugene of Savoy smashed the French and Bavarian allies. The happy prospect of an early victory turned into the nightmare possibility of protracted war.

Before Blenheim it seemed possible that the Porte might intervene on the Franco–Hungarian side. The secretary of Baron Charles Ferriol d'Argental, the French ambassador in Constantinople, had hurried to tell Rákóczi that a force of 10,000 Turkish troops was being prepared to march to the aid of the Hungarians. Rákóczi replied: "I am disturbed because to accept this offer is as dangerous as to turn it down. . . . The aid of such a neighboring power might lead us into thralldom that in time to come may not be dissimilar to German oppression."[11] Rákóczi eventually decided it would be more hazardous to reject the offer but wanted to attach strict conditions to acceptance. He communicated these conditions to the French government through Ferriol's secretary. They stipulated that King Louis should inform the Porte that he had taken Rákóczi and the Hungarians under his protection, that the Porte should undertake not to extend Ottoman frontiers at Hungary's expense, that the Turkish troops should be incorporated into Rákóczi's army rather than operate under a separate Turkish command, that these facts should be communicated to the Turkish troops in a manifesto from the sultan, that Rákóczi would hire 4,000 janissaries and 2,000 cavalry each for Hungary and Transylvania, and that in return Rákóczi would offer the sultan annually an agreed "gift" of money.[12]

The possibility of Ottoman troops reappearing on the Great Hungarian Plain, even as allies, made it imperative for Rákóczi to offset their potential threat to Hungary's territorial integrity by obtaining broader European recognition and assistance. Besides this obvious reason of state, Rákóczi's attention had been caught by the brilliance of the military feats of Charles XII of Sweden. Early in 1704 he sent an emissary to the Swedish king to recommend the conclusion of an alliance between Sweden, Poland, Prussia and Hungary. Prussia, it soon turned out, was interested only in the pacification of Hungary so that Habsburg forces tied down there would be released for use against France. Rákóczi had little more success with Charles XII. Realizing that a major war was in the making between the Swedish soldier-king and Russia, and hoped to persuade the Porte to make war on Russia with which the Ottoman Empire's long-critical relations had led to serious border clashes in the area of Azov. If Russia were at war with the Porte, the burden would be lifted from Charles XII who, according to Rákóczi's designs, could then turn against Leopold I in the west. With this in mind, in May 1705 he sent Charles another emissary, Pál Ráday, the head of his chancellery and his closest adviser. Ráday quickly ascertained that the Swedish king was not about to abandon his war with Russia or willing to conclude an alliance with the Islamic Porte, but he was not averse to an Ottoman attack on Russia at the same time as his own offensive.

As Rákóczi's northern European projects disintegrated, he focused his attention more and more on the Porte, his last resort. Rákóczi agonized over whether to seek Ottoman assistance without substantial reassurance that Hungarian interests would be protected. He was well aware that, apart from France, the powers were still unwilling to consider the Ottoman Empire part of the concert of Europe, as Charles II's rejection of an alliance with Constantinople had reminded him.[13] Ottoman aid at the expense of alienating western Europe was too high a price to pay lightly, for the main drive of Rákóczi's foreign policy was to secure recognition of Hungary's independence by as many states as possible.

The defeat at Blenheim and the failure of his northern European designs were not the sole complications Rákóczi had to contend with. In Constantinople a palace coup had removed one grand vizier and installed another who was unfriendly toward the French cause.[14] Rákóczi realized that he would not be able to set the terms for eventual Ottoman aid but would rather have to solicit it. Early in 1705 he entered into correspondence with the pashas of Temesvár and Belgrade, whose counsel on Hungarian questions weighed heavily in Constantinople. He also chose a special envoy, András Török, who was to go to the Ottoman capital. Török was instructed to congratulate the new grand vizier on his accession, to assure him that Rákóczi's government intended to remain on the best possible terms with the Sublime Porte and to affirm that Rákóczi's Hungary would act as a "bastion" against German penetration of the Ottoman Empire. He was to remind him that the Porte had been aiding Hungary against the Habsburgs for two centuries and to express Rákóczi's hope for similar assistance now. Török was to tell the grand vizier that Hungary was not seeking direct Ottoman military aid but to request permission for Hungary to recruit soldiers in the Ottoman districts adjacent to their common frontier.[15] The instructions reveal Rákóczi's latest ideas and hopes and contain the principles that were to govern his policies virtually to the end of his administration. They are otherwise insignificant because, for reasons not quite clear, the emissary was never dispatched.

The cautiousness and limitations of Török's instructions underline Rákóczi's apprehension about the Turks, even after he had realized that they were the last resort to which he could turn for help. The Scylla of Habsburg despotism and the Charybdis of an Ottoman reconquest of central Hungary were the alternative reefs between which Rákóczi had to steer the Hungarian ship of state. His worst nightmare was that Vienna and Constantinople could reach an accord to partition Hungary between them. His circumspection was by no means misguided, for Hungary's only firm ally, France, was not moved by altruistic motives. It, too, acted for reasons of state. French policymakers saw the Hungarian War of Independence as an effective Austrian diversion. In reality, French policy in Constantinople was primarily directed not to seeking Ottoman aid for Rákóczi but to forcing Austria to commit more troops in Hungary to wage an Ottoman war. Since massive Ottoman military aid was not forthcoming, the French pushed for a limited commitment of men to help Rákóczi to tie down Habsburg troops.[16] Ferriol offered Hungarian territory to the Porte as recompense for its alliance. Not aware that such an unacceptable offer had even been made, Rákóczi continued to cooperate loyally with the French.

In August 1705 a Hungarian envoy, Ferenc Horváth, was sent to Ferriol in Constantinople, which he reached in September. He was instructed to gain first-hand information about the chances of fomenting a Russo–Turkish war.[17] Although the French were more interested in a Habsburg–Ottoman conflict, Ferriol was also empowered to encourage the Porte to put pressure on Russia to come to terms with Sweden. Louis XIV believed it was to the Habsburgs' benefit to have the war between Russia and Sweden drag on.[18] In this respect the common policy of France and Hungary favored a Russo–Ottoman war.[19]

As Rákóczi's reluctance to seek major Ottoman aid weakened and he began to make his first tentative moves in this direction, a bizarre incident helped to propel him toward contacts with the Porte. In the fall of 1705 Rákóczi was visited at his residence by one Ali Bey, who identified himself as a messenger from Gazi-Girei, khan of the Crimean Tatars and Sultan Ahmed III's grand vizier.

Ali Bey bore a letter of greeting from the khan which also apparently made reference to friction between the Tatars and the Russians. The Porte's message was transmitted orally as Ali Bey claimed that official contact had to be initiated by Rákóczi.

He informed Rákóczi that the Porte was interested in involvement in a war as a means of keeping discipline over the military. He offered Rákóczi military aid in return for resumption of a tribute that Hungary had not paid since 1683, when Kara Mustafa, Ahmed II's grand vizier, had launched the campaign that culminated in the siege of Vienna.

Rákóczi rejected payment of tribute on the grounds that the Hungarians had risen to regain their freedom not to exchange one slave-master for another. He pointed out that it was possible that Austria and Hungary might reach an accord and then move jointly against the Porte.[20] Rákóczi finally decided to send Ali Bey back to Constantinople in the company of János Pápai, who was to take the Hungarian counterproposal to the Sublime Porte.[21]

According to Rákóczi's instructions, his envoy was to negotiate on the basis of Ali Bey's message. He was to deal only with the grand vizier and could inform Horváth and Ferriol of his mission only under conditions of complete secrecy. Pápai was to tell the grand vizier that the Hungarian Assembly had resolved to pursue the war against the Habsburgs and to seek the Porte's recognition of Rákóczi as prince of Transylvania and its declaration that both Hungary and Transylvania were under Ottoman protection. Pápai had to obtain the Porte's undertaking that it would not extend the empire's frontiers beyond those set by the Treaty of Karlowitz and its permission for Rákóczi to hire 8,000 Albanian and 4,000 Turkish troops. In return he would offer the Porte an annual "gift" of 30,000 talers in respect of Hungary and 40,000 in respect of Transylvania, and assurances that no peace would be concluded without its knowledge and no German troops would be allowed to cross Hungary. Finally, Pápai was urged to do his utmost to persuade the grand vizier to make war on Russia while Rákóczi in turn would induce Charles XII to launch a simultaneous attack. If these conditions were unacceptable to the Porte, the envoy was to remind the Turks of the possibility of an alliance between Hungary and Austria. He was also to offer no territorial concessions.[22] János Pápai set out on October 28, 1705, together with Ali Bey and a small escort. At about the same time Gáspár Pápai was sent with Mihály Bay to the Crimea to inform Khan Gazi-Girei of Hungary's intentions in Constantinople.[23]

János Pápai began to be suspicious about the authenticity of Ali Bey's mission even before they reached Constantinople. When they arrived in Craiova in the principality of Walachia on November 10, the Turkish officials there found Ali's papers were not in order and he was not extended the least courtesy or aid that his alleged rank would have warranted. Pápai's diary is full of complaints during the rest of their month-long journey about Ali, who used every trick in the book to slow their progress and drain Pápai's resources. Once they were in the Ottoman capital, Ali promised every day that Pápai would be presented to the grand vizier and every day the appointment was postponed on increasingly flimsy pretexts. Already losing patience, Pápai on December 26 referred to Ali as *"canis filius"* (son of a dog). On January 3, 1706, sixty-eight days after setting out and a month and ten days after reaching Constantinople, Pápai, who still had not seen any Ottoman official, finally exhausted his patience for good. Referring to Ali in his diary, he wrote: "Now that I have become aware of all his falsehoods, I have sent word to him not to hamper or trick me any more. I know now that he can be of no assistance to me." When at last on January 10, 1706, Pápai had his first audience with the Porte's grand dragoman, he mentioned the Ali affair to the official who denied any knowledge of the man's existence.[24] Interestingly enough, however, Ali set out again for Hungary on February 24, 1706, amid rumors that his mission was to make peace between Rákóczi and the Habsburgs. So Pápai continued to be in doubt whether Ali was an agent of the Porte or a clever scoundrel. The whole affair was also embarrassing to Ferriol who was censured by the French government because Ali was arranging diplomatic contacts between the Hungarians and the Porte rather than doing so himself. To clear himself in his superiors' eyes, Ferriol denounced Ali Bey as a rogue and asked Pápai to testify to his mendacity. Pápai refused to do his mentor this favor, saying: "How could I confirm the Turk's falsehood publicly when even today I am not sure about it after all? When the grand dragoman's son escorted me to an audience with the deputy grand vizier, he asked me not to say a word to the deputy about the Turk because it wouldn't be well received."[25]

The truth about Ali Bey's role may remain a mystery forever. Rákóczi claimed he was convinced that Ali Bey's embassy was *bona fide* because he was familiar with too many intimate details about the Porte's past policy toward Hungary. Rákóczi believed it was the major setbacks his troops suffered at the end of 1705 that caused the Porte to reconsider its offer to come to Hungary's aid and the easiest way for the Ottomans to back off was to denounce Ali and disclaim the proposals he had made to the Hungarians.

Historians are at odds on the matter. Kálmán Benda asserts that in the eighteenth century a number of Turkish impostors with false credentials posed as ambassadors to collect gifts from their hosts. On the other hand, he admits, it was not unusual for the Porte to break off negotiations on the pretense that its emissary was a fake. Some of these "shams" were even imprisoned or executed.[26] For his part the historian Béla Köpeczi believes that Ali Bey was a self-styled ambassador.[27] The warm welcome given Gáspár Papai and Mihály Bay by Khan Gazi-Girei, however, lends support to the authenticity of Ali Bey's stated mission.[28]

The whole record of Rákóczi's two envoys in Constantinople, János Pápai and Ferenc Horváth, is a pathetic exercise in futility. But, then, one can only wonder what Rákóczi based his concept of international relations on. How could he or his spokesmen have the temerity to offer Charles XII to "persuade" the Porte to attack the Russians, or tell the Porte that they would prevail on the Swedes to invade Russia or on France to stay out of the war? If the concept behind Rákóczi's demarches was a delusion, even sorrier were their results. Pápai and Horváth stayed in Constantinople for years, waiting, negotiating, making promises, entreating, coaxing with gifts, corresponding, in the vain hope that, if only the Porte could be made to see circumstances and its own interests properly, if only there were a sudden change among the officials, their recommendations would be heeded and their mission would succeed. Their hopes never flagged, even though Ottoman officials told them constantly and unequivocally that they were not prepared to establish official contact with Rákóczi or them. The grand vizier never received either Hungarian, even in secret. They were unable to obtain any satisfactory response to such a relatively minor request as that the Porte preclude Austrian troops from crisscrossing its territory, in particular the pashalik of Temesvár. Habsburg forces could move through supposedly neutral Ottoman lands with such impunity that they could have come up on the Hungarians' rear at any moment. General Jean-Louis Rabutin de Bussy, the Austrian commander, for instance, marched a major military unit across Ottoman territory on March 19, 1706, without incident.[29] The Hungarian diplomats likewise complained to no avail about insurgent Serbs, allied with the Habsburgs, who fought ferociously and then withdrew into Ottoman territory to regroup and make renewed forays against Hungarian troops and civilians alike. The Hungarians' repeated requests for permission to buy gunpowder or saltpeter were turned down on the ground that the sale would violate the Treaty of Karlowitz. Even a private merchant who offered on February 26, 1705, to sell the Hungarians saltpeter and ship it to Orsova on the Hungarian border was unable to obtain a permit.[30] The envoys' plea that the princes of the Danubian states should not sell provisions or supplies to the Austrians fell on deaf Ottoman ears. Numerous requests to be allowed to hire volunteers in the Ottoman lands were denied.[31]

Such rebuffs and the Hungarians' daily treatment should have alerted them that the Porte was not about to help the Hungarian cause. If they were not enough, Alexandros Mavrokordatos, the grand dragoman, the Hungarians' main contact in the Ottoman administration, told them quite candidly on several occasions what the Porte's policy really was. On December 28, 1706, Mavrokordatos told Pápai: "The Porte wishes to keep the holy peace[32] scrupulously, unless the other party breaks it. Up till now the Porte has found no reason to disrupt the peace.... The Porte is pleased that you are here but it is not pleased to treat with you when the [Holy Roman] Emperor's ambassador is in attendance.... Your presence is not displeasing to the Porte.... If it did not wish to accept you here, you would be expelled."[33] Two months later Rákóczi had Pápai press the Porte to receive an official mission (solemnis legatio) from him with proper dignity. The grand dragoman turned it down on the ground that the Porte was unwilling to infringe the Treaty of Karlowitz. Pápai strove valiantly to convince the Ottomans that openly and officially dealing with Rákóczi as the sovereign prince of Transylvania was not a treaty infraction.[34] The Porte's counterargument was: "Countries and provinces are possessed on the basis of covenants and treaties. In accordance with the last armistice treaty [Karlowitz], Transylvania is a possession of the Germans except insofar as they cede it to the prince [Rákóczi]. At present his possession is still in abeyance, so it cannot yet be considered the prince's realm. For their part, the Turks have no claim on or grievance against Transylvania while the treaty runs. Beyond that, the Sublime Porte is your friend, your case is under advisement, your men are welcome here and elsewhere, and the pashas of the marches have been commanded to remain on good terms with the prince."[35]

In spite of the Porte's persistent indifference toward his cause, Rákóczi sent to Constantinople a new envoy in the person of the prominent Szekler nobleman Mihály Henter. Pápai presented him to the deputy grand vizier on January 3, 1708. Henter brought the farthest-reaching proposals from Rákóczi yet. He told the Porte that Transylvania acknowledged its feality to the sultan, that Rákóczi was ready to dispatch an official delegation to express this fealty publicly and that, if his delegation would be received, it would bear suitable gifts and further proposals.

Henter received no response to his urgent embassy until May 16 and even then it was negative. The deputy grand vizier told him: "The canon of our faith requires that ambassadors should be received only from a prince who rules freely, for a principality has to be a territory under his jurisdiction where no other has sway and he has absolute dominion. Full honors shall be rendered to such ambassadors as their due. Under the present circumstances these honors cannot be given either to the prince or to his state."[36] He told the Hungarians that in future Rákóczi should approach Ibrahim Pasha of Belgrade, not the Sublime Porte, on all matters to do with the Ottoman Empire. "Do not be dismayed that we have entrusted this mission to the pasha of Belgrade," he added. "This is our usual practice, as you well know."[37] It is true that it was common for the Porte to communicate with foreign powers through certain pashas of its marches, as the pasha of Buda had been the customary contact with the Holy Roman Emperor in earlier times, but since the Porte had been dealing directly with Rákóczi's envoys in Constantinople for several years, this was a sign that Hungarian affairs were becoming of even more peripheral interest than they had been.

It is an intriguing question why the Porte dealt with Rákóczi's emissaries in Constantinople for such a long time. For it is a fact that, apart from the grand vizier himself, all sorts of Ottoman officials received the Hungarians in secret and talked with them, albeit unofficially. The two wars in progress (the Great Northern War and the War of the Spanish Succession) were full of the unexpected and there was no knowing where their erratic courses might lead. In such changeable circumstances it was always possible that Rákóczi's cause might, at least partially, succeed. In view of this, the Ottomans did not wish to close the door on him completely. Unofficial contact with the Hungarians was a constant reminder to Vienna that the Porte could always discomfit it by strengthening its links with Rákóczi. Good relations with France, which the Porte was anxious to preserve, were partly conditional on not treating its protégé, Rákóczi, too harshly. It was the general practice of the Porte to be slow to make decisions and this, too, was a factor. By keeping the Hungarian envoys in Constantinople, the Porte wished to hinder the eventuality of peace between the Hungarians and the Habsburgs. Finally, it is very clear from the detailed account of his negotiations with various Ottoman officials in Pápai's diary that the Turks were deeply interested in news and chatter from the diplomatic community in Constantinople, about which they always inquired closely. The Hungarians were always being asked for such intelligence as the disposition of the Habsburg and Hungarian troops or the latest tidings from Russia or the French. It was hardly surprising, then, that, though the Porte would not treat with the Hungarians officially, nor did it wish to see them depart.

The Hungarian mission was welcome as long as it caused no major diplomatic embarrassment and did not press too hard for official recognition. In this state of limbo, the Hungarians for their part used every tactic they could to gain leverage. One such maneuver was the repeated warning that, if they did not receive official recognition, Pápai would leave. The Porte had nothing to learn from the Hungarians about diplomatic cunning and diversionary ploys, so Pápai was frankly informed on April 3, 1706, and on April 12 and many times thereafter that he was free to go home whenever he wished. But to forestall his abrupt departure, since the Porte did not really wish him to leave, he was also reminded that he needed to obtain a certificate of dismissal beforehand. When at last Pápai came to the conclusion that he could not accomplish Rákóczi's mission and applied for his certificate of dismissal, it was not forthcoming. Still waiting for it on June 21, he exclaimed to the grand dragoman: "I don't know what to make of it: you neither let us go nor negotiate with us." The Porte continued to blow hot and cold. When in exasperation Pápai simply turned his back on the Ottoman officials and stopped calling on them, the grand dragoman summoned him and on September 2 disarmingly remarked: "I have not seen you for so long! Why have you not called?"[38]

Rákóczi's Ottoman policy and his emissaries' efforts in Constantinople received no official recognition from the Turks and failed miserably. The French ambassador was accorded full honors and dignity but French policy was no more successful than the Hungarians'. France's representative directed his efforts in the same direction as Pápai, Horváth and Henter. Unlike them, however, he was received by the grand vizier and so could make his representations in Rákóczi's behalf directly to the head of the Ottoman government rather than to secondary officials.

In April 1706 Ferriol urged the grand vizier to accede to the Hungarians' requests, pointing out that Pápai was intending to return to Rákóczi's camp. The grand vizier remained noncommittal. He explained that, in spite of all the well-reasoned arguments, the Ottomans were bent on keeping peace with Austria and Russia. He dismissed the supposed Russian threat to the Ottoman Empire by saying that Peter the Great was "disturbed and a little mad" and would come to a bad end anyhow.[39] On May 31 Ferriol again met the grand vizier and recommended that the Porte extend its protection to Hungary, offer Rákóczi aid and prohibit Habsburg troops from crossing neutral Ottoman territory. He asked the vizier to receive Rákóczi's emissaries, who had been in Constantinople for six months to present the same proposals and had yet to be given an audience by him. The Turk excused himself on the rather transparent pretext that the Hungarians' credentials were addressed to his deposed predecessor and not to him. "But we will see,"[40] he concluded, continuing to procrastinate in the wonted Ottoman manner and leaving the Hungarian affair in the same limbo it had been in so long.

Following this audience, Ferriol drafted a memorandum to the grand vizier on the desirability of a Russo–Ottoman war. The note reproached the Porte for dismissing the "mad" tsar so lightly. He was quite normal but power-hungry and ambitious, and had to be stopped before it was too late. The memorandum warned of the danger of Russian designs on the Crimea and Constantinople itself, and described the Porte's Orthodox subjects in the Balkans as a subversive element. Significantly, it suggested that they would take Russia's part not only because of their religion but also because of other "common interests." It claimed that Russia had broken several articles of the Russo–Ottoman Treaty of Constantinople of 1700 and this would justify an Ottoman offensive against the tsar. An Ottoman victory was assured in view of Russia's recent defeats in the Great Northern War.[41]

Pápai and Ferriol both had the initial impression that the memorandum had had an impact on the Porte but they soon realized that the Ottomans were intransigent. The French ambassador concluded that the Porte was showing no enthusiasm for war because it served its interest for the conflicts in Europe to drag on. They would exhaust the belligerents, leaving the Ottoman Empire in a relatively stronger position.[42]

Pápai, whose grasp of the functioning of the Ottoman government was less than Ferriol's, surmised that the Porte had failed to act because of its treaty obligations to Austria and Russia. He was convinced, however, that a Russo–Ottoman war would break out as soon as Turkey found a real *casus belli*.[43]

By the spring of 1707, with no Ottoman recognition or support in sight, Rákóczi had decided to respond favorably to diplomatic overtures from Russia.[44] Peter I had been kept abreast of the progress of Franco–Hungarian diplomacy in Constantinople by his ambassador there, Pyotr A. Tolstoy.[45] It seems that the tsar was even aware of Rákóczi's qualms about the Turks. On May 1, 1707, he offered Rákóczi protection against both Austria and the Ottoman Empire. In return, Rákóczi was to use his good graces with Louis XIV to have the French king intercede to bring peace between Sweden and Russia.[46]

The Russian initiative, which had been begun in March 1707, led to a modification of the Hungarian envoys' assignment in Constantinople. Pápai was instructed in April to stop urging the Porte to make war on Russia.[47] After a formal treaty was signed between Hungary and Russia in September, Pápai was further advised to do his utmost to prevent the outbreak of any such conflict.[48]

The Russo–Hungarian entente did not mean that Pápai was to cease his efforts to recruit 12,000 troops sorely needed to prop Rákóczi's declining military fortunes. With Russian protection for Hungary, Rákóczi no longer feared an Ottoman onslaught and the presence of Turkish troops would have been all the more desirable.[49] Pápai's renewed endeavors still came to nothing. After more than two years in Constantinople and still no success visible, Pápai finally came to a conclusion not unlike Ferriol's own.

It came home to him that the Porte simply did not want to go to the aid of France and Hungary. A victorious France and a francophile Hungary could lead to French hegemony in Europe and this was not in the Porte's interest.[50] Both Ferriol and Pápai concluded that Constantinople had decided against intervening in their behalf because of its perception of the European balance of power.

These two experienced diplomats, who had often bought the favor of officials, recognized that religious and cultural differences between the Ottoman Empire and their respective countries had little to do with shaping the Porte's foreign policy. A Levantine state just like a European state was prompted to act by the principle of the balance of power.

Franco–Hungarian attempts to appeal to Islamic prejudices against the Balkan Orthodox were seen by the Porte for what they were: a political ruse to propel the Ottoman Empire into war. Notwithstanding, the Porte itself was not above using such a device for its own political ends. The Porte's refusal to extend either recognition or aid to the Hungarians finally led to Pápai's recall on September 3, 1708.[51] Henter had left three months earlier, on June 2, his mission no less a failure. Although Horváth stayed on in Constantinople as the Hungarians' unofficial legate, Pápai's recall signaled the end of Rákóczi's Ottoman orientation. The Porte's continuous apathy toward Rákóczi fed suspicions that the Turks were inclined to come to terms with Austria to partition Hungary.[52]

In February 1709, in mistaken anticipation of an imminent Russo–Swedish truce, Rákóczi proposed to Peter I that the tsar should attack the Ottoman Empire and establish an eastern empire of his own. He asked the tsar to guarantee Poland's and Hungary's freedom so that European peace might be restored.[53] Rákóczi's call for war against the Porte was a volte-face, yet he was consistent in his perception of Ottoman policy, for he still feared a return of Ottoman domination over Hungary. Until 1708 he had encouraged the Ottoman Empire to attack Russia in order to deflect the full force of Ottoman power away from Hungary. After 1708 for the same reason Rákóczi urged Peter the Great to make war on Turkey. Either way Rákóczi hoped in the meantime to be able to restore Hungary to the position it had enjoyed in the fifteenth century and Transylvania to its position in the sixteenth and seventeenth centuries, so that together they would dominate East Central Europe. He realized that otherwise either Russia or the Ottoman Empire would be master in the southeast European area. Up to 1708 Rákóczi had favored the Porte, with which Hungary could have shared Eastern Europe, and warned it that it must defeat Russia to safeguard its sphere of influence. France, too, for its own political reasons, favored Ottoman ascendency.

Neither Rákóczi nor Louis XIV was successful in his attempt to court the Porte's favor. Nor was their vision of their respective countries' role in Europe fulfilled. By 1711 the Hungarian War of Liberation was over and French defeat was in the offing. The only power that won a war that year was Sultan Ahmed III's Ottoman Empire.

*   *   *   *   *

Rákóczi left Hungary on February 21, 1711. While he was in Poland for negotiations with Tsar Peter I, his commander in chief, Count Sándor Károlyi, reached an accommodation with the commander in chief of the Habsburg forces, another Hungarian aristocrat, Count János Pálffy. The ensuing Treaty of Szatmár was signed on April 30. Like the other compromises between the dynasty and the Hungarian estates, the treaty recognized the king's rather broad prerogatives and reestablished Hungary's feudal constitutional government. The majority of the Hungarian population, especially the serfs, derived no benefit from it.[54]

The treaties that signalized the Peace of Utrecht of 1713 redrew much of the map of Europe, but they were silent about

Hungary. The goal of Ferenc II Rákóczi's foreign policy had been the very opposite: to secure Hungary's position and development by making them a European issue. The treaties' silence was the clearest indication of the failure of that policy. The only consolation his compatriots may have taken was that without their perseverance in battle against Habsburg power dynastic absolutism may have continued to weigh on Hungary. The Szatmár compromise at least restored the constitutional guarantees the Hungarian estates had enjoyed through the centuries; it yielded nothing else.

NOTES

1. K. Benda–F. Maksay (eds.), *Ráday Pál iratai 1707-1708* [Pál Ráday's Papers, 1707-1708] (Budapest, 1961), p. 21; E. Molnár, *Magyarország története* [History of Hungary] (Budapest, 1967), I, p. 316.

2. B. Köpeczi, *A Rákóczi-szabadságharc és Franciaország* [The Rákóczi War of Independence and France] (Budapest, 1966), pp. 66-67. The greatness of Rákóczi's prestige in East Central Europe can be gauged by the fact that he was considered a potential candidate for the Polish throne. *See* A. Kamiński, *Konfederacja sandomierska wobec Rosji w okresie poaltrąsztadzkim, 1706-1709* [The Confederation of Sandomierz vis-à-vis Russia in the Period after Altranstädt, 1706-1709] Wrocław, 1969), pp. 35-37, 72-74, 79-92, and 134.

3. Ferdinand I (1526-1564) was the first in the unbroken line of Habsburg succession to the Hungarian throne but the first Habsburgs elected to wear St. Stephen's crown were Albert II (1437-1439) and his posthumous son László (Ladislaus) V (1452-1457).

4. O. Jászi, *The Dissolution of the Habsburg Monarchy* (Chicago, 1961), p. 55.

5. B. K. Király, *Hungary in the Late Eighteenth Century: The Decline of Enlightened Despotism* (New York, 1969), pp. 238-39.

6. For the current Marxist interpretation of the Treaty of Szatmár *see* B. Köpeczi–A. Várkonyi (eds.), *Rákóczi tükör: Naplók, jelentések, emlékiratok a szabadságharcról* [Rákóczi Mirror: Diaries, Reports, Memoirs of the War of Independence] (Budapest, 1973), I, p. 29.

7. B. Hóman–Gy. Szekfű, *Magyar történet* [Hungarian History] (Budapest, 1935-1936), IV, p. 74.

8. Prince Gábor Bethlen of Transylvania led his troops toward Bohemia in 1620 to aid the Czechs, but failed to arrive in time before their defeat at the Battle of the White Mountain. Gy. Szekfű, *Behlen Gábor* (Budapest, 1929), pp. 111-13.

9. B. Köpeczi, *II. Rákóczi Ferenc* (Budapest, 1976), pp. 89-110. On the Hungarian War of Independence and Europe, *see* B. Köpeczi (ed.), *A Rákóczi-szabadságharc és Európa* [The Rákóczi War of Independence and Europe] (Budapest, 1970), pp. 5-32.

10. For Rákóczi's views on the nature of war, *see* Ferenc II Rákóczi, *II. Rákóczi Ferenc emlékiratai* [Memoirs of Ferenc II Rákóczi] (Budapest, 1951), pp. 64-65. For a Marxist analysis, *see* Á. R. Várkonyi, "A nemzet, a haza fogalma a török harcok és a Habsburg-ellenes küzdelmek idején

THE SUBLIME PORTE 147

(1526-1711)" ["The Idea of Nation, Fatherland, during the Turkish Wars and Anti-Habsburg Struggles (1526-1711)"] in [Anon.], *A magyar nacionalizmus kialakulása és története* [The Formation and History of Hungarian Nationalism] (Budapest, 1964), pp. 27-30.

11. Réflections de M. Dessaleurs, Apr. 1, 1705, in: Ministère des Affaires Étrangères, *Correspondance des Affaires Politiques* (hereinafter cited as CAP), *Hongrie*, X; Rákóczi's instructions to Ráday, Jan. 27, 1704, in K. Benda—T. Esze (eds.), *Ráday Pál iratai 1703–1706* [Pál Ráday's Papers 1703-1706] (Budapest, 1955), p. 122; E. Kovács, *Magyarok és lengyelek a történelem sodrában* [Hungarians and Poles in the Course of History] (Budapest, 1973), p. 189.

12. K. Benda (ed.), *Pápai János Törökországi naplói* [János Pápai's Turkish Diary] (hereinafter cited as *Pápai Naplói*) (Budapest, 1963), p. 14. See also Köpeczi–Várkonyi, *op. cit.*, pp. 227-29.

13. M. Asztalos, *II. Rákóczi Ferenc és kora* [The Age of Ferenc II Rákóczi] (Budapest, 1934), pp. 159, and 166; K. Benda, "II. Rákóczi Ferenc török politikájának első évei" ["The First Years of Ferenc II Rákóczi's Turkish Policy"], *Történelmi Szemle* [Historical Magazine], II 1962, p. 191.

14. *Idem.*, p. 195; *Pápai Naplói*, pp. 9-14; Köpeczi, *A Rákóczi-sbabadságharc és Franciaország*, p. 66; Asztalos, *op. cit.*, pp. 144-47.

15. *Pápai Naplói*, p. 16.

16. Ferriol to Louis XIV, Dec. 29, 1705, *CAP*, *Turquie*, XL; L. Rousseau, *Les relations diplomatiques de la France et de Turquie au XVIIIᵉ siècle* (Paris, 1908), p. 188; Köpeczi, *A Rákóczi-szabadságharc és Franciaország*, pp. 66-67.

17. Benda—Esze, *op. cit.*, p. 444.

18. Louis XIV to Ferriol, Aug. 6, 1703, *CAP*, *Turquie*, XL.

19. While Benda only suspects that Ferriol carried out anti-Russian agitation in 1704, Shutoy is categorical. *Cf.*, Benda–Esze, *op. cit.*, p. 444, n. 2, and V. E. Shutoy, "Pozitsiya Turtsii v gody severnoy voyny 1700-1709" ['The Position of Turkey during the Years of the Great Northern War 1700-1709"] in M. B. Grekov and B. D. Korolyuk (eds.), *Poltavksaya pobeda* [The Victory at Poltava] (Moscow, 1959), p. 108.

20. Rákóczi to Ferriol, Mar. 4, 1706, *CAP*, *Hongrie*, X.

21. *Pápai Naplói*, p. 23

22. *Idem*, p. 22.

23. K. Thaly (ed.), "Bay Mihály és Pápay Gáspár naplója tatárországi követségükről (1705-1706)" ["The Diary of Mihály Bay and Gáspár Pápay of Their Embassy to Tartary"], *Századok* [Centuries], 1873, IX, p. 610.

24. *Pápai Naplói*, p. 45. The Grand Dragoman (chief interpreter) of the Porte was a Phanariot, Alexandros Mavrokordatos, at the time of Pápai's mission. The Grand Dragoman had much broader authority than his title implies, wielding considerable influence in the Ottoman administration, particularly over the empire's international affairs. Pápai presented his credentials to the deputy grand vizier on January 21, 1706.

25. *Idem.*, pp. 45-48, 67, 95-98.

26. *Idem.*, p. 24.

27. Köpeczi, *A Rákóczi-szabadságharc és Franciaország*, p. 130.

28. Ferriol to Torcy, Dec. 27, 1705, *CAP*, *Turquie*, XLIII; G. Veinstein, "Missionaires jésuites et agents français en Crimée au début de XVIIIᵉ

148   ISLAMIC AND JUDEO-CHRISTIAN WORLD

siècle," *Cahiers du Monde Russe et Soviétique*, 1969, pp. 414, 424. For the Tatars' anti-Russian policies, *see* Shutoy, *op. cit.*, pp. 112-17; B. H. Sumner, *Peter the Great and the Ottoman Empire* (Hamden, Conn., 1965), pp. 11-12. For biographical sketches of Gazi-Girei and Devlet-Girei, *see* H. H. Howorth, *History of the Mongols* (London, 1880), Pt. 2, Div. I, pp. 568-70, and 571.

29. Protests about Austrian troops crossing Ottoman territory in *Pápai Naplói*, pp. 130, 134, 139, 140. On Bussy de Rabutin, *ibid.*, p. 150; N. Szávai (trans.), "J. L. Bussy de Rabutin: Emlékiratok a magyarországi háborúkból" ["J. L. Bussy de Rabutin: Recollections of Wars in Hungary"] in Köpeczi–Várkonyi, *op. cit.*, I. pp. 286-309.

30. *Pápai Naplói*, pp. 207, 209, and 215.

31. *Idem.*, p. 220.

32. The Porte referred to the Treaty of Karlowitz variously as the "holy peace," "peace" and "armistice."

33. *Pápai Naplói*, p. 203.

34. *Idem.*, pp. 87-88.

35. *Idem.*, p. 219

36. *Idem.*, p. 256.

37. *Idem.*, pp. 256-58.

38. *Idem.*, pp. 116, 121, 151, 177, 179, and 200.

39. Ferriol to Louis XIV, Apr. 15, 1706, *CAP, Turquie*, XLIII. Rousseau, *op. cit.*, p. 179.

40. *Pápai Naplói*, p. 143.

41. Mémoire présenté à la Porte par MM. Pápay et Horvát, Apr. 13, 1706, *CAP, Turquie*, XLII. These Franco–Hungarian memoranda are identified as French only by Shutoy, *op. cit.*, p. 109. A recent American publication claims they form the "germinal ideas" of the famous forgery, "Peter I's Testament"; *see* O. Subtelny, "'Peter I's Testament': A Reassessment," *Slavic Review*, December 1974, pp. 664-69.

42. Ferriol to Louis XIV, April 22, 1706, *CAP, Turquie*, XLIII.

43. *Pápai Naplói*, pp. 135-37.

44. J. Sternberg, "Russko-vengerskiye otnosheniya perioda poltavskoy pobedy" ["Russo-Hungarian Relations during the Time of the Victory of Poltava"] in Grekov–Korolyuk, *op. cit.*, p. 72.

45. Subtelny, *op cit.*, p. 665; Shutoy, *op. cit.*, p. 109.

46. Peter I's instructions to David Korbea, Apr. 21, 1707, in *Pisma i bumagi imperatora Petra Velikago* [Letters and Papers of Tsar Peter the Great] (St. Petersburg, 1907), V, p. 597.

47. Rákóczi to Pápai, Apr. 12, 1707 in Benda–Maksay, *op. cit.*, p. 151.

48. *Pisma i bumagi . . .*, VI, pp. 73-78; Rákóczi to Pápai, Nov. 3, 1707, in Benda–Maksay, *op. cit.*, p. 323; K. Thaly (ed.), *II. Rákóczi Ferencz leveleskönyvei 1708–1709* [Correspondence of Ferenc II Rákóczi 1708-1709], "Archivum Rákóczianum" (Budapest, 1873), II, pp. 152-54.

49. Rákóczi to Gáspár Pápai, Apr. 12, 1708, in Benda–Maksay, *op. cit.*, p. 405.

50. János Pápai to Rákóczi, Feb. 1, 1708, in *Pápai Naplói*, p. 377.

51. *Idem.*, p. 265.

52. S. Károlyi, *Önéletírása és naplójegyzetei* [Autobiography and Diary] (Pest, 1865), II, p. 492.

53. A. V. Florovsky, "Russo-Austrian Conflicts in the Early 18th Century," *The Slavonic and East European Review*, 1969, p. 109.

54. Köpeczi–Várkonyi, *op. cit.*, pp. 343-52.

A. Z. Hertz

MUSLIMS, CHRISTIANS AND JEWS IN
SIXTEENTH-CENTURY OTTOMAN BELGRADE[1]

From prehistoric times until the present, the promontory over-
looking the confluence of the Sava and Danube rivers has been
a favorite spot for human settlement. This location was defended
on two sides by formidable streams and made even more inac-
cessible by the heights rising sharply from the shore. Here a
relatively secure life combining fishing, agriculture and livestock raising was possible. Furthermore, the inhabitants of this
headland enjoyed substantial advantages in trade. These commercial opportunities were, of course, related to unparalleled
access to both the Sava and Danube, but in addition Belgrade
lay directly on the main Balkan land route linking Central
Europe and Asia Minor. For these same reasons, Belgrade has
also always been an extremely valuable military position. More
often than not, it has been the site of a major fortress coveted
by a long succession of warlike peoples. Celts, Romans, Byzantines, Bulgars, Serbs and Hungarians were only some of the
conquerors who held this stronghold in the course of its turbu-
lent history. In 1521 Belgrade fell to the Ottomans who, with
the exception of three periods of Habsburg rule, maintained a
Turkish Garrison here until 1867. Upon the Ottoman conquest,
the defeated Hungarian soldiers were permitted to return home
and the Serbian townsmen were deported to a village near Istanbul. In their stead, an Ottoman force occupied the citadel and
Turks, Vlachs, Gypsies and Jews were encouraged to settle in
the town. Such population transfers were a common practice
designed to cut the ties with the past and strengthen the sultan's control of the newly-won possession. From the fall of
Belgrade to the final Ottoman subjugation of Hungary (1541),
the city earned its nickname *darülcihat* or "the gate of holy war."

Belgrade became the principal launching pad for several Ottoman campaigns into Central Europe. At the same time, it was the capital of the Ottoman province (*sancak, liva*) of Semendire (Smederevo) which occupied more or less the same territory as Serbia before 1878.

This present study is based almost exclusively upon an unpublished Ottoman domesday book (*defter-i mufassal*) housed in the Prime Ministry Archives in Istanbul (*tahrir defteri 517*). Seven hundred and fifty-five pages in length, the register attempts to survey every form of human settlement in the *liva-i Semendire*. A full twenty pages (363–381) are devoted to the population and agrarian production of Belgrade as recorded by the official census taker (*defter emini*) Bali Mustafa at some time shortly before September 2, 1570 (1 rebiyülâhır 978).

The Ottomans were hardly concerned with obtaining a complete statistical picture of the entire population which might reveal sex and age structure and the many other demographic facets central to the concerns of a modern census bureau. Rather, they sought to provide a fairly accurate assessment of the state revenues to be derived from the populace within the context of the existing tax law. This fiscal legislation consisted of the particular code applicable to the province (*kanunname*) supplemented by specific decrees (*emr-i şerif*) authorizing exemptions for special groups performing government service. For example, fifty-two of the one hundred and ninety-one adult male Gypsies of Belgrade possessed just such a document recognizing their existence as a corporation of tax-exempt state servants (*cemaat-i müselleman*). As such, they were "free from *haraç, ispence* and other extraordinary taxes and customary dues" in return for their labor as blacksmiths on the vessels of the Ottoman fleet docked in the harbor of the lower fortress. Similarly, in the 1530s seventy-two Vlach households had enjoyed comparable privileges in exchange for guarding the imperial powder magazines.[2] It was, therefore, essential for Bali Mustafa to assign each potential taxpayer to his proper classification. With the exception of the civilian Muslims, all other groups whether ethnic, religious or vocational were perceived as constituting *cemaats* (congregations, corporations, assemblies, religious communities, military units). Thus, the Jews of Belgrade were the *cemaat-i Yahudiyan* and the artillerymen of the upper fortress the *cemaat-i topçuyan*. To complete this inventory of the tax-paying and the tax exempt, it sufficed to record the adult male population. Children and women were not enumerated except for those few Christian widows liable to taxation as household heads. Accordingly, the census results were generally expressed not in terms of the total number of individuals inhabiting a given quarter (*mahalle*), but by the total number of households or *hane*. For this reason, the present data can offer no information regarding family size which renders impossible any exact computation of the total population.

Despite this drawback, the 1570 census preserves a plethora of information regarding the city and its inhabitants. Geographically, Bali Mustafa divides Belgrade into three basic units—the town itself (*varoş*), the upper fortress (*kale-i balâ*), and the lower fortress (*kale-i zir*). Although in terms of location and function the upper fortress formed the core of Ottoman Belgrade, the *varoş* was the real focus of urban life. Bounded by the Danube on one side, the Sava on the other side and by the upper fortress in the middle, the *varoş* extended south into the country where town life quickly gave way to agriculture. The *varoş* boasted an active market place (*câ-i pazar*), public baths, the government storehouse (*ambar-i hassa*) and nine different mosques. Here lived most of the merchants and artisans, and all of the farmers. Here, as in the other two sections of the city, Muslims formed the overwhelming majority of the population. Bali Mustafa counted 481 Muslim households. In addition, for tax purposes, he separately identified 15 *imams*, 16 *müezzins* and 1 *sipahi* who were probably also family heads. Accordingly, the *varoş* housed well over five hundred Muslim households distributed throughout fifteen separate *mahalles* inhabited exclusively by their coreligionists. Almost invariably bearing Islamic names, the Muslims of Belgrade cannot be assigned an ethnic classification. The domesday data, therefore, generally furnishes no clues which might allow us to determine whether these families were actually Turks, or Muslims of another ethnic origin. In any case, such ethnic or national consciousness did not exist in sixteenth-century Belgrade. Doubtless, all Muslims felt themselves to be part of the ecumenical Islamic community which found its most striking political expression in the empire of the Ottoman sultan.

Gradually, the testimony of both historical documents and linguistic research is prompting a reevaluation of the Ottoman role in the Balkans. Contemporary historians are no longer satisfied with the assumption that the half millennium of Turkish rule can be judged from our knowledge of the last one hundred and fifty years. Thus, some attention to the question of Balkan commerce will reveal the very great differences between the sixteenth and nineteenth centuries. Specifically, the stereotype of the Balkan merchant under the Ottomans demands that he originate from one of the subordinate ethno-religious groups. Indeed, contemporary Belgrade contained a substantial colony of Ragusan merchants whose special status required that they be omitted from the domesday book. Recent research has revealed much about their activities that would appear to justify the traditional view of Balkan traders.[3] Yet, all of the Belgrade merchants (tacir) and boatmen (sefinei) actually enumerated in our census were Muslims. The substantial role of these Muslim businessmen is corroborated by the contemporary account books of the Ottoman customs house at Buda. On the basis of this material, it is clear that Muslim merchants and boatmen dominated domestic commerce on the Ottoman Danube and enjoyed a monopoly of the very important grain trade.[4] Furthermore, every last one of the approximately one hundred entries indicating shipments from Belgrade to Buda or Pest also records the name of a Muslim merchant or ship's captain. Although wheat was the staple, barley, rye, rice, grapes, figs, chickpeas, dried fruit, honey, olive oil, vinegar, pepper, flax and flour were all traded by Belgrade's Muslim merchants who also dealt in textiles, dyestuffs, leather goods, clothing, hardware, confections (helva), prepared meats and livestock. Along with the merchants of the Ragusan enclave, these Muslim traders helped make sixteenth-century Belgrade one of the more significant centers of Balkan commerce.

If data on the ethnic origin of the Muslim townsmen is lacking, information on the division of labor is abundant. Of the 513 adult male Muslims of the varoş over two hundred are identified by trade, official position or profession.[5] One hundred and sixty of these men were engaged in commerce, transport, services and crafts, while the remainder occupied religious and governmental posts. With the exception of agriculture, smithery, stonemasonry and tanning, Muslims virtually monopolized every

civilian job category. In this respect, the picture presented by
the *defter* conforms with the results of linguistic research. For
almost a century, philologists have concerned themselves with
the phenomenon of Ottoman loan words in the languages of
southeastern Europe. No Balkan language has borrowed more
heavily from Ottoman-Turkish than Serbian and nowhere in
Serbian are "Turkisms" more common than in the realm of urban
life, artisanry and trade.[6] Evidence of this kind is clearly indicative of the massive cultural influence of one civilization upon
another. This process is well illustrated by the social relationships reflected by the 1570 census. In this light, the Ottoman
presence in Serbia can no longer be regarded as sterile. After
all, the medieval South Slavs had had little interest in town
life. Preoccupied with the raising of livestock and agriculture,
they preferred to live in many small villages.[7] The Belgrade
which emerged in the first century of Turkish rule was, consequently, very much a product of Ottoman civilization.

After the Muslims, the next largest community of the *varoş*
was that of the Christians (*cemaat-i gebiran*). Bali Mustafa
counted two hundred and twelve such households distributed
throughout seven *mahalle*s. Although the Ottoman census here
too does not specify ethnic group, the earlier history of the city
would suggest the presence of large numbers of Vlachs. Confir-
mation of this supposition may be sought in onomastic analysis,
for the domesday book generally provides both the name of
the taxpayer and that of his father. Still, Vlach anthroponyms
are exceedingly difficult to distinguish from South Slavic personal names. Centuries of interaction, intermarriage, a common
faith and parallel subjection to identical third-party influences
had lessened the differences between originally distinct peoples.
Nonetheless, historical documents very like the present domesday book have furnished us with anthroponyms of individuals
forming groups specifically identified as Vlach. Just such name
lists were published by Karel Kadlec in his classic study on the
Vlachs and the Vlach law.[8] A comparison of the Christian
(*gebiran*) names from the present *defter* with the Kadlec material reveals that more than two-thirds of the Belgrade anthroponyms may be considered to be Vlach. Among these appellations are a very great many which the Vlachs shared with the
South Slavs and some which they did not. Thus, *Boğdan, D'ure,*

İstepan (*Stepan*), *Istoyan* (*Stoyan*), *Marko, Nıkola,* and *Radoye* are personal names which may be viewed as either Serbian or Vlach. *Filip, Kuman, Mane, Manoylo, Maruş, Mire, Pavel, Radu, Radul* and *Rafil* are clearly Vlach. Finally, the very common "Peter" almost invariably appears in a Vlach form as *Petre* and only once in its Serbian guise *Petar*.[9]

Whatever the difficulties of ethnic analysis, the picture is clear with reference to occupation or profession. In this respect, it is apparent that almost all the Christians of the *varoş* were engaged in agriculture with special emphasis on wheat and grape must. In addition, two kinds of barley (*şair, arpa*), rye, honey, fruit and vegetables were cultivated on a relatively large scale. Added to the canonical tithe[10] on this produce, the *defter* reveals taxes on seventeen separate mills (*resm-i asiyap*) and another levy on vineyards (*resm-i dönüm-i bağan*). In contrast to most other villages of the county (*nahiye*), Belgrade paid none of the dues relating to stockbreeding (*âdet-i ağnam, bid'at maa bojıt', resm-i ağıl*). Accordingly, the town's needs for meat, animal fat and hides were satisfied by rural producers. Despite this omission, the detailed assessment for the Christian community of Belgrade indicates a scale of agriculture sufficient to monopolize almost all of its labor. Through their efforts, the Christian peasants of the *varoş* made the city one of the more important agricultural centers of Ottoman Serbia.

Apart from farming, only eight other professions were practiced by thirteen Christian townsmen. Bali Mustafa recorded three Christian tailors and two each of priests, tilemakers, bakers, and stonemasons. In addition, there were one carpenter, one matmaker and one quarryman. Although the *defter* fails to identify Christian tanners, one of the Christian quarters is in fact labelled "district of the tanners."[11] Here, the names of thirty-seven adult males appear without any job classification. Many of these individuals were, doubtless, involved in the preparation of hides. Clearly, the vocational spectrum of the Christian community was relatively narrow. Assuming the domesday book to be comprehensive, Belgrade's Christians must have satisfied many of their commonplace needs through recourse to Muslim artisans.

Although the third group in size, the one hundred and ninety-two adult male Gypsies[12] of the *varoş* were without doubt the most enigmatic component of the population. Two peculiarities justify this designation of mystery. First, the Belgrade Gypsies formed a mixed Muslim and Christian community. Second, their Christian names were for the most part markedly Vlach.

In as much as a characteristically Muslim name indicates Islamic faith, ninety-seven of the Gypsies surveyed were Muslim and the remainder Christian. Nonetheless, the line between the two faiths could not have been sharp, for in several instances members of the same family bore names normally associated with the two different religions. Thus *Yovan* and *Ali* were both sons of *Grade*, and *Istepan* the brother of *Kurt*. Similarly, *Bolko*, *Gazanfer* and *Kurt* were all sons of *Pıryak* (*Prijak*). Data of this kind suggests a process of conversion from Christianity to Islam. This conclusion is supported by the frequent appearance of the Muslim name *Abdullah*, "the servant of God." In all thirty-six cases, it appears as a subinscription denoting the name of the registrant's father. As such, it was doubtless the common Ottoman hypocoristic glossing over a Muslim convert's "infidel" descent. This impression of easy transition from one faith to the other is corroborated by nineteenth-century observers. According to Ami Boué, the Gypsies "change their religion with as much ease as their domicile . . ." and François Pouqueville opined: "Ready to follow all religions, the Bohemians (Gypsies) have not any religion at all."[13] Whatever the worth of these flippant assessments of Gypsy piety, the structure of the census suggests that they were regarded as distinct from the other Muslims and Christians. At that time, as in the nineteenth century, they were not accepted by either community.[14]

The Vlach character of the non-Islamic Gypsy anthroponyms is especially salient. Again employing the Kadlec list as a yardstick, we discover the correspondence of close to fifty of the almost seventy different names. Many of these appellations are common to more than one Balkan people. Others are more distinctive, e.g., *Dorkun* (*Drokun*), *Bobe*, *Bota*, *Buta*, *Kalana*, *Korda*, *Kuman*, *Manoylo*, *Mire*, *Murşa*, *Petre*, *Radul* and *Yarul*. In addition, "Gabriel" appears neither in its Ottoman form *Gebrail* nor as the Serbian *Gavrilo*, but as *Gevril*.

The domesday book conforms to the Balkan stereotype in associating Belgrade's Gypsies with metalwork. As indicated above, fifty-two of them serviced the Ottoman Danube fleet and performed whatever smithery was needed in the fortress. But for one locksmith, their kinsman in the *varoş* were registered without any information regarding their profession. Any assessment of Gypsy agriculture or livestock raising is absent. Consequently, the hundred and forty non-service adult male Gypsies paid none of the agrarian dues and tithes rendered by the Christian peasants of the *varoş*. At the same time, *ispence*—the customary (*örfi*) poll- or gate-tax—was not levied upon these civilian Gypsies of Belgrade.[15]

Subject to the same freedom from *ispence* and agricultural taxes was the Jewish community of the *varoş*. Together with the sixteen adult male Jews of the town of Semendire, the twenty adult male Jews of Belgrade are the only ones which the domesday book records. On this basis, permanent Jewish residence in the other towns and villages of the *sancak* may be ruled out. Although the census preserves no indication of the manner in which the small Jewish community earned its livelihood, contemporary Hebrew sources point to local commerce and Danube trade. Thus, among the published *responsa* of the Sephardic Rabbi Samuel of Medina (*circa* 1506–1589), appears one case relating to sixteenth-century Belgrade Jews. In this legal process, Ruben, Simon, Levy, and Yehuda are all mentioned in connection with the leasing and exploitation of a shop, warehouse and residence constituting part of the *vakıf* properties located in the city.[16] Similarly, the published (1599) judicial decisions of Rabbi Samuel ben Moses Kalai (*circa* 1500–1582) include a record of the official proceedings of a Belgrade Jewish communal court. Meeting on November 3, 1547, this body convened to hear testimony relating to a brigand attack upon Jewish merchants travelling by boat from Belgrade to Buda. In addition to this information concerning the existence of Jewish Danube merchants, the protocol prepared by the inquiry makes specific mention of the presence of a synagogue in Belgrade.[17] Equally significant, both the cases cited refer to Jewish travel or trade between Belgrade and Ottoman Buda where there was a far larger Jewish settlement.[18] Finally, the appearance of two cases relating to Belgrade among *responsa* published in Salonica and Venice indicates that Belgrade's small Jewish community also maintained ties with other centers of Jewish life. In this respect, it would be nice to classify the Belgrade Jews as Ashkenazim, Sephardim or Rumanyots. Unfortunately, the personal names preserved in our *defter* are biblical anthroponyms common to all three traditions.

Abandoning the *varoş*, Bali Mustafa continued his survey in the upper fortress where six hundred and fifteen cannon and mortar of all sizes held the heights for the sultan.[19] Here, the overwhelming majority of the population consisted of the various units of the Ottoman armed forces. Nonetheless, one civilian *mahalle* of seventeen Muslim households surrounded the mosque of Sultan Süleyman (*cami-i şerif-i hazret-i hudavendigâr*). Twelve of these noncombatants practiced eleven different trades. There were two *müezzins* and one *imam*, tailor, saddler, barber, merchant, carder, carpenter, shoemaker, iron boot-tip maker and button maker. The services which they were able to provide the garrison were supplemented by several soldiers who were also artisans. Thus, the Janissaries (*müstahfazan*) had four carpenters (*neccar*) and both the *azaps* and *martolos* had one tailor each. Altogether, the Ottoman garrison here consisted of 541 men of whom 380 were Muslim and 161 Christian. The 230 Janissaries were exclusively Muslim. Their commander Nashuh was also the governor (*dizdar*) of the entire upper fortress. The artillerymen were separated into a Muslim unit of thirty-six and a special Christian contingent of ten commanded by a Christian *serbölük*. The four bombardiers (*kumbaracı*) were all Muslim, but the twenty-one *limancı* (military stevedores) were of both faiths. In this instance, there are two examples of Christian officers (*seroda*) commanding Muslim enlisted men. The combined unit of marines, caulkers and carpenters (*cemaat-i azaban ba kalafatçıyan ve neccaran*) was formed by one hundred Muslims and forty-seven Christians serving side by side within the same *odas*. Finally, of the ninety-three *martolos*, eighty-six were Christian and only seven were Muslim. Hudaverdi, the *ağa-i martolosan*, was a Muslim, but four of his six officers (*seroda*) were Christian. Again, here, two Muslim soldiers served in *odas* commanded by Christian officers.

Common service and personal contact prove the existence of far friendlier inter-faith relations than prevailed in later centuries. Certainly, the barrier between Muslims and Christians in the contemporary Turkish army was not insuperable. The succeeding period witnessed fewer Christians in the Ottoman armed forces. This phenomenon has generally been ascribed to the competition of Muslims who forced their way into traditionally Christian units (e.g., the *martolos*). However, the Christian military service reflected in the domesday book is clearly indicative of an environment favorable to Islamization. Is it not as probable that the gradual decrease of Christians in the Ottoman army was the product of conversion? According to this view, exactly those Christian elements (e.g., the Vlachs) with a tradition of military service would be the most susceptible to Islam. Their desertion would tend to exhaust the military skills of the Christian community. This process would ultimately render the remaining Christians less qualified to serve and less willing to regard the army as a viable career.

Between the water and the heights, a relatively flat strip of shoreline accommodated the lower fortress. Here, an exclusively Muslim population inhabited both the lower town and a citadel known as Bölme (barrier). The latter was held by a janissary garrison of forty-one which included one *imam* and one *müezzin*. In addition, Bölme boasted a civilian population of fifty households grouped around the Hasan Ağa mosque and another three families living near the Bölme landing (*iskele*). The remainder of the lower fortress stretching as far as the harbor was occupied by three civilian quarters. Here, seventy-three households worshipped in the *cami-i şerif-i hazret-i padişah*. Bali Mustafa recorded little of their activities. There were four *imams*, five *müezzins*, and two *vakıf* officials (*kaim*). More secular needs were served by two boatmen, two porters and one merchant, perfumer, barber, carpenter and butcher. If these were indeed the sole tradesmen, the lower town could not rival the commercial activity of the *varoş*.

The enumeration of Belgrade complete, Bali Mustafa had entered into the domesday book the names of 1,654 inhabitants. 582 of those registered formed part of the Ottoman garrison. The remainder were civilians representing households (823), or inscribed as individuals (249). As this last distinction appears fiscal and not demographic, it is preferable to treat the entire civilian population as one unit consisting of 1,072 households. Although the total number of persons constituting each household will never be known, some historians familiar with Ottoman domesday research have fastened upon five as a reason-

able fiction.[20] Adherence to this arbitrary convention will not
guarantee authenticity. It will, however, preserve the possibility of comparison with other sixteenth-century towns whose
population has been calculated on the same assumption. On
the basis of five persons per household, Belgrade's civilian population was in the neighborhood of 5,360 individuals distributed
as follows: Muslims 3,240; Christians 1,060; Gypsies 960; Jews
100. To the total civilian population, Ömer Lutfi Barkan generally adds ten per cent. This addition is designed to cover
"certain army units, the entourage of high civilian and military
officials, the Janissaries, the employees and servants of the imperial court for certain towns and finally the slaves" all of whom
tend to be omitted from the domesday books.[21] However, the
Belgrade census does include the Muslims (421) and Christians (161) of the Ottoman garrison. For this reason, Barkan's
ten per cent will not be employed. Instead, two noncombatants
for each member of the military will be added to the civilian
population. This addition (1,164) is an estimate including soldiers' families and other dependents, as well as the unregistered
categories detailed by Barkan. Accordingly, our calculation of
Belgrade's civilians will rise to 6,524 distributed as follows:
Muslims 4,082; Christians 1,382; Gypsies 960; Jews 100. If
soldiers and civilians are considered together, Belgrade's total
population was:

Muslims	4,503
Christians	1,543
Gypsies	960
Jews	100
Total	7,106

Employing the identical method of calculation, we may now
turn to the same domesday book to compare Belgrade's population with that of the other major towns of the *sancak*:

Semendire (Smederevo)—		Užice—	
Muslims	3,366	Muslims	2,955
Christians	970	Christians	220
Gypsies	80	Total	3,175
Jews	80		
Total	4,496		

Valjevo–		Rudnik–	
Muslims	2,420	Muslims	655
Christians	280	Christians	965
Total	2,700	Total	1,620

Belgrade's status as the province's largest center is immediately apparent. Like Belgrade, Semendire, Užice and Valjevo were predominantly Muslim towns. Although largely Christian, Rudnik had a substantial Muslim minority. In this context, Belgrade was clearly typical of urban life in sixteenth-century Serbia. From other Ottoman provinces, similar domesday data reveals the population (1571–1580) of some selected cities. Thus, Belgrade was more populous than Monastir (5,918), in the same category as Sofia (7,848), but far behind Sarajevo (23,485) and Bursa (70,686). Of course, all these towns were dwarfed by Istanbul's agglomeration of seven hundred thousand. Like Belgrade, Istanbul, Bursa, Edirne, Ankara, Tokat, Konya, Sarajevo, Monastir, Skopje, Sofia, Siroz and Larissa were largely Muslim. Christians predominated in Athens, Sivas, Trikala and Nicopolis, and Jews constituted the majority in Salonica.[22] Among Ottoman towns, Belgrade was of relatively modest size. Nonetheless, it was a full participant in an Ottoman urban civilization that has left a deep and lasting mark on Balkan culture.

Appendix

Occupations

ağa (3M*)	Head of a military unit, *cemaat*
alemdar (1M)	"Standard bearer," military rank
arabai, arabacı (4M)	Teamster or cartwright
attar (1M)	Perfumer or druggist
azap, kalafatçı, neccar 100M, 47C+)	Marine, caulker, carpenter
baçdar (1M)	Toll-collector
bakkal (7M)	Grocer
bezzaz (3M)	Linen draper
canbaz-i esb (3M)	Horse dealer

* M = Muslim
+ C = Christian

cebei, cebeci (4M)	Armorer
cerrah (2M)	Surgeon
çilingir (2M, 1M Gypsy)	Locksmith
çizme-duz (4M)	Bootmaker
debbağ (4M, 37C)	Tanner
dizdar (2M)	Castle warden; fortress commander
düğmei (2M)	Maker or seller of buttons
dülger (2C)	Carpenter
emin (1M)	Government official; steward; custodian; trustee
gülâbi (1M)	Rosewater maker; julep maker
habbaz (2M, 2C)	Baker
halife (3M)	Deputy head of guild
hallaç (1M)	Carder
hamami (1M)	Keeper of a public bath
hâmil (3M)	Porter
hayyat (10M, 4C)	Tailor
helvai (4M)	Confectioner
ilbad (12M)	Carder
imam (21M)	Muslim prayer leader
kâhyai (2M)	Trade guild warden
kaim (5M)	*Vakıf* official
kalafatçı (*see, azap*)	Caulker
kalai (7M)	Tinker; tinsmith
kasap (25M)	Butcher
kâtip (2M)	Clerk; scribe; secretary
kazgani (6M)	Coppersmith; cauldron maker
kefşger (14M)	Shoemaker
kethüda (4M)	Deputy commander of military unit, *cemaat*
kumbaracı (5M)	Bombardier
kuşçu (1M)	Bird dealer; falconer
kürekçi? or kürkçü? (1M)	Oarmaker / Furrier
limancı (3M, 18C)	Military stevedore
martolos (7M, 86C)	Militiaman
muy-tab (2M)	Hair-rope maker
muzeduz (1M)	Bootmaker

müezzin (26M)	One who calls Muslims to prayer
müsellem (52MC) Gypsies)	Tax-exempt state servant (here ironworkers)
müstahfaz (271M)	Garrison soldier; Janissary
naibelşeri' (1M)	Judge
nakarazen (2M)	Kettledrummer
nalbent (5M)	Blacksmith; farrier
nalça-ger (2M)	Maker of iron boot-tips
nassah (1M)	Tailor
neccar (8M)	Carpenter
nefyei (2M)	Matmaker
pop (2C)	Orthodox priest
saka (1M)	Water carrier; Janissary rank (corporal)
saraç (7M)	Saddler
sefinei (8M)	Boatman
semerci (1M)	Packsaddle maker
senktraş (1M, 2C)	Stonemason
ser-bölük (31M)	Commander of approximately ten Janissaries
ser-oda (12M, 6C)	Commander of approximately ten soldiers, marines, etc.
ser-traş (6M)	Barber
ser-topçuyan (1M)	Commander of the artillerymen
seyyaf (1M)	Maker or seller of swords
sipahi (2M)	Cavalryman
tacir (12M)	Merchant
taşçı (1M, 1C)	Quarryman
tave-gir (2C)	Brickmaker or tilemaker
tellâl (6C)	Town-crier; commercial broker
topçu (36M, 10C)	Artilleryman; gunner
turşucu (1M)	Maker and seller of pickles
voyvoda (1M)	Mayor or city governor
zer-ger (1M)	Goldsmith

NOTES

1. Research for this paper was supported by a grant from the National Endowment for the Humanities to the Ottoman Domesday Research Group of the Institute on East Central Europe, Columbia University.
2. B. Djurdjev, "Belgrade," *Encyclopaedia of Islam*[2], I, p. 1164.
3. J. Tadić, *Dubrovačka arhivska gradja o Beogradu: knjiga, I, 1521-1571. Gradja za istoriju Beograda*, Belgrade, 1950; R. Samardžić, "Belgrade,

centre économique de la Turquie du nord au XVIᵉ siècle," in *La ville balkanique XVᵉ-XIXᵉ siècles, Studia Balcanica III*, ed., N. Todorov (Sofia, 1970); V.Čubrilović, ed. *Istorija Beograda*, I (Belgrade, 1974), chapter IX, "Ragusians in Belgrade in the 16th and 17th centuries," pp. 423-51.

4. L. Fekete–G. Káldy-Nagy, *Rechnungsbücher türkischer Finanzstellen in Buda (Ofen), 1550-1580: Türkischer Text*, Budapest, 1962, p. 749.

5. For a view of occupations in Belgrade as a whole, *see* Appendix, with the alphabetical list of vocations.

6. M. Mladenović, "Die Herrschaft der Osmanen in Serbien im Licht der Sprache," *Südost-Forschungen* 20 (1961), pp. 159-203; A. Knežević, *Die Turzismen in der Sprache der Kroaten und Serben*, Meisenheim am Glan, 1962, pp. 397-407; A. Škaljić, *Turcizmi u srpskohrvatskom jeziku*, Sarajevo, 1966; F. Miklosich, "Die türkischen Elemente in den südost- und osteuropäischen Sprachen," *Denkschriften der kaiserlichen Akademie der Wissenschaften: philosophisch-historische Classe* 34-35, Vienna, 1884-1885.

7. J. Cvijić, *La péninsule balkanique: géographie humaine*, Paris, 1918, p. 257.

8. *Valaši a valašské právo v zemích slovanských a uherských*, Prague, 1916, pp. 451-68.

9. That the Ottoman scribes were sensitive to this precise distinction is clear from recently published domesday material, *see* G. Bayerle, *Ottoman Tributes in Hungary According to Sixteenth Century Tapu Registers of Novigrad*, The Hague–Paris, 1973, p. 138.

10. Earlier domesday material defines the tithe or *öşür* as one seventh or one eighth of the grain harvested and a full one tenth of vegetables and grape must. See B. McGowan, "Food Supply and Taxation on the Middle Danube (1568-1579)," *Archivum Ottomanicum* 1 (1969), p. 190.

11. *Mahalle-i debbagin der varoş*.

12. For tax reasons, the adult male Gypsies like the Jews and members of the Ottoman military were enumerated *neferen* (as individuals) and not by *hane* (household). Despite this peculiarity, there were probably one hundred and ninety-two Gypsy households in the *varoş*.

13. Quoted by A. G. Paspati, *Etudes sur les Tchinghianés ou Bohémiens de l'Empire ottoman*, Constantinople, 1870, p. 13 n.1.

14. *Idem*, pp. 12-13.

15. On this particular exaction, *see* H. Inalcık, "Ispendje," *The Encyclopaedia of Islam²*, IV, p. 211.

16. A. Hananel–E. Eškenazi, eds., *Evrejski izvori za obšestveno-ikonomičeskoto razvitie na balkanskite zemi prez XVI vek*, Sofia, 1958, I, pp. 219-20.

17. *Idem*, pp. 468-71.

18. L. Fekete, "Budin," *The Encyclopaedia of Islam²*, I, p. 1285, refers to seventy-five Jewish households in Ottoman Buda (*circa* 1550). However, recently published Ottoman census material (1546) indicates approximately two hundred and twenty adult male Jews divided among a total of ninety-nine households. See G. Káldy-Nagy, *Kanuni devri Budın tahrir defteri, 1546-1562*, Ankara, 1971, pp. 10-11, and 14-15.

19. For a 1536 inventory of armaments and munitions of Ottoman Belgrade, *see* H. Šabanović, *Turski izvori za istoriju Beograda*, Belgrade, 1964, pp. 283-84.

20. Ö. L. Barkan, "Essai sur les donnés statistiques des régistres de recensement dans l'Empire ottoman aux XVᵉ et XVIᵉ siècles," *Journal of*

the Economic and Social History of the Orient I (1958), pp. 9-36; *idem.*, "Quelques observations sur l'organisation économique et sociale des villes ottomanes des XVIe et XVIIe siècles," *Recueils de la Société Jean Bodin,* VII, La Ville: deuxième partie, Institutions économiques et sociales, Brussels, 1955, p. 293, n. 1.; T. Halasi-Kun, "Sixteenth-Century Turkish Settlements in Southern Hungary," *Belleten* 28 (1964), p. 68; the problem of the "household divisor" is surveyed by McGowan, *op. cit.,* pp. 157-164. Employing a somewhat different method, he suggests that the household divisor in late sixteenth-century Semendire *sancak* was in fact 4.59. This very complicated question may also be pursued in three separate articles on Serbia in *Household and Family in Past Time,* eds., P. Laslett–R. Wall, Cambridge, 1972, pp. 335-427.

21. Barkan, "Quelques observations...," p. 293 n.1.
22. *Idem.,* pp. 292, and 295.

V. MUTUAL CULTURAL IMPACTS

Ü. Ü. Bates

THE EUROPEAN INFLUENCE ON
OTTOMAN ARCHITECTURE

This paper will explore in a preliminary way the nature of the European impact on Ottoman architecture. The evolution of public architecture in the Ottoman Empire, which was a major power in Europe for almost 600 years, is clearly influenced by European, particularly Mediterranean, cultural sources. This paper will not attempt to list presumably borrowed traits or architectural elements shared by Ottoman and European buildings. Rather it will take up a more fundamental problem which is to understand the political function of monumental architecture in Ottoman society, and thereby better see what specific selective pressures could have influenced its growth. In short, architecture is erected by people. People do not respond to "influences," they respond to particular problems and attempt to realize specific objectives. Keeping this in mind, the paper will offer a number of generalizations in order to very broadly and briefly describe the nature of European influences in three periods of Ottoman history.[1] These three periods are: 1. the formative years of the Ottoman state, 1300–1450; 2. the so-called Classical Age, 1450–1650; and 3. the period of decline, 1650–1900.

These periods correspond to internal political, economic and social changes in the Ottoman Empire, which necessarily altered the nature of European–Ottoman relations. The discussion of European impact on Ottoman architecture will be limited to the most conspicuous and monumental Ottoman building of all periods: the mosque. Evolutionary changes can be shown more readily in one type of building, rather than trying to demonstrate architectural transformations selectively among diverse types of structures erected to answer a variety of needs.

Islamic ideology exerted a very strong, even vital force on the art and architecture of the Ottomans.[2] Many art historians have considered it to the exclusion of all else. There is considerable justification for this viewpoint. The religious or ideological differences separating the Ottomans and Europe probably have determined, more than any force, the limits to direct artistic exchange. Ideology and the symbolism of the architectural form also limited the transference of architectural plans, just as political boundaries impeded the movement of architects and artisans. On the other hand, our focus cannot simply be on differences and barriers to artistic interaction. The Greco-Roman architectural tradition was a common heritage, from which both the Judeo–Christian world in the West and the Muslim world of the Ottoman East derived their models.[3] Obviously, the process of adaptation and assimilation of this heritage was strongly shaped by the internal structure of each world but their shared forebears and continued mutual interaction cannot be overlooked.

The Ottomans were at all times in direct confrontation with some European power. One of the functions of public or monumental archictecture is political; that is, architecture serves as a symbol of power and of governmental commitment to particular objectives and policies. In architecture, the Ottomans developed and made use of a universal language readily comprehensible to Europeans. Of course, what was being communicated by the sultan and his government to Europe and to Ottoman subjects changed periodically as conditions changed. It is apparent from the accounts of European travellers to Ottoman lands that the messages recorded in architecture were understood.[4] Let us now turn to specific examples from three periods, and attempt to analyze the extent and nature of European impact on each selected building.

The first monument from the formative period of Ottoman architecture that we shall look at is the Mosque-Medrese, or school of higher learning, of Murat I Hudavendigâr in Bursa. Murat was the grandson of Osman, the founder of the dynasty. He acceded to the throne in 1360 at Bursa but did not remain in this city long. He personally carried the campaigns into the Balkans that had started during the reign of his father, Orhan Bey. By conquering the Balkans, Murat believed, Asia Minor would become vulnerable to the Ottomans. In 1366 Murat des-

...did in Bursa which however still remained *dār al-saltana*.
...rne under the patronage of Murat II became resplendid wit...
...pices, medreses, *dār al-hadīth* (the first in Ottoman architec...
...e), and a *mavlawikhāne*. He further built hostels, bridges...
...mams, mosques and *haneqahs* in the environs of Edirne.[1]
...s immense architectural activity concentrated in Rumeli...
...ked the renewed commitment of the Ottomans to Europe,...
...their desire to establish roots in this part of the world. The...
...re of European influence on Ottoman architecture in this...
...native period is, then, that the Ottoman state was in the...
...cess of claiming land and population in Europe, and the...
...ction of their architecture was to confirm and further this...
...cy.

...ultan Mehmet II, the son and successor of Murat, considered...
...self the Ottoman version of Alexander the Great, a world...
...queror, this time moving from East to West.[13] The conquest...
...Constantinople in 1453 was not the beginning of an era for the...
...kans, but the culmination of the efforts of the Ottomans to...
...blish themselves there as the leading power.[14] The conquest...
...natolia was a trivial matter after this event. It had completed...
...ocess which had started with Orhan Bey in 1345. From now...
...the Ottoman sultan no longer referred to himself merely...
...ghazi or bey but as the padishah of Islam. The Ottoman...
...ishah was the central institution of the Islamic empire.
...he policy of centralization became apparent after the con-...
...st of Constantinople, when the city was designated the...
...tal of the empire. Until then the Ottoman sultan had main-...
...ed multiple seats in the cities of Bursa, Edirne and to some...
...nt in İznik. This reflected the power of local interests. The...
...version of Istanbul to the sole center echoed more than simply...
...movement of administrative offices to a new site. The real...
...ge was in the decline of local political and economic inter-...
...as the central authority became stronger.
...he policy of centralization in the Ottoman Empire is reflected...
...rchitectural activities following 1453. The sultan was no...
...er patron of scattered or single buildings in several cities,...
...of immense *külliyes* or complexes composed of a central...
...que and its charitable, educational and pious dependencies...
...he best locations of Istanbul. The gathering of so many...
...lings fulfilling various functions within one enclosure is

ignated Edirne as the second capital after Bursa, and by developing this city as a center, he attracted it to *ghazis* as well as other volunteers and soldiers of fortune from Anatolia. These men were to be later used in the attacks on the Balkans. According to Gibbons, Murat was largely successful in his projects: if Osman gathered his people together, and if Orhan formed the Ottoman state, it was Murat who founded the empire.[5]

Also in 1366, in celebration of his sons' circumcision ceremonies, Murat began the building of an unusual but monumental mosque-medrese in Bursa. The commemoration of this religious building in Bursa celebrated implicitly the *ghaza* being carried out in Europe from the frontier city of Edirne. The construction was completed in 1385. The Mosque-Medrese of Murat is the first major building in Ottoman architecture which clearly draws on western, more precisely on Mediterranean styles. The main factors underlying the overt European influence on this build-in are three-fold: Foremost among these is the fact that the Ottomans were then expanding over the Balkans but not in Anatolia, and therefore, a considerable amount of its population was situated in this area. Moreover, the *devshirme* institution in the Ottoman army, or conscription of non-Muslim youths was inaugurated under Murat I. The majority of *devshirme* youths necessarily came from the Balkans, and they formed, thus, a new and important stratum in the Ottoman state. A second factor is that Italian cities and colonies, particularly Venice, entered into trade relations with the Ottomans around this time. Finally, we cannot forget that for political reasons, the Ottomans were not in direct communication with the Islamic East. Now let us turn to the particulars of this Mosque-Medrese of Murat.

The building is two-storied: the first floor is a mosque with adjoining rooms that served as *zaviye* (hospice). Upstairs are the medrese cells and classrooms. Although medrese and *zaviye* buildings adjoining a mosque were common enough in Anatolia, superimposition of units serving various functions within one imposing structure was unique and innovative. Until the Ottoman era, the Anatolian-Islamic structure, whether religious or secular, retained predominantly horizontal lines, and projected a traditional facade or other architectural symbols which made the identification of a building's function comparatively easy. In the case of Mosque-Medrese of Murat there is an obvious deviation from the established modes. The multi-storied building reminds one of palatial Mediterranean structures, such as Venetian palaces.

The façade of Murat's building contains two stories of galleries or loggias that are directed to the street, but more importantly to the landscape of Bursa valley. Such "opening up" of the building for viewing is unfamiliar in earlier Anatolian-Islamic architecture, but common to the Mediterranean secular architecture.[6] The Mosque-Medrese has the "textile"-like effect of colorful wall texture, accomplished by alternating rows of brick and stone layers, blind arches, diamond, hexagon and checkerboard patterns that enrich the areas around galleries or windows. Although such wall texture had been familiar in Byzantine architecture since the eleventh century, it is most widespread in parts of the Balkans, extending its geographical limits to Venice. Whether an Italian or Dalmatian architect was responsible for the Ottoman structure is now impossible to document. What is certain though, there was enough interest in the Balkans to emulate its architecture in Bursa. It is significant that Ottoman architecture was experimenting with new types of structures for religious buildings, and was very responsive to Western models at this time. Here the elements adopted are not simply decorative but of fundamental structure and shape.

In this period of Ottoman expansion into the Balkans there was an overt effort to stimulate a movement of Islamic settlement westward, as well as to incorporate local populations into the Empire. The Ottomans entered into close trade relations with Italian cities in the late fourteenth century, especially with Venetians who maintained a preferred status until near the end of the sixteenth century. Anatolian textiles and rugs made their appearance in Italian painting in the early fifteenth century, and a distant relationship between Ottoman İznik ware and Italian maiolica pottery has also been postulated.[7] It seems that direct artistic exchanges did take place between Italy and Ottoman Turkey. The Mosque-Medrese of Murat I in Bursa is an Islamic building in Mediterranean garb.

There is another compelling reason for the increasingly Western orientation of Ottoman architecture. With the Mongol invasion of Anatolia in 1243, the end of the Abbasid Caliphate in 1258, and collapse of the Seljuqs of Rum in 1307, the Islamic

states were no longer even symbolically uni[...] leader, they were left divided and weak. Va[...] in western Anatolia, the Ottomans among th[...] with eastern Islamic lands severed. Until th[...] especially Iran, had provided models, archit[...] Anatolian archictecture. Now, Ottomans and[...] cipalities in western Anatolia found thems[...] the manpower and cultural resources of the[...] Ottomans too, drew heavily on available loc[...] Anatolia and the Balkans. The Ottoman ar[...] losing its essential Islamic character, in[...] West became more meaningful to the newl[...] Most important, it announced to all the shif[...] tion of the state. It replicated the nature [...] during the reign of Murat I; one actively e[...] and trade relations to the West.

Murat I attempted to borrow and assimil[...] tural elements because he was particularly [...] kans. However, when Bayezit I succeeded to[...] he developed a foreign policy based on alli[...] of Egypt and other Muslim rulers.[8] The th[...] Timur from the east, most probably, com[...] rulers to unite and form a common frontier.[...]

Architecture during this time reflected [...] or traditional Islamic outlook. The Ulu Ca[...] of Bursa built by Bayezit between 1390 a[...] dition of Friday mosques of the Seljuqs, n[...] the "Western" look of the Mosque-Medrese[...]

In 1402 Timur had come and gone, takin[...] him as captive, leaving the Ottomans in[...] struggling for existence. However, by the ti[...] the throne in 1421, the Ottomans were or[...] ready to resume their campaigns to Europe[...] the examples of his forefathers, married th[...] tian princes from the Balkans or from Byz[...] wives' dowries to his ever-growing estate. A[...] ranks with the Ottomans once again in Ed[...]

Sultan Murat II transformed Edirne int[...] the ghazis, but also into one that was a mi[...] gateway to Europe. He spent many years [...]

clearly a symbolic expression of the power of the sultan. Moreover, it expresses the fact that he exercised authority by presiding over a highly specialized and ranked administrative bureaucracy.

The complex dedicated by the conqueror Sultan Mehmet in Istanbul is the first of grandiose dimensions, and with an orderly layout, organized symmetrically and differentially structured horizontal and vertical uses of space within a rectangular enclosure of approximately 200 by 300 meters.[15] The diversity of functions that various buildings served in the dependencies of the mosque suggests that the Byzantine concept of philanthropy as one of the most important of the many virtues expected of an emperor may have influenced Mehmet II in the organization of his architectural undertaking.[16]

The mosque situated in the center of the vast layout, collapsed during the earthquake of 1766 and was later rebuilt along slightly different lines. According to contemporary drawings and descriptions of the first mosque, the dominant theme of the building was the immense dome, echoing the one that covered Hagia Sophia in the same city. That the dome should become a significant element to such a degree was more than accidental.

The cathedral of the former Christian state, Hagia Sophia, Church of Holy Wisdom (built in 532–535) was at once upon the fall of Constantinople converted into an Imperial Friday mosque to serve the religion of the new state. Once converted into an imperial mosque, Hagia Sophia became the foremost model for mosque architecture. In part this is due to its symbolic association with the triumph of Islam. Hagia Sophia came to be seen as an almost miraculous architectural achievement in terms of space, dome and imposing exterior. It kindled the technical and artistic imagination of generations of Ottoman architects. Hagia Sophia was the pinnacle of the architectural tradition that the Ottomans inherited in northwestern Anatolia. In order to use Hagia Sophia as a mosque, icons and other signs of the Christian church and Byzantium were removed, and finally a small mihrab niche was built at a slant toward Mecca within the enormous apse. Also four minarets were added later. The architectural shell, that magnificent technical and artistic achievement was left intact. In addition, the church of Pantokrator (built between 1118–1124) or the Zeyrek Cami, served as the first medrese in the city.[17] The question to be raised here, why a 6th century structure and not more recent Byzantine structures were chosen by the Ottoman sultan to become the model for his royal mosque in Istanbul?

The historian of Mehmet II, Neshri while discussing the Sultan's architectural and artistic undertakings affects an offended tone.[18] The ruler seems to have displeased his fellow Muslims, especially the ulema. The ulema took offense without doubt in the close interest the young sultan displayed in European, that is in non-Muslim matters, such as "western" sciences and arts. He also housed European artists in his palace. Gentile Bellini, for example, was invited to make portraits of Mehmet and spent some time in Istanbul. There was also a learned Jewish doctor from Italy who served as his secretary.[19] No other Ottoman sultan before the nineteenth century indulged himself so openly with Europeans. Westerners must have also noticed Mehmet's hospitable behaviour toward European artists, because some wondered whether he was a Christian in disguise, or his Christian mother's influence on him was so great.[20]

His library was well furnished with Greek classics as well as Islamic literature, medicine, geography and history.[21] He composed poetry under the name Avni. Mehmet recognized the importance of commerce for his state, and preserved Italian colonies in Pera, granting them trading licenses. If we view Mehmet as a Renaissance man in the contemporary sense we can understand why he chose Hagia Sophia of the sixth century to serve as model for his and future Ottoman royal mosques and not later Byzantine edifices.

Sultan Mehmet was interested in the arts of East and West. He sought to incorporate in his royal buildings the past current ideas from Islam and the conquered eastern Roman world as well as from contemporary Italy. His mosque and the surrounding buildings were meant to reflect his universal kingship. It is not recorded that Mehmet ever brought an architect from Europe although it is mentioned that he attempted twice to have Italians build a bridge over the Golden Horn.[22]

In Italy about this time architects were researching Roman architecture, like their Ottoman counterparts, in order to represent "an ordered cosmos" in terms of architecture, "presiding over a homogeneous, geometrical order."[23] The Renaissance architect in the West introduced intentionally classical members: pilasters, columns and colonnettes, geometrical relationships, and a strong emphasis on spatial centralization and symmetry. The very elements that the Ottoman architect applied to the mosque and its dependencies of Mehmet II in the newly conquered Istanbul. The most logical sources of inspiration for the Ottomans were found in the Roman and early Byzantine architecture. There is a parallelism in the architecture of the West and the Ottomans who derived their elements from similar types of buildings and resources.

It is correct to say that the great domed mosques of the Ottomans, built after the fall of Constantinople, are unthinkable without Hagia Sophia.[24] On the other hand, the Ottoman mosque is by no means a blue-print reproduction of the Byzantine church. Hagia Sophia has a pronounced horizontal axis leading toward the apse. The central nave is screened off from the sides and is dominated by the dome. This wide nave provided room for the liturgical processions as well as the procession of the emperor and his retinue while the people were restricted to the side aisles and galleries. The mosque does not require such an isolated section since no processions are present in the liturgy of Islam. The central area is not separated because ideally everyone worships God on equal terms in the mosque. In Hagia Sophia the enormous piers supporting the home are hidden behind the screen of columns. The dome seems not to be resting on any material object, but as if floating over the central area. The worshipper is denied the intelligibility of the building.[25] There are no similar illusionary effects in the Ottoman building; the architectural structure is laid bare to the eyes, the relationships between members of architecture are clear and intelligible.[26] The characteristic of the Ottoman mosque is that every part of a building should appear as clear, easily recognizable and as rather independent forms. The same concept is also true for the Renaissance building.[27] The Ottoman mosque is clearly indebted to the Christian building, and by extension to the western architecture; yet it does not imitate it. The mosque answers its own needs. Its architecture is selective in the elements it borrows from western architecture.

At the peak of its political power, in the sixteenth century, how did the Ottoman Empire respond to Europe in terms of the architecture? What were the messages that Ottoman architecture directed to Europe? We can draw some conclusions about the importance of architecture in the political process. For this purpose the paper will focus on one royal mosque built in Edirne toward the end of the classical era, in the late sixteenth century.

Edirne, since its conquest in 1352 by Süleyman Pasha, son of Orhan Bey had become the second most important city of the Ottomans. After 1453 the Ottomans paid little attention to their first capital city Bursa but maintained a palace and spent long periods of time in Edirne.[28] The importance of Edirne was more than its gardens or its comfortable palaces, it was because of its strategic position as a gateway to Christian Europe.

Selim II was the first Ottoman sultan who was not engaged in large-scale war with the East, either within Anatolia or Iran. Before he came to the throne in 1566 as a successor to Süleyman the Magnificent, he had concluded peaceful treaties with Safavid Iran. He turned his attention to Europe where the Ottoman cause began to take a turn for the worse for the first time.

As economic and military setbacks continued, Sultan Selim searched for new sources of revenues. Against the advice of his grand vizier Sokullu Mehmet Pasha, he approved an attack on Cyprus, which was taken in 1571 from the Venetians. However, the fears of Sokullu were realized. The European forces united against the Ottomans and there was even talk of a crusade against Islam. The revenues received from Cyprus were far from being adequate to replace the naval forces of the Ottomans which were destroyed in the Mediterranean by the united Italian cities. The French and Austrians pressed harder for commercial favors from the Ottomans. Against the backdrop of such financial and political disasters Sultan Selim sought to commemorate himself and his reign in the form of a mosque and its dependencies grander than his father's. The site that was chosen was Edirne, actually on the road leading from Edirne to the West. The Selimiye mosque was meant to be a symbol of power, a sign of unshaken centralized Ottoman government under the leadership of the sultan, against the threatening European forces.

The mosque was built by the greatest Ottoman architect Sinan during the years 1569 and 1574. It is probably Sinan's personal accomplishment, and represents the highest point of Ottoman architecture. The mosque, framed by four slender minarets can be seen from any point in Edirne. It rises to unrivalled height and compactness.

Starting around the middle of the eighteenth century there is a change in the attitude of the Ottoman Empire toward Europe. The Ottomans seem to have realized their weakened condition. Still unshakenly Muslim and Ottoman, nevertheless, there is an attempt to acquire certain tools from the West which would ensure survival: such as printing technology, military training, medicine and engineering. Mahmut II (1808–1839), the most daring sultan since Mehmet II in his westernization abolished the Janissaries, established an educated officers' class, and he himself publicly donned a "European-looking" hat and trousers. He ordered his photographs to be displayed in every official building. For all he did, he was nicknamed "gâvur padishah" (infidel padishah), and major structural changes were never carried out.

The attempts to introduce novel elements from the West into architecture likewise remained at the surface. The basic layout of the mosque did not change, although ornamental innovations did take place. The medrese existed side by side with Western style schools. Palaces or kiosks were built in European styles, but the internal divisions into "haremlik" (women's quarters) and "selâmlık" (men's quarters) were still retained. On the other hand, for the first time in Ottoman architectural history there is direct imitation of European art, although imitations do not penetrate very deep. Now let us turn to the consideration of two royal mosques, one built in the eighteenth and the other in the nineteenth centuries.

The first royal mosque is the Nuri-Osmaniye or Light of Ottomans, begun under the patronage of Mahmut I and completed by Osman III in 1755. Sultan Mahmut after he squelched the Patrona Halil uprising, managed to bring relative peace in the country, and in relations with the West. Trade agreements were signed with Sweden and Spain, and those with France were renewed. For his royal mosque "it was said he wanted to have a building in the western manner but was dissuaded from such a folly by the ulema."[29] Nevertheless, the influence of western baroque elements are obvious in this edifice, and the result is that it is one of the most interesting mosques in Istanbul.

The domed square space of the mosque interior conforms with the traditional plan. However, in the elevation of the structure European influences are to be seen: the emphatic and plastic curve of the arches on lateral walls that support the dome; the projecting cornices; round or lobed arches of the many windows; the fluidity of architectural members. instead of being treated separately, and finally paintings of naturalistic flowers on the walls. The architect, a non-Muslim Simeon Kalfa, was the first of Greek, Armenian or European trained royal architects educated in "western ways." He designed a courtyard that must have pleased Sultan Mahmut and caused the ulema to shudder. Instead of the established square or rectangular courts of Otto-man mosques, Nur-i Osmaniye has a horse-shoe ground plan. Closely set slender columns carry the elegant, slightly horse-shoe shaped arches of the arcading. The approaches to the mosque are by means of ramps and broken staircases. Nur-i Osmaniye is the first mosque on which elements from baroque architecture are imposed. It is a major commitment by a ruling sultan to the recognition of contemporary western culture, par-ticularly that of a region over which they themselves did not rule.

Sultan Mahmut II who was sincerely interested in European "culture" celebrated the abolition of the Janissaries by building a royal mosque between 1822 and 1826 which he called Nus-retiye or Divine Victory. The mosque rose at the end of the parade route for the New Army which had replaced the Janis-saries, and had been set up along European lines.

The Nusretiye mosque when compared with the Nur-i Osmaniye is a much more successful example in which tra-ditional Ottoman and European elements are combined. The exterior of the building has a light and elastic appearance instead of the sprawling and pyramidal forms of classical Ottoman mosques. Two very thin minarets bracket the harmonious out-line of the mosque. Well integrated members of the mosque curve, undulate and form a fluid whole. The monumentality of the former Ottoman mosques is no longer present, but there is the concession of an impoverished Empire to Europe whose influ-ence is increasingly stronger. It is to the great credit of the Armenian royal architect, Kirkor Balian, that he could combine traditional Islamic and western elements in such an elegant manner.

This brief survey of European influences on Ottoman architecture comes to several concluding points:

1. The Ottoman Empire, by the virtue of having occupied a considerable part of Europe, was necessarily responsive to European stimuli which contributed to the shaping and evolution of its architecture.

2. The type of response to Europe on the part of the Ottoman patron and his architect differed from period to period, and depended mainly on the political conditions of the time.

3. During the formative years of Ottoman architecture, the influence of the Christian-Western world was stronger; it affected the choice of construction material, the taste of the patrons, and provided "modes" for specific buildings. The major inspiration for early Ottoman architecture was derived from local Greco-Roman, Byzantine and contemporary eastern Mediterranean architecture. The architecture that evolved during this early period was functional in terms of Islamic and Ottoman society, and at the same time intelligible to the Christian population in Ottoman lands.

At the peak of its power in the fifteenth and sixteenth centuries, the Ottoman Empire could not ignore Europe. Its architecture contained the symbols of power and of a centralized empire ruled by the padishah. The dome, more than any other architectural element, signalled these concepts to Europe where it was correctly interpreted.

Finally in the eighteenth and nineteenth centuries when diplomatic interaction with Europe was predicated on the technical and economic supremacy of the West, imitation of western institutions, especially in education began. At this time, too, European architectural elements began to affect the very fabric of the Ottoman architecture in a way reflecting the dependency of that society on the West.

NOTES

1. There are two art historical studies on the problem of European influence on Ottoman architecture, both in Turkish. Both works deal with the 18th and 19th century architecture: D. Kuban, *Türk barok mimarisi*, Istanbul, 1954; A. Arel, *On sekizinci yuzyılda Istanbul mimarisinde batılılaşma süreci*, Istanbul, 1975.

2. R. Ettinghausen, "Muslim Decorative Arts and Painting; Their Nature and Impact on the Medieval Arts," in: S. Ferber (ed.), *Islam and the Medieval West*, Binghamton, New York, 1975, p. 6.

3. O. Grabar, "Islamic Architecture and the West; Influences and Parallels," in: *idem*, p. 60.

4. Almost every European who travelled to or through Istanbul and Edirne and wrote about his visit praises or condemns Ottoman architecture and often compares it with Christian structures in his homeland or in Istanbul. Among the most extensive and critical descriptions of buildings by a visitor is that by Lady Montagu, *Letters of the Right Honourable Lady M——y W—— Montagu, Written during her Travels in Europe, Asia and Africa*, 4 vols., London, 1763.

5. H. A. Gibbons, *The Foundation of the Ottoman Empire; A History of the Osmanlis up to the Death of Beyazid I (1300-1403)*, Oxford, 1916, p. 125.

6. Constantinople became the site of an architecturally similar structure about this time. The so-called Tekfur Sarayı on the Golden Horn is also a rectangular block-like Bursa building, and has multiple windows on several tiers. What is surprising about this Byzantine palace is that it has been called "Un-Byzantine but western." R. Krautheimer, *Early Christian and Byzantine Architecture*, revised edition, Baltimore, 1975, pp. 473-75.

7. A. Lane, "Ottoman Pottery from Isnik," *Ars Orientalis*, 2 (1957), pp. 268, and 281.

8. Gibbons, *The Foundation of the Ottoman Empire*, p. 182.

9. Bayezit, to strengthen his position in the Balkans, placed a strong Ottoman colony in Üsküp and many conversions followed in Bosnia in 1399. Gibbons, *The Foundation of the Ottoman Empire*, p. 183.

10. Neshri, *Kitab-i cihan-núma. Neşri tarihi*, II, Ankara, 1957, p. 661.

11. *Neşri tarihi*, p. 667.

12. *Idem*, p. 679.

13. F. Babinger, *Mehmed der Eroberer und seine Zeit. Weltensturmer einer Zeitenwende*, München, 1953, pp. 450, and 546. Babinger further suggests that Mehmet must have been familiar with Ahmedi's *Iskendername*, and Greek version of *Alexander's Campaigns* by Flavius Arrianus, copies of which were found in the Topkapı Sarayı Library during his reign.

14. S. A. Fisher-Galati, *Ottoman Imperialism and German Protestantism, 1521-1555*, New York, 1972, p. 1.

15. For a very competent discussion and illustrations of this mosque and its dependencies *see*: G. Goodwin, *A History of Ottoman Architecture*, Baltimore, 1971, pp. 121-131. More controversial studies on the same mosque are: M. Agaoğlu, "Fatih Mosque at Constantinople," *The Art Bulletin* 12 ii (1930), pp. 179-96; and R. M. Riefstahl, "Selimiye in Konya," *The Art Bulletin*, 12 iv (1930), p. 311-21.

16. D. J. Constantelos, *Byzantine Philanthropy and Social Welfare*, New Brunswick, 1968, pp. 28, and 43.

17. A. Adnan-Adıvar, *Osmanlı Türklerinde ilim*, Istanbul, 1943, 2, p. 321.

18. *Neşri tarihi*, pp. 709-11.

19. Adıvar, *Ilim*, p. 201.

20. Babinger, *Mehmed der Eroberer*, p. 451.

21. Adıvar, *Ilim*, pp. 201 ff.

22. Babinger, *Mehmed der Eroberer*, pp. 552-56.

23. C. Norberg-Schulz, *Meaning in Western Architecture,* tr. A.M. Norberg-Schulz, New York, 1975, p. 226.

24. *Idem,* p. 137.

25. Krautheimer, *op. cit.,* p. 225.

26. Goodwin, *A History of Ottoman Architecture,* p. 170.

27. Norberg-Schulz, *op. cit.,* p. 251.

28. A. H. Lybyer, "Constantinople as the Capital of the Ottoman Empire," *Annual Report of the American Historical Association for the Year 1916,* I, p. 382.

29. Goodwin, *A History of Ottoman Architecture,* p. 383; T. Allom–R. Walsh, *Constantinople and the Scenery of the Seven Churches of Asia Minor,* London, 1836–1840, p. 12.

P. B. Golden

THE OĞUZ TURKIC (OTTOMAN/SAFAVID) ELEMENTS IN GEORGIAN: BACKGROUND AND PATTERNS

Introduction

The presence of Ottoman Turkish loanwords in the languages of the non-Turkish peoples once under the dominion of the Sublime Porte, one of the measures of the Ottoman impact in these areas, has long attracted the attention of philologists. The Ottoman elements in the languages of the Balkans and Central Europe, areas that were seats of Ottoman power and the focal points of prolonged contention between the Sultans and the European powers, have, in particular, been the objects of detailed investigations.[1] The collation of the results of these studies (one of the principal desiderata of Ottoman Studies) with the data drawn from local sources, the accounts of European and Ottoman travellers and the extraordinarily rich material currently being extracted from the massive body of Ottoman socioeconomic documents (*defters*, *vakıfnames* etc.)[2] and its setting into the context of the traditional political narrative, will one day enable us to trace the impact of the Ottomans on these lands on a microcosmic scale. Such a study will not only reveal much about the interaction of the Ottomans, on every level, with the peoples of these territories, but ultimately should greatly enrich our knowledge of the nature of societies in confrontation and interaction.

It is only recently that studies employing the sophisticated modes of philological analysis familiar to Ottoman-Balkan or Ottoman–Hungarian researches have appeared which deal with areas of the Ottoman Empire in which the cultural, societal or religious backgrounds were similar to that of the Ottomans (*e.g.*, the Arab lands).[3] Still less explored is a third area, one which, in terms of the various cultural layers that may be delineated in it, is extremely complex: The Caucasus.

With the exception of most of the Armenian lands and parts of Western Georgia, Ottoman rule here was not as stable as elsewhere nor of equal impact throughout the region. Societies here were at different stages of development, ranging from pagan and semi-pagan clan and tribal organizations to highly sophisticated and relatively urbanized Christian and Muslim political entities with ancient traditions and a sense of identity. This region, a traditional bone of contention between the empires to its East and West for more than a millennium before the advent of the Ottomans, was also a crossroads between the civilizations spawned by these empires as well as a gateway to or defense line against the "Peoples of the North."[4] This was (and remains) an area of enormous ethnic complexity, a fact recognized by the medieval Islamic geographers who termed "Mount Qabx" the "Mountain of Tongues" (*Jabal al-Alsun* or *Jabal al-Alsinah*).[5] Thus, the tenth century Arab polyhistor, al-Mas'ûdî, noted that some 72 different languages and peoples flourished in the North Caucasus.[6] In Transcaucasia, in contrast to the jumble of tongues in the North, three separate and distinct politico-cultural units took shape. In the South lay Christian Armenia, Indo-European in speech (but with a considerable Caucasian substratum) and receptive to the cultural winds blowing from East and West.[7] In the East was situated a patchwork of entities, pre-Islamig Ağvan/Alvan (Albania), Adharbayjân of the Islamic geographers, fragments of whose early medieval history have been preserved in the account of Movsês Dasxuranc'i/Kałankatvac'i.[8] This has always been an area with a complicated linguistic history (Caucasian, Iranian and now largely Oğuz Turkic) which became Islamicized and has at all times been profoundly influenced by Persian culture. Finally, in the West, lies Georgia, predominantly Orthodox Christian (as opposed to the Monophysitism of neighboring Armenia) and speaking a language belonging to the K'art'velian subgrouping of the rather loosely defined "Caucasian" language family.[9]

It is to Georgia, in particular, that I wish to turn. An assessment of the Ottoman linguistic impact here must first be prefaced by some important background points of orientation.

This is made necessary by the fact that some of the axioms for determining an Ottoman loanword in Balkan Slavic, Greek, Albanian, Rumanian or Hungarian do not hold true for Georgian. Thus, leaving aside pure Turkic words, the overwhelming bulk of Islamic culture words (words of Arab or Persian origin) found, for example, in a Balkan Slavic language almost always point to Ottoman. Indeed, the Balkan and Central European association with the Islamic world was virtually exclusively Ottoman. Similarly, although all of these countries experienced considerable contact with the peoples of the Turkic-Eurasian steppes during the Middle Ages, it is only in Hungary (nomadic in origin, profoundly and continuously influenced by Turkic peoples from "pre-conquest" (*honfoglalás előtti*) times through the Middle Ages) that we find any significant strata of Turkic loanwords antedating the Ottoman period.[10]

In contrast, the Georgian experience with respect to exposure to and interaction with Turkic and Islamic societies may best be described as multi-tiered, reflecting Georgia's ongoing interaction with various elements of the Turkic and Islamic worlds since the early Middle Ages. Hence, a given Turkic, Arabic or Persian term in Georgian may have a rich history antedating the Ottoman period. Moreover, even during the Ottoman period, the Ottomans were not the sole source of Islamic culture-words or even Turkic loan-words in Georgian. They had strong competition from their foremost rivals in the East: the Safavid State in Iran. The latter arose out of a Ši'ī sectarian movement which gained wide support amongst the Oğuz Turkic tribesmen of Iran and parts of Anatolia. These tribes are usually lumped together under the collective designation *Qızılbaš* (*Kızılbaş*). The Safavid dynasty, whatever its ultimate ethnic origins,[11] employed Oğuz Turkic as an official language (*cf.* several documents of Shâh Ismâ'îl written in the early sixteenth century which are linguistically indistinguishable from Ottoman).[12] Finally, it should be noted that in terms of ethno-linguistic classification, the Oğuz Turkic tribal components of both the Ottoman and Safavid states were identical. The Oğuz tribes as they entered the Near and Middle East in the eleventh century (under the Seljuq aegis), formed a solid belt extending from the westernmost, Anatolian "ğâzî line" to Central Asia. The tribes, however, did not always remain in compact groups.

Rather, fragments splintered off as they progressed westward. Thus, tribal groupings bearing the same name can be traced, even today, in checkerboard fashion all across the region. This phenomenon is confirmed by toponyms.[13] As a consequence, the problems encountered in determining whether a given Turkic word of clear Oğuz origin (as opposed to Qıpčaq and other Turkic elements also present in Georgian) is Ottoman or Safavid are considerable. All of these factors make it necessary to back-track somewhat and briefly explore the implications for our study of Georgia's complicated political history.

Contacts With the Turkic and Islamic World
Prior to the Fifteenth Century

The Georgian lands, like their neighbors in Transcaucasia, frequently found themselves the objects of unwanted attention from the neighboring "super-powers." Consequently, parts of the disunited Georgian realm were placed into the political and cultural orbit of the "super-powers" or their allies. In the early seventh century, for example, the Byzantine Emperor Heraclius, locked in a life and death struggle with Sâsânid Iran, formed an alliance with the Turkic Qazars whose raids into Transcaucasia and involvement in local politics became a permanent feature of the region's history until the late eighth century. The Georgians had barely had time to recover from the Qazar siege and taking of T'bilisi in 628 when the Arabs, replacing the Sâsânids, appeared on the scene and T'bilisi (*Tiflîs* in Arabic) was transformed into an amîrate in the Umayyad Caliphate.[14] The western Georgian lands, Ap'xazet'i (with its Georgian-speaking ruling elite and mixed populace) and Imeret'i, however, found themselves in the Qazar–Byzantine orbit. Leon II of Ap'xazet'i (whose maternal grandfather was the Qazar Qağan) was able to take advantage of temporary rifts in the otherwise stable Qazar–Byzantine alliance, to break out of the Byzantine orbit (with Qazar support) and become independent in the late eighth century.[15] Turkic influences, via the Qazars, were felt in early medieval Georgian lands and a remembrance of this is reflected in anthroponymy (*cf.* the name *Xazara*).[16] Turkic titles (*qağan, tarqan, jabğu*) are mentioned in Georgian historical sources for this period (*cf., K'art'lis C'xovreba*). Georgian–Arab relations

(and hence Arab cultural influences) were far more complicated. The Georgian territories, at this time, were a patchwork
of rival, native holdings and Muslim amîrates, both of whom
periodically showed signs of rebelliousness against the Caliphate.
By the early ninth century, the amîr of Tiflîs (Isḥâq b. Ismâ'il,
Sahak in Georgian) had established a *de facto* independence
and remained in "revolt" against the central government (according to the *Ta'rîx al-Bâb* preserved in Münneccimbaşı) until
ca. 853 when he was defeated and executed by Buğa the Turk
(who was also not immune to the centrifugal forces rampant in
the area).[17] Subsequent attempts to keep the region under the
authority of the central government (*cf.* the expedition of Abu'l-
Qâsim in 914) only slightly retarded the total collapse of Caliphal control.[18] Thus, by the mid-late tenth century, direct Arab
cultural influence from the Caliphal center was greatly reduced,
but the Muslim amîrs in and around Georgia provided a source
of constant contact and interaction.[19]

The struggle of rival Georgian dynasts, in the eleventh century, to achieve political unification of the country, was played
out against a backdrop of Byzantine and local Muslim involvement. The process was almost completed (T'bilisi, however, remaining under a Muslim amîr and the Kaxet'ian principality
unwilling to join the fold)[20] when a new and very serious com-
plication appeared on the scene: the Seljuq Turks. The first,
major Seljuq assault came during the reign of Alp Arslan in
1064 and was followed by another attack in 1067–1068.[21] This,
however, was only a prelude. Following the Byzantine collapse
at Manzikert in 1071, the new Seljuq Sultan, Malikšâh (1072–
1092), despatched expeditions against Georgia in 1073–1074 and
1076. These marauding incursions soon became annual affairs
and some of the invaders began to settle in abandoned lands.
The culmination of these raids was the *didi t'urk'oba* (lit. "the
Great Turkdom"), a massive series of Turkish invasions which
ravaged the land *ca.* 1080. The Georgian king, Giorgi II, was
forced to pay the *xarâj* and to join his army to the Seljuq bands
operating in those areas not under his direct rule (this did not
save his own lands from plunder). The result of this was the
massive depopulation of some regions and the presence of Turkish tribesmen throughout the land. Giorgi's ineffectiveness led
to a coup d'état in 1089 in which he was toppled and replaced

by his son Davit'.[22] The latter, called *Aǧmašenebeli* (the "Re-storer/Rebuilder"), in the course of his long reign (1089–1125) was able to stem the Seljuq tide and give a new and more posi-tive form to the Turkic influences in Georgia. The Georgian kingdom, able to benefit from the Crusades and the decline of both Byzantium and the Seljuq state, experienced a period of considerable territorial expansion, transforming itself in the process into a "Caucasian monarchy."[23] After conducting a series of military reforms, Davit', who in 1097 had already ceased paying the *xarâj*, began in 1101 a series of campaigns aimed at driving the Seljuq tribesmen from his lands. The effort was ex-hausting and Davit' feeling the need for extra forces (and a standing army) turned to his father-in-law, *Atrak* (*At'raka, Otrok*, of the Rus' chronicles), son of the famous Šaruqan (*Saraǧanis dze* in Georgian) who with his horde of 40,000 Quman families was induced, in 1118, to enter Georgia in service to the crown. They were settled in depopulated Inner K'art'li, Heret'i, Northern Armenia and the border zones. Although some of the Qumans ultimately returned to the North Caucasian steppes, others be-came sedentarized, converted to Christianity and were assimi-lated.[24] This population movement, conducted on a grand scale (even allowing for the exaggeration typical of medieval sources) left, perforce, its imprint as we can judge from the Qıpčaq loanwords in Georgian (*see* below).

Muslim influence (in either Arabo–Persian or Turkic garb) was also important during this period. Following his great vic-tory over the Seljuqs at Didgori in 1121, Davit', in 1122, at last took T'bilisi (which, after the long period of Muslim rule had, like other towns in Georgia, a strong Islamic character). Davit' 's subsequent conquests in Armenian lands and the successful con-clusion of his long campaign against the Muslim state of the Širvânšâhs (completed in 1124[25]) transformed Georgia into a truly Transcaucasian monarchy. The urban areas of this greatly expanded realm had large Muslim elements which exerted an influence on Georgian culture.

Georgia, due to its imposing military strength, political, eco-nomic and matrimonial ties, remained intimately connected with the neighboring Muslim states and statelets. The decades follow-ing Davit' 's death were taken up with the struggles of his successors to retain many of the non-Georgian lands won in his wars of conquest. The medieval Georgian kingdom reached the zenith of its power under Queen T'amar (1184–1212) who, in many respects, brought to fruition the work of Davit' Ağmašenebeli. Georgia had become one of the most formidable powers in the Near East. The state structure of the Georgian monarchy while retaining many of its native forms (*i.e.*, the *uxuc'esis* etc.) had also taken over institutions from the Seljuq state: the office of *vazîr* (in Georgia there were five *vaziris*, the highest offices of the state, who also formed a council, the *savaziro*); the Turkic *atabeg* office etc.[26]

T'amar's successors, Giorgi Laša (1212–1223) and his sister Queen Rusudani (*Rusudan mep'e*, 1223–1247) were both more given to debauchery than affairs of state. Thus, when the Mongol tide swept through, punctuated by the ravagings of the fleeing Xwârizmšâh Jalâl ad-Dîn, Georgia collapsed as rapidly as its neighbors.[27]

As in the preceding period, Georgia, caught up in the web of pan-Mongol and then Ilxanid politics, was open to considerable Turko-Mongolian influence some of which has remained in the vocabulary of Modern Georgian. Indeed, during certain periods, Turko-Mongol names, customs etc. became fashionable in Georgian high society.[28] Ilxanid rule, however, also gave subtle (and sometimes overt) encouragement to the centrifugal forces that were always present in the aristocracy and for this Georgia would pay dearly. When Ilxanid rule collapsed in the course of the first half of the fourteenth century, it was followed by the double scourges of Timur Leng and the Black Death. Of somewhat longer duration (but decidedly reduced in scale) were the attacks of Türkmen tribes (the Aq Qoyunlu and Qara Qoyunlu) who constituted Georgia's principal link with the Turkic world in the early fifteenth century.[29] Royal authority had, meanwhile, undergone serious buffeting. A respite was granted by the relative peace of the fifteenth century and the fact that their dynamic, new neighbor, the Ottoman state, was still largely busy with Constantinople and European affairs and the Safavids were only just beginning to stir. Georgia, however, was unable to overcome the feudal divisions that had so long plagued her despite the clear warnings signaled by the Ottoman moves on the Abxaz coast in 1451 and their subsequent taking of the Byzantino–Georgian state of Trebizond.[30]

Ottomans and Safavids in Georgia

In the sixteenth–eighteenth centuries, the now completely disunited Georgian lands found themselves alternately or simultaneously ravaged by the Ottomans and Safavids (the battle of
empires here was, in many ways, similar to the Ottoman–Habsburg struggles in Hungary). To the complex tangle of Ottoman–
Safavid relations in this region were added the expansionist
policies of the burgeoning Russian state which established a
foothold in the North Caucasus and periodically maintained contact with various Georgian dynasts.[31] The tribes of Dağıstan,
many of which had become Muslim, frequently raided the Georgian territories, often being summoned thither by the Muslim
superpowers. Entire regions of Georgia were for relatively long
periods under direct Ottoman or Safavid rule. Not infrequently,
the local representatives of either the Ottoman or more particu-
arly the Safavid administration were native Georgian dynasts
nominally adhering to Islam. Indeed, the role of the Georgians
and other peoples of the Caucasus (Armenians and "Circassians"
Čerkes–the Georgians are also frequently called by this term)
was quite extensive in the Safavid state.[32] To a certain extent,
it can be said that the Caucasian elements, the Georgians in particular, played a role in Safavid politics analogous to that of the
Balkan peoples in the Ottoman state. The Georgians constituted one of the principal sources of the *quls*, the military slaves
of the Safavid rulers, identical in this respect to the *kuls* of the
Ottoman Janissary Corps and Palace Administration. The Safavid *Qullarağası* was usually a Georgian.[33] Georgian *quls*, however, were not limited to the Safavid realm. Caucasian slaves .
were highly regarded in the Ottoman state and figured prominently in the affairs of the Porte. Indeed, Ottoman Iraq was
dominated by the Georgian Mamlûks.[34]

As might be expected, given the geopolitics of the region,
Ottoman influence tended to be stronger in the western Georgian
lands and Safavid influences in the East. Ottoman documenta-
tion bears this out. The text of the sixteenth century Ottoman
Defter-i mufassal-i vilâyet-i Gürcistân (published by S. Jik'ia[35])
employs the term *Gürcistân* ("Georgia") but deals only with
the western regions: Borjomi, Axalc'ixe, Adigen, Aspindza, Axalk'-
alak'i, Samc'xe, Javaxet'i and the Kars region, *i.e.* lands in the

Samc'xe Saatabago.[36] The Ottoman–Safavid Armistice of 1554 recognized the Ottoman spheres as being the Kingdom of Imeret'i and the principalities of Guret'i and Mingrelia. Safavid spheres were the kingdoms of K'art'li and Kaxet'i and part of the Samc'xe Saatabago.[37] Safavid documents for the region have also been published as well as local documents reflecting Safavid influences.[38] The latter can be measured, to a certain extent, by a comparison of the Georgian code of laws, the *Dasturlamali*, compiled by Vaxtang VI in the early eighteenth century with the Safavid *Tadhkirat al-Mulûk* stemming from the same period.[39]

The story of the Ottoman–Safavid rivalry as played out in the Caucasus, a rivalry that was soon enmeshed in local Georgian dynastic politics, is too long and complicated a narrative to be related here. From the earliest stages, however, certain patterns emerged: 1) as was noted above, Western and South-western Georgia tended to establish close ties with Istanbul and Turko-Georgian dynasts are found here. Eastern Georgia tended to be more in the Safavid sphere with the resultant dynastic ties and cultural influences 2) continuing feudal and dynastic divisions prevented any really concerted effort against the invaders, Ottoman or Safavid 3) the various dynasts, on occasion, attempted to use the neighboring Muslim super-powers against their domestic enemies 4) when one of the super-powers was either temporarily weakened or distracted elsewhere, the other usually seized the opportunity to expand its authority in Georgia 5) on the whole, the Safavids appear to have made a greater effort to incorporate their Georgian holdings into the main body of their realm. The Ottomans, for the most part, preferred a looser tributary relationship.[40] Finally, we should note that, in addition to being an important source of slaves, the country was periodically subjected to devastating raids which led to the depopulation of many regions. This was a particular feature of Safavid policy. Thus, when Shâh 'Abbâs I (1589–1629) decided to embark on his military reforms which would, he hoped, undercut the power of the Qızılbaš tribal chieftains, it was to the Caucasus that he turned for manpower. *Ğulâm*s were obtained through fearful raids which saw thousands led off into captivity in Persia proper (where their descendants live to this day).[41]

The centuries-old Georgian administrative structure was not

uninfluenced by these events. Thus, when *Rostom Mep'e* (King Rostomi), otherwise known as Xusrau Mîrzâ, a Bagratid prince raised in Persia and a convert to Islam, became the Safavid viceroy of T'bilisi (ruling from 1632–1658), he carried out a reorganization of the administration which mixed Georgian and Safavid usages.[42] Many of the Turkic and Arabo–Persian titles and offices given in the *Dasturlamali* undoubtedly derive from his reforms.

Although the Ottoman–Safavid struggle for Transcaucasia ended with the collapse of the Safavids in the first quarter of the eighteenth century, the ethno-political patterns remained unaltered. The Afšars and Qajars who succeeded the Safavids in Iran were also Oğuz Turkic in origin and hence the Turkic influences emanating from both East and West in Georgia remained constant. With the Safavid collapse, the Ottomans moved in and briefly established themselves in Eastern Georgia. They were dislodged in 1735 when Nâdir Shâh, aided by rebellious Georgian dynasts (who soon turned on him as well) took T'bilisi from them. Unfortunately for the Georgians, the experiences of Shâh 'Abbâs I's reign were soon repeated and the country was again drained of manpower to fuel Nâdir's wars. Georgia was saved from further exactions only by Nâdir's death in 1747.[43]

The strength of both of the great Muslim powers of the Near East was now ebbing. Thus, it was not to them but to the Russian empire that the tattered remnants of the Georgian polity ultimately fell in the early nineteenth century.[44]

As has been sketched above, for some three centuries Georgia found itself in direct, intimate contact with two essentially Turkic imperial entities. Georgians served both Sultan and Shâh in the army, administration and harem. The Turkic impact was felt at every level of society. Thus, it is hardly accidental that many of the eighteenth century manuscripts of the *Sitqvis kona* ("Bouquet of Words"), the famous Georgian lexicon of Sulxan-Saba Orbeliani (1658–1726), the greatest figure in the development of Modern Georgian and Georgian lexicography, contain supplements with Turkic wordlists.[45]

To round out our preliminary remarks, we must now turn to a brief review of the patterns of borrowing in Georgian in the pre-Ottoman period.

Patterns of Borrowing: The Pre-Ottoman Period

The eighth century Georgian chronicler, Leonti Mroveli, in his *History of the Georgian Kings* (*C'xovreba k'art'velt'a mep'et'a*), the earliest chronicle in the collection of medieval Georgian historical sources known as the *K'art'lis C'xovreba*, notes that in ancient times "six languages were spoken in Georgia: Armenian, Georgian, Qazar, Assyrian, Hebrew and Greek."[46] This statement (which is not to be taken absolutely literally) points to those patterns of cultural interaction already prevalent at that time and to a multi-lingualism and receptivity to surrounding cultures that is a feature of Georgian history. We can still discern in Modern Georgian the traces of the influences noted by Mroveli: Armenian, Semitic (largely Syriac in Pre-Islamic times and Arabic subsequently), Turkic and Greek. To this listing Iranian must be added.

Georgian shares a sizable vocabulary with Armenian (claimed as indigenous by both) as well as direct Armenian loanwords,[47] *e.g.*: Georg. *t'argmani* "to interpret, translate; translation" (clearly of Semitic origin, *cf.* Heb. *Targum*) ~ Arm. *t'argmanel* "to translate," *t'argmanut'iwn* "translation"; Georg. *vačari* "merchant, trader;" *vačroba* "to trade. bargain" ~ Arm. *vačarel* "to sell" (<Pahlavî *vâzâr*, Mod. Pers. *bâzâr*, a culture-word which has ranged far and wide, *cf.* Hung. *vásár* "market, fair" in a form suspiciously close to the Georgian).[48] Direct Syriac loanwords may be seen in: *k'ark'aši* "scabbard, sheath, quiver" < Syr: *karkâšâ; zet'i* "oil" < Syr. *zeitâ* (*cf.* also Georg. *zeit'uni* with the same meaning from Arabic *zaytun*); *zogi* "some" < Syr. *zaugá* "pair" (≤ Grk. zeugos "yoke").[49]

Byzantine Greek loanwords are quite common in Medieval Georgian literature and are helpful in resolving some of the problems of early Medieval Greek phonology.[50] Some have survived in Modern Georgian. *cf. martvili* "martyr" <Grk. mártyr; *Egvipte* "Egypt" < Grk. Aigyptos. Some other words, although ultimately of Greek origin pose problems as to the route by which they entered Georgian, *cf. tomari* "scroll, roll" ≤ Med. Grk. Tomárı[o]m < Tômos, but Arm, *tomar* and Osm. *tomar*).

From Pahlavî, from which there are numerous loanwords with extensive derivations in Georgian, we may cite just a few illustrations: *tomi* "race, tribe" <Pahl. *tôm* < *tohm* "an egg, seed, sperm"; *tani* "body, form, figure" <Pahl. *tan* "body"; *nišani* "sign, mark, token" (with numerous derived forms: *danišvna* "to appoint, engage, betroth"; *dasanišnavi* "marriagable, to be appointed"; *nišnoba* "engagement, betrothal"; *agnišvna* "to note, record, denote"; *agsanišnavi* "to be noted"; *mnišvneloba* "meaning, sense, significance, importance"; *šenišvna* "to observe, remark, notice" etc.) <Pahl. *nišân* "sign, mark."

Arabic and New Persian elements are found in considerable numbers in Georgian of the Pre-Ottoman period *e.g.*: *abrešumi* "silk" < Pers. *abrišam, abrešum*; *alqa* "cordon, circle, ring" < Ar. *ḫalqah*; *nobaťi* "tocsin, alarm-bell; turn of the watch, sentry" < Ar. *nawbat*;[51] *čoxa* "cassock" < Pers. *čoxâ* (borrowed also into Osm. *çuha* and thence into Balkan Slavic and Hungarian; *xaraji* "tribute" (*daxarjva* "to spend," *damxarjveli* "spender" etc.) < Ar. *xarâj* "tribute"; *xati* "picture, illustration, image, icon," *xatva* "to draw, paint" etc. < Ar. *xaṭṭ* "line, stroke, writing, calligraphy"; *lašḱari* "army" (*lašḱroba* "to make war"; *gamolašḱreba* "to set out on a campaign" etc.) < Pers. *laškar* "army"; *pasuxi* "answer" < Pers. *pâsux*; *jašuši* "spy" < Ar. *jâsûs*[52] (this form may have entered Georgian via a Turkic intermediary, *cf.* Osm. dial. *çaşıt-, çaşut- Tarama sözlüğü*, Ankara, 1965, II, pp. 833–834; Qıpçaq *jašut-* or *čašut-*: *Kitâb al-Idrâk li-lisân al-Atrâk*, ed. A. Caferoğlu, Istanbul, 1931, Arabic text p. 43). This brief sampling indicates the wide areas covered by these borrowings.

The Pre-Ottoman Turkic elements stem from several periods and different Turkic peoples: Qazars, Seljuqs, the Turkic tribes associated with the Ilxanids and the Qıpčaq Qumans. From the Qazar period we find titles and names (noted in the *K'arťlis C'xovreba*): *xakan, jibğu, ťarxan* and *Bluč'an*.[53] Seljuq borrowings also tend to be in the area of politico-administrative-military affairs, *cf. aťabagi* < Selj. Turk. *atabeg* "a military chief in the ruler's entourage, to whom the ruler entrusts the education and care of his son . . .";[54] *uji* < Selj. Turk. *uj* "border"; *jari* "army" < Selj. Turk. *čeri* etc.[55] Probably coming from Qıpčaq Quman are: *K'oč'* as in *ḱoč'ad svla* "to wander"; *ḱoč'ad mivali* "nomad" < *köč–* 'nomadize" (*cf.* K. Grønbech, *Komanisches Wörterbuch*, København, 1942, p. 149 *köč–* "nomadisieren, fortziehen"); *ťoḱmač'i* "smith" < Qıpč. *°tökmäči* (*cf.* Osm. *dökmeci* "founder,

metal-worker") and perhaps other terms such as *qanči* "vulture"
(Turk. *qan* "blood" + the nomen actoris suffix -*či*); *qarači*
"Gypsy, dark-complexioned person" (Turk. *qara* "black" + -*ač*,
-*č*, a suffix indicating "similarity to" *qarač, cf. B. Atalay,
Türk Dilinde ekler ve kökler üzerine bir deneme, Istanbul, 1941,
p. 21. The form *qarači* is found only in *Čağatay* now, *see* V.
Radloff, *Opyt slovaria tiurkskix narečii* SPb., 1893–1911, ii 1,
c. 162; which if it is unique to the latter would indicate that
qarači probably entered Georgian during the Mongol period).
Georgian *t'alp'ak'i* "cap, cowl" is probably a form of Qıpčaq
qalpaq (Radloff, *Opyt slovaria tiurk. nar.*, ii 1, cc. 268–69 Crimean, Qazan, Qırğız, Teleut, Osm. "eine Art Mütze...") with
a q/t alternation. The *Kart'lis C'xovreba* mentions two Qıpčaq
terms for "brave warriors who fight in the front ranks": *čalaš*
and *dasnačtda*.[56] The former is clearly Turkic *čalıš* (Radloff,
Opyt slovaria tiurk. nar., iii 2, cc. 1882–1883 Uyğur, Osm.
Teleut, Altay, Lebed "sich abmühen, sich Mühe geben,
sich einer Sache widmen, arbeiten"); the latter term is unclear.

In the Mongol Period still other terms of Turkic or Mongol
(usually via a Turkic intermediary) origin entered Georgian:
iaraği[57] "weapon, tool, implement" cf. Osm. *yarak*; *qaeni* "Great
Khan" < Mong. *Qa'an* ≤ *Qağan*; *ulusi* "nomad encampment"
< Mong. *ulus* "nation, people, state."

The Oğuz Turkic Elements In Georgian
Abbreviations, Sources

Limitations of space preclude the full listing of sources and
the various forms, variations etc. Below is a brief, representative
sampling of the most frequently consulted works. As all of the
latter have their entries arranged alphabetically, page numbers will not be cited here (except for the entries in Kakuk).

Georgian:
  E. Cherkezi, *Georgian–English Dictionary* (Oxford, 1950)
  M. Tschenkéli, *Georgisch–Deutsches Wörtenbuch*, fasc. 1–26
     (Zürich, 1960–1974)
  M. Kankava, *Mokle k'art'ul'-rusuli lek'sikoni* (T'bilisi, 1965)
  A. Torotadze, *Mokle rusul-k'art'uli lek'sikoni* (T'bilisi, 1969)
  N. Č'ubinašvili, *Rusul-k'art'uli lek'sikoni*, i–ii (T'bilisi,
     1971–   )

I. Abuladze, *Dzveli k'art'uli enis lek'sikoni* (T'bilisi, 1973)
   for pre-eleventh century vocabulary
Dast. = *Dasturlamali: see* n. 39
Iraqî Ar. = Iraqî Arabic:
   1. J. van Ess, *The Spoken Arabic of Iraq* (Oxford, 1938²)
      glossary
   2. H. al-Bakrî, *Dirâsât fî 'l-Alfâz al-'âmmîya al-Mawṣilîya*
      (Baġdâd, 1972)
Syr. Ar. = Syrian Arabic: T. Halasi-Kun, "The Ottoman Ele-
      ments in the Syrian Dialects," *Archivum Ottomanicum*
      1 (1969), 5 (1973)
Kakuk = S. Kakuk, *Recherches sur l'histoire de la lange Os-
      manlie* (*see* n. 1; Kakuk is cited to indicate that the
      same or kindred term is found in Hungarian and one or
      more of the languages of the Balkans during this period).

There are nearly 300 root terms (exclusive of derivatives) of
Oğuz Turkic origin in Georgian. The number of Arabic and
Persian words shared by Ottoman and Georgian which are not
found in Abuladze (the bulk of which probably date to the
Ottoman–Safavid period) and hence may have entered via Ottoman or Safavid Turkish is somewhat more than 300. Our concern will be primarily with Oğuz Turkic. The Oğuz Turkic elements in Georgian fall into two large categories: 1) words of
Oğuz Turkic etymology (these, where criteria are available, may
be subdivided into Ottoman and Safavid Turkish[58]) 2) words
of Arabic or Persian origin which have entered Oğuz Turkic and
were thence introduced into Georgian. Criteria for establishing
this latter category are either linguistic (*i.e.*, the Arab or Persian
word has undergone some change and appears in Georgian in
its Oğuz Turkicized garb) or circumstantial (*i.e.*, older Islamic
governmental etc. institutions have been modified in Ottoman
or Safavid practice and appear in Georgia in this modified
form). It would go far beyond the scope of this introductory
paper to present all the Oğuz Turkic lexical material here (this
I plan to do in a study which will appear in the *Archivum Ottomanicum* 9 (1977). What follows is a sketch, with representative
illustrative material, of the semantic groupings of the Oğuz
Turkic loanwords (including relevant words of Arab or Persian
etymology) in Georgian and comparisons (by no means com-

plete) with Ottoman loanwords in the other non-Turkic languages of the Ottoman Empire. What is most striking about this material is that it is not (as was largely true of the Pre-Ottoman Turkic elements in Georgian) limited to governmental and other institutional terminology, but touches on virtually every level of life. In short, we may speak of a symbiosis, on the linguistic level, which undoubtedly reflects a broader, societal symbiosis. A brief perusal of the material drawn from other regions of the Ottoman Empire indicates a similar pattern (and most often the same words are borrowed). One of the desiderata of Ottoman studies would be the collection and collation of all the Ottoman lexical elements in the languages of the non-Turkic peoples of the Empire. As was indicated in my introductory remarks, this data, used in conjunction with our other sources, would greatly facilitate an accurate assessment of the Ottoman impact. It is hoped that the following will give some indications of the richness of this material with respect to Georgian.

The Oğuz Turkic elements in Georgian may be divided into eight broad categories: 1) *government* (incl. titles, offices, symbols of authority, areas of economic life under government control, *e.g.* weights, measures, coins and taxes) 2) *the military/ military technology* 3) *social and economic life* (incl. family, kinship, dwellings, the home and accessories, economic terms, occupations, tools, implements, utensils, clothing, comestibles, games, entertainment) 4) *health, illness, medicines* 5) *animals* 6) *colors* 7) *expressions and interjections* 8) *miscellanea.*

1. The Ottoman and Safavid impact is especially extensive in the area of government. A comparison of the fourteenth century Georgian law code, the *Xelmcip'is karis garigeba* ("Ordering of the Royal Court") composed just prior to the period of Ottoman–Safavid domination of the land, with the eighteenth century *Dasturlamali* (< Arabo–Pers. *Dastur al-'Amal,* all citations are from the Surguladze ed., *see* n. 39) written after more than two centuries of intensive contact, is very instructive. Although the *Xelmcip'is karis garigeba* is not lacking in "foreign elements" (*cf. at'abagi* < Selj. Turk. *atabeg; alami* "royal standard" < Ar. *'alam; veziri* < Ar. *wazîr; ejibi* "chamberlain" < Ar. *ḫajîb;* numerous titles with *amir-* etc.), the *Dasturlamali* contains a much greater number of Ottoman/Safavid terms which either replaced older Georgian terms or denoted new or slightly dif-

ferent institutions: *garigeba* "a setting in order" *i.e.* "a law code" has become *Dasturlamali*; the *mandaturt'uxuc'esi* ("Master of the *mandaturis*"; *mandaturi* "lower ranking police-palace official") is now the *ešikağasbaši; beglarbegi* ("a provincial ruler" in Safavid usage, *cf.* also Osm. *beğlerbeği/beylerbeyi*, a title borne by Giorgi XI); *memandarbaši* "Receiver of Guests" at the court (< Pers. *mehmândâr* "a host, an officer appointed to receive and entertain an ambassador or foreign sovereign" + Turk. *baš* "head, chief"); *qap'ič'ibaši* ("Master of the *qap'ičis,*" *qap'ič'i*, *cf.* Osm. *kapıcı* "gatekeeper"); *qorč'ibaši* ("Master of the *qorč'is,*" < Turk. *qorči* "guard") etc. Many of the taxes cited in the *Dasturlamali* are of Oğuz Turkic origin: *kuluxi* "a wine tax payable in kind" (< Osm. *kulluk* "slavery"); *geč'anbaži/* var. *geč'anbaši* "a crossing tax" (< Turk. *gečen* "crossing + Georg. *baži* "duty, custom-duty" ~ *cf.* Osm. *bac*); *qonaxluği* "a hospitality tax imposed on the nomadic tribes" (*cf. konak* "halte, station; journée de chemin," *see* Kakuk, pp. 245–46; also Iraqi Ar. 2 *qonâğ*); *k'eč'abaši* "a tax on sheep imposed on the nomadic tribal population" (< Osm. *keçe* "felt" + *baži* which by popular etymology and influenced by Turkic has become *baši*); *odunaxč'a* "a tax on the nomadic tribes at one *abazi* per household" (< Turk. lit. "wooden coin" *odun* + *aqča*) etc.

Other terms that may be noted are: *č'auši* "courier, sheriff's officer" (< Osm. *çauş, cf.* Kakuk, pp. 100–102, Iraqî Ar. 2, Syr. Ar.); *elči* "ambassador" (< Osm. *elçi*, Kakuk, p. 140, Syr. Ar.); *sanjaxi* "district, a Sanjak" (< Osm. *sancak*, Kakuk, p. 348); *uzbaši* "commander of a hundred soldiers" (< Osm. *yüzbaşı*, Kakuk, p. 426; Iraqî Ar. 1 *yôzbaši*); *jalat'i* "hangman, executioner" (< Osm. *cellât* ≤ Ar. *jallâd, cf.* Kakuk, p. 92). Other terms not as widely travelled but found in Georgian are: (*Dast.*) *salbaši* "Master of the Rafts" < Osm. *sal* "raft" + *baš*); (*Dast.*) *tut'xuč'i* "collector of a tax on the sheep of the nomadic tribal population (the *tut'xu*)" = Turk. **tutquči* (< Turk. *tut-* "hold, seize" + suffix *-qu* + *či*). Of particular interest are terms of Mongol origin relating to the police apparatus which appear to have entered Georgian via Ottoman or Safavid Turkish: *taruğa* "chief of police" (*cf.* Osm. *daruga*); *iasauli* "police official" (*cf.* Osm. *yasavul* ≤ Mong. *jasağul*[59]).

The Ottoman system of measures of distance and units of capacity has also left its imprint on Georgian: *ağač'i* < Osm.

ağaç "a league"; *aršini* "a measure of about 71 cm." < Osm. *aršın* "measure of *ca.* 28 inches or 68 cm." (*cf.* Kakuk, p. 44); *oqa* "unit of weight" < Osm. *okka* "weight of 400 dirhems or 2–8 lbs." (Grk. ounkía which entered Osm. via Arabic, *cf.* Kakuk, pp. 308–309); *bat'mani* "unit of weight *ca.* 8 kg." < Osm. *batman* "weight varying from 2 to 8 *okes.* 5–30 lbs." (≤ Ar. *wazn* "weight" via Pers. *vaznân, cf.* M. Räsänen, *Versuch eines etymologischen Wörterbuchs der Türksprachen,* Helsinki, 1969, pp. 65, and 73).

2. Terms relating to the military and military technology are also numerous. A few of the entries under this category are: *bairaği* "flag, banner, standard" and its bearer the *bairağtari* < Osm. *bayrak* (*cf.* Kakuk, p. 61 also Iraqî Ar. 1, Syr. Ar.); *gemi* "ship" < Osm. *gemi* (*cf.* Kakuk, pp. 159–60); *katarğa* "galley" < Osm. *kadırga* (*cf.* Kakuk, p. 202 and H. and R. Kahane–A. Tietze, *The Lingua Franca in the Levant, Turkish Nautical Terms of Italian and Greek Origin,* Urbana, 1958, p. 526); *t'op'i* "gun, rifle" < Osm. *top* "ball, gun, cannon, artillery"; *t'op'č'i* ("gunner" <Osm. *topçu*); *t'op'č'ibaši* "Chief of Gunners" < Osm. *topçubaşı* (*cf.* Kakuk, p. 399, Iraqî Ar. 2; Syr. Ar.); *qumbara* "bomb" < Osm. *kumbara* (≤ Pers. *xum-pâra, cf.* Kakuk, p. 252); *dambač'a* "pistol" < Osm. *tabanca* (≤ Pers. *tapanča*); *č'axmaxi* "cock in gun," *č'axmaxis p'exi* "trigger" < Osm. *çakmak* (*cf.* Syr. Ar.); *p'alia* "fuse" < Osm. *falya* (≤ Ital. *falla, cf.* Räsänen, *Versuch.* p. 143); *ialk'ani* "sail" < Osm. *yelken.*

3. Very few kinship or family terms entered Georgian. There are only two that may be cited here: *baba* (var. *babai*) "father" found only in the Guret'ian, Imeret'ian and Mingrelian dialects < Osm. *baba; bağana* "child"[60] < Osm. dial. *bağana* etc. "yeni doğmuş çocuk üç yaşma kadar olan çocuklara verilen genel ad..." (*Türkiye'de halk ağzından derleme sözlüğü,* Ankara, 1965, ii, pp. 473–474). With regard to the home and dwellings in general, the following entries are worthy of note: *ojaxi* "household, family" with numerous Georgian derivatives (*e.g., meojaxe* "family man or woman," *daojaxebuli* "dere-e Familie gegründet hat," *saojaxo* "domestic" etc.) < Osm. *ocak* "hearth, family line, home..." (*cf.* Kakuk, p. 306; Iraqî Ar. 2); *ot'axi* "room, chamber" *cf.* Azeri *otag; oda* "dwelling house" *cf.* Osm. *oda* "room"

(*cf.* Iraqî Ar. 1); *č'ardaxi* "open-air building on four columns" < Osm. *çardak* (*cf.* Kakuk, p. 89; ≤ Pers. *čârtâq*[61]). Occupational terms borrowed into Georgian include, among others: *qač'aği* "brigand, bandit" < Osm. *kaçak* "fugitive, deserter, runaway" (*cf.* Iraqî Ar. 2 − *qačâǧ*); *k'urk'č'i* "furrier" < Osm. *kürkçü*; *javairč'i* "jeweller" < Ar. *jawâhir* "jewels" + Turk. nomen actoris suffic -*či*; *t'erdzi* "tailor" <Osm. *terzi* (≤ Pers. *darzî*, *cf.* Kakuk, pp. 394–95); (*Dast.*) *quluxč'i* "servant, one who serves" < Osm. *kullukçu* (*cf.* Kakuk, p. 252); (*Dast.*) *qalionquorč'i* "water-pipe guard" < Pers. *qalyân* "water-pipe" + Turk. *qorči*; *ek'imi* "doctor, physician" < Osm. *hekim* (≤ Ar. *ḥakîm*); *ek'imbaši* "quack" < Osm. *hekim-başı*.

Turkish terms for tools and implements apparently had a prestige quality attached to them for they replaced or stood side by side with a number of native terms in the languages of peoples under Ottoman domination. In Georgian we may cite a few of our entries: *č'ak'uč'i* "hammer" < Osm. *çekiç* (*cf.* Iraqî Ar. 2, Syr. Ar.); *t'oxmaxi* "hammer" < Osm. *tokmak* (*cf.* Iraqî Ar. 1); *burği* "gimlet" (*cf.* verb *burǧva* "to bore") < Osm. *burgu* (Iraqî Ar. 2, Syr. Ar.); *dugma* "hook" < Osm. *düğme* (Serb.–Cr., Iraqî Ar. 2); *qut'i* "box" < Osm. *kutu* (*cf.* Kakuk, pp. 256–57. Iraqî Ar. 2, Grk. koutí < koutíon < kýtos); *šuša* "glass" < Osm. *şişç* "bottle" (Iraqî Ar. 2); *t'ep'ši* "plate" < Osm. *tepsi* "small tray" (*cf.* Kakuk, p. 393; Iraqî Ar. 2, ≤ Pers. *tabšî*); *t'asqašuǧi* "scoop, ladle" = Osm. *tas* "cup, bowl"(*cf.* Iraqî Ar. 2) + Osm. *kaşık* "spoon"; *t'uluxi* "water-skin"; *t'uluxč'i* "water-carrier" < Osm. *tuluk* (dial. form of *tulum* "skin made into a bag to hold water"); *č'ant'a* "satchel, bag" Osm. *čanta* (Iraqî Ar. 1, Syr. Ar.). The Turkish imprint is equally observable in clothing and sundry apparel: *p'ap'uči* "slipper" < Osm. *pabuç* (*cf.* Kakuk, p. 317), Iraqî Ar. 2, Syr. Ar.); *qauxi* "turban" < Osm. *kavuk* (*cf.* Kakuk, p. 228); *č'ek'ma* "boot" < Osm. *çekme*; *araxč'ini* "cap" < Osm. *arakçın* (*cf.* Kakuk, pp. 41–42. Iraqî Ar. 1 ≤ Arabo–Pers. *'araqčîn*); *peštamali/peštemali* "apron" < Osm. *peştemal* (*cf.* Kakuk. p. 328. ≤ Pers. *pêšdâman* or *puštmâl*).

Turkish cuisine became particularly widespread in lands under their rule and still influences the cuisine of the Balkans, Hungary and the Arab lands. In Georgian we find: *airani* "buttermilk" < Osm. *ayran*; *bak'mazi* "eingedickter Fruchtsaft" < Osm. *pekmez* (*cf.* Kakuk, p. 324); *basturma* "sauer eingelegtes Fleisch

für Spiessbraten" < Osm. *pastırma* (*cf.* Kakuk, pp. 319–20. Iraqî
Ar. 2, Syr. Ar.); *boza* "e. dem Bier ähnliches Getränk" < Osm.
boza (*cf.* Kakuk, p. 78. Syr. Ar.); *bozartʾma* "a lamb dish" *cf.*
Azeri *bozartma*; *bozbaši* "a soup with lamb meat" *cf.* Azeri
bozbaš; čixirtʾma "chicken or mutton broth made with egg
yolk and vinegar" *cf.* Azeri *čığırtma; qaurma* "dish of chopped
meat" < Osm. *kavurma* (Iraqî Ar. 2); *tolma* "mutton rissoles
cooked in vine leaves" *cf.* Osm. *dolma.* Of foodstuffs, we may
note: (*Dast.*) *čaltʾukʾi* "unhusked rice" < Osm. *çeltik; pʾortʾoxali*
"orange" < Osm. *portakal* (Iraqî Ar. 2, Syr. Ar.).

Games and entertainments include: *alčʾu* "Rücken des Spiel-
knöchels. Ausdruk des Gewinnens beim Knöchelspiel" < Osm.
alçı (*cf. Tarama sözl.,* i. p. 92, ≤Mong. cf. Räsänen. *Versuch.*
p. 16); *duduki* "Rohrpfeife, Art Schalmei mit 9 Löchern" < Osm.
düdük; čibuxi "pipe" < Osm. *çubuk* (Grk.).

4. Oğuz Turkic terms for human and animal health and infirmi-
ties were also borrowed into Georgian: *jansaği* "healthy" *jansa-
ğoba* "health" < Osm. *can sağlığı; dambla* "Lähmung, Paralyse"
< Osm. *damla.*[62] The equine illness *damaği* "Gaumengeschwulst
(Pferdekrankheit)" < Osm. *damak.*[63] Although Georgian has a
native term for "crazy," *giži* (ult. of Iranian origin) it has also
borrowed the Turkish *deli* "verrückt" and preserved it in its
original meaning (*cf.* specialized secondary meanings developed
in the Balkans, Kakuk, pp. 120–21 "soldat turc, hardi, téméraire").

5. As might be expected, terms relating to horses and things
equestrian have entered Georgian from Oğuz Turkic: *čortʾi*
"trot" < Osm. dial. *çort;*[64] *dušaqi* "Fussfessel, Spann-strick, -kette
für Pferde"/*dušaqoba* "(dem Pferde) Fussfesseln..." < Osm.
dušak; iorğa "ambler" < Osm. *yorga; jidao* "withers" < Osm.
cıdav; uzangi "stirrup" < Osm. *üzengi; tʾavla* "stable" < Osm.
tavla (≤ Ar. *ṭawîlah*) etc.

Many of the borrowings dealing with animals again reflect
areas of interest to the nomad: *qočʾi* "wether" < Osm. *koç; šišagi*
"ein-bis zweijähr. weibl. Schaf: < Osm. *şişek;* (Dast.) *čebičʾi/
čepʾičʾi* "one year old goat, kid" < Osm. *çepiç* (≤Pers. *čapiš,
čapuš*); *tana* "calf, one-two year old calf" < Osm. *dana; kʾopaki*
"cur"/*kʾopʾakoba* "curishness" < Osm. *köpek.*

6. Relatively few terms for colors were taken into Georgian from Oğuz Turkic: *ala* "Flecken auf dem Mond" < Osm. *ala* "spotted, speckled"/*alabula* "Schmutz, Unrat" < Osm. *ala bula* "motley"; *qirmizi* "crimson" < Osm. *kırmızı* (if it is not directly from Ar. *qirmizî*); *abanozi* "Ebenholz" *cf.* Osm. *abanoz* "ebony" (< Ar. *abanûs.* ≤ Grk. ébenos).

7. Expressions and interjections: *alaverdi* "Trinkspruch, mit dem man e-n andern auffordert, aus demselben Trinkgefäss und auf denselben Toast zu trinken" *cf.* Osm. *Allâh verdi* "God has given"; *at'adan-babadan* "von altersher, seit undenklichen Zeit" *cf.* Turk. *atadan-babadan* "from (the time of) fathers and forefathers"; *bašusta* "jawohl, mein Herr!" < Osm. *baş üstüne!*; (Pšav and Kaxet'ian dial.) *dostoğriv* "pfeilschnell" < Osm. *dosdoğru* "straight, straight ahead, perfectly correct";[65] *iaxšiol* "Your health!" < East. Anatol. Azeri *yahši/yaxši ol!*; *ap'erum* "bravo" < Osm. *aferum, aferim* (≤ Pers. *âfarîn*) etc.

8. Miscellanea: *alaša* "Kühne, frei heraussprechende Frau" *cf.* Osm. *alaşa* "wild, unbroken ...".; *armağani* "gift" < Osm. *armağan* (*cf.* Iraqî Ar. 2, Syr. Ar.); *baiquši* "Eule, Kauz; (komischer) Kauz, ungeselliger Kerl, Brummbär" < Osm. *baykuş* "owl" also (*Derleme sözl.*, ii, p. 581) "mecâzen, sersem, aptal, uğursuz (kimse)"; *boğč'a/boxč'a* "Bündel, Futteral" < Osm. *bohça* (*cf.* Kakuk, p. 75. Iraqî Ar. 1, Syr. Ar.); *borji* (Guret'ian, Imeret'ian dial.) "First, Termin" (Kaxet'ian dial.) "Geldschuld" < Osm. *borç*; *boši* "weich (lich); schwach, locker" < Osm. *boş*; *bulaqi/bulaxi* "source" < Osm. dial. *bulak*; *dinji* (with numerous derived forms) "composed, quiet, sedate" < Osm. *dinç*; (Pšav. K'is. dial.) *duzi* "Feld in einer Ebene" < Osm. *düz*; *iara* "sore" < Osm. *yara*; *juja* "dwarf" < Osm. *cüce*; *sira* "row, series, rank" < Osm. *sıra*; *t'arsi* "unheilbringend(er) Mensch, unruhiger Mensch ..." < Osm. *ters* "reverse or back or a thing ... peevish, contrary, surly, wrong-headed ...".; *tusaği* "prisoner" < Osm. *tutsak*; *t'ut'uni* "pipe tobacco" < Osm. *tütün* etc.

Georgia has been in constant and close contact with a variety of Turkic peoples during the past 1400 years. As has been briefly illustrated through the representative samplings of Turkic loan-words borrowed during this time, the most far-reaching contacts appear to have occurred during what we have termed the Ottoman–Safavid period, a phenomenon reflected in a large body of loanwords covering virtually all areas of life. The Ottoman impact is of especial importance, for Ottoman civilization influenced not only Georgia, but the other major Turkic power that shared partial hegemony with the Ottomans in Transcaucasia, *i.e.* the Safavids. Inevitably, the question arises as to why Georgian society in the Ottoman–Safavid period proved so much more open to these external influences? The answer to this question is inextricably bound up with a larger issue, namely: why was Ottoman civilization able to establish the kind of all-pervading symbiosis with the conquered peoples that has been alluded to in the foregoing pages. A satisfactory answer will be forthcoming only after the many lacunae in our knowledge of the social history of the "conquered lands" have been filled in. Hopefully, this brief sketch has underlined the importance of the question and provided some fresh data that may ultimately contribute to its solution.

NOTES

1. The literature is much too extensive to be fully cited here. Among the most recent works, mention should be made of S. Kakuk, *Recherches sur l'histoire de la langue Osmanlie des XVIᵉ et XVIIᵉ siècles. Les éléments osmanlies de la langue hongroise* (The Hague–Paris, 1973) which has a thorough bibliography of the question. The classic work still remains: F. Miklosich, *Die türkischen Elemente in den südost-und osteuropäischen Sprachen,* I-II (Wien, 1884) and his *Die türkischen Elemente in den südost- und osteuropäischen Sprachen. Nachtrag,* I-II (Wien, 1888-1890).

2. For a bibliography of published Ottoman tax-registers, *see* G. Bayerle, *Ottoman Tributes in Hungary* (The Hague–Paris, 1973), pp. 172-73. For the use and examples of other types of Ottoman socio-economic material *cf.* D. Kal'di-Nad' (Káldy-Nagy), "Tureckie pravovye knigi mukata'a kak istoričeskie istočniki," *Vostočnye Istočniki po Istorii Nardov Iugo-vostočnoi i Central'noi Evropy,* ed. A. S. Tveritinova, I (Moskva, 1964); M. T. Gökbilgin, *XV-XVI asırlarda Edirne ve Paşa livası Vakıflar—mülkler—mukataalar* (Istanbul, 1952); M. E. Düzdağ, *Şeyhülislâm Ebussuûd Efendi fetvaları ışığında 16. asır Türk hayatı* (Istanbul, 1972).

3. *See* the pioneering work of T. Halasi-Kun, "The Ottoman Elements in the Syrian Dialects," *Archivum Ottomanicum* I (1969), pp. 14-91, and 5 (1973), pp. 17-95.

4. C. Toumanoff, "Armenia and Georgia," *The Cambridge Medieval History,* IV, part I: *The Byzantine Empire: Byzantium and Its Neighbors,* ed. J. M. Hussey (Cambridge, 1966); D. Obolensky, *The Byzantine Commonwealth* (London, 1971), pp. 33-34. M. F. D. Allen, *A History of the Georgian People* (reprint: New York, 1971), p. 76.

5. V. F. Minorsky, *A History of Sharvân and Darband* (Cambridge, 1958), p. 91; Ş. Erel, *Dağıstan ve Dağıstanlılar* Istanbul, 1961), pp. 1-2.

6. Al-Mas'ûdî, *Murûj adh-Dhahab wa Ma'âdin al-Jawhar*, ed. C. Pellat (Beirut, 1966), I, p. 209; *cf.*, also Ibn al-Faqîh, *Kitâb al-Buldân*, ed. M. J. de Geoje (Leiden, 1885), pp. 25-295; Yâqût, *Mu'jam al-Buldân* (Beirut, 1957), IV, pp. 300 etc.

7. In general, *see* S. Der Nersessian, *The Armenians* (New York–Washington, 1970) and N. Adonc, *Armeniia v époxu Iustiniana* (SPb., 1908), pp. 2-3; on Armenian origins *see* G. Kapancian, *Istoriko-lingvisti-českie raboty* (Erevan, 1956); C. Toumanoff, *Studies in Christian Caucasian History* (Georgetown, 1963), pp. 48 ff.

8. *The History of the Caucasian Albanians by Movsês Dasxurançi*, trans. C. Dowsett (London, 1961); *cf.* also K V. Trever, *Očerki po istorii i kul'ture kavkazskoi Albanii* (Moskva–Leningrad, 1959).

9. G. A. Klimov, *Kavkazskie iazyki* (Moskva, 1965), esp. pp. 38-48.

10. The literature here is very extensive. For the "pre-conquest" and "conquest" periods, *see* Gy. Németh. *A honfoglaló magyarság kialakulása* (Budapest, 1930) and L. Ligeti (ed.) *A magyarság őstörténete* (Budapest, 1943). For the Pečenegs and Qumans in Hungary, *see* bibliographies in Gy. Moravcsik, *Byzantinoturcica* (Berlin, 1958²), I, pp. 87-94; L. Rásonyi, *Tarihte Türklük* (Ankara, 1971), pp. 327-33. On the Turkic loanwords in Hungarian, *see* G. Bárczi–L. Benkő–J. Berrár, *A magyar nyelv története* (Budapest, 1967), pp. 280-84; Z. Gombocz, *Die Bulgarisch-Türkischen Lehnwörter in der ungarischen Sprache in den Mémoires de la Société Finno-Ougrienne* 30 (1912) and the new data on post- Bulğaro/Oğuric loanwords in T. Halasi-Kun, "Kipchak Philology and the Turkic Loanwords in Hungarian," *Archivum Eurasiae Medii Aevi* 1 (1975). It should be noted that the Slavic-speaking Bulgarians of today, although partly Turkic in origin, have preserved surprisingly little of their pre-Ottoman Turkic vocabulary. Bulğar Turkic (a form of Oğuric) appears to have been almost totally effaced with the advent of Christianity to Bulgaria in the mid-9th century and the subsequent slavicization of the Turkic ruling element. On Bulğar Turkic *see* O. Pritsak, *Die Bulgarische Fürstenliste* (Wiesbaden, 1955).

11. *See* Minorsky's comments in *Tadhkirat al-Mulûk*, ed. trans. V. F. Minorsky (London, 1943), pp. 12-18, 187-95. R. M. Savory, "Safavid Persia," *The Cambridge History of Islam* (Cambridge, 1970), I, pp. 394-99; H. Laoust, *Les Schismes dans l'Islam*, (Paris, 1965), pp. 261, 263-65; P. M. Holt, *Egypt and the Fertile Crescent 1516-1922* (London, 1966), pp. 33-36. On Ottoman–Safavid polemics *see* J. R. Walsh "The Historiography of Ottoman–Safavid Relations in the Sixteenth and Seventeenth Centuries," *Historians of the Middle East*, eds. B. Lewis–P. M. Holt (London, 1962); E. Eberhard, *Osmanische Polemik gegen die Safaviden im 16. Jahrhundert nach arabischen Handschriften* (Freiburg, 1970). On the heterodox movements amongst the Anatolian Oğuz tribes, *see* M. F. Köprülü, *Osmanlı imparatorluğunun kuruluşu* (Ankara, 1972²), esp. pp. 98 ff., 141 ff.; H. Inalcık, *The Ottoman Empire, The Classical Age 1300-1600* (London, 1973), pp. 194-97.

12. L. Fekete, "İlk Sefevî şahlarının Türkçe çıkartılmış iki senedi," *Ağmosavluri P'ilologia*, 3 (1973), pp. 290-93.

13. Köprülü, *Osm. imp. kur.*, pp. 85-92, 128; D. E. Eremeev, *Étnogenez turok* (Moskova, 1971), esp. pp. 83-89. For a detailed analysis of the Oğuz tribes *see* F. Sümer, *Oğuzlar* (Ankara, 1967), pp. 193-363. For Oğuz tribal names as toponyms in Transcaucasia, *see* R. A. Guseinov, "Tiurkskie

ètničeskie gruppy XI-XII vv. v Zakavkaz'e," *Tiurkologičeskii Sbornik 1972* (Moskva, 1973), p. 381.

14. Movsês Dasxuranc'i, trans. Dowsett, pp. 81-88; *K'art'lis C'xovreba*, ed. S. Quaxč'išvili (T'bilisi, 1955), I, pp. 225, 374-75. On the Arab conquests, *see* I. Javaxišvili, *K'art'veli eris istoria* (T'bilisi, 1965), II, pp. 73-75. For the treaty of the Arab commander Habîb b. Maslamah with the inhabitants of Tiflîs, *see, al-Balâdhurî, Futûh al-Buldân*, ed. Riḍwân M. Raḍwân (Cairo, 1959), pp. 204-205.

15. *K'art'lis C'xovreba*, ed. Qauxč'išvili, I, p. 251; Javaxišvili, *K'art'veli eris ist.*, II, pp. 82, 92-93; Z. V. Ančabadze, *Iz istorii srednevekovoi Abxazii* (Suxumi 1959), pp. 101-105; Toumanoff, *Studies*, pp. 256-401.

16. M. Jik'ia, "T'urkuli carmomavlobis ant'roponimebi K'art'ulši," *Aḡmosavluri P'ilologia* 3 (1973), p. 212.

17. Minorsky, *Hist. Sharvân and Darband.* (Arabic text), p. 3, trans. p. 25. Buḡa was recalled by the caliphal government when it was learned that he had been negotiating with the Qazars (*K'art'lis C'xovreba*, ed. Qauxč'išvili, I, pp. 256-57).

18. *K'art'lis C'xovreba*, ed. Quaxč'išvili, I, pp. 262-63; Javaxišvili, *K'art'-veli eris ist.*, II, pp. 104-105. N. A. Berdzenišvili–V. D. Dondua, *et alii, Istoriia Gruzii* (Tbilisi, 1962), I, p. 130.

19. Aside from the amîr of Tiflîs the most important of the local Muslim dynasts were the Šaddâdids who figure prominently in the history of Eastern and Western Transcaucasia, *see* V. Minorsky, *Studies in Caucasian History* (London, 1953), chaps. I-II.

20. Berdzenišvili–Dondua *et al., Ist. Gruzii*, I, pp. 134-45; Toumanoff, *CHM*, IV/1, pp. 618-19.

21. *K'art'lis C'xovreba*, ed. Quaxč'išvili, I, pp. 306-309; Ibn al-Athîr *Al-Kâmil fî't-Ta'rix*, ed. C. J. Tornberg (Beirut reprint, 1965-1966), X, pp. 38-40; N. Lûgal (Turk. trans.), *Sadruddin ebu'l Hasan 'Ali ibn Nâsir ibn 'Ali el-Hüseyin, Ahbâr üd-Devlet is-Selçukıyye* (Ankara, 1943), pp. 24 ff.; M. H. Yınanç, *Türkiye tarihi, Selçuklular devri* (Istanbul, 1944), pp. 57-59; M. D. Lordkipanidze, *Istoriia Gruzii XI-načala XIII veka* (Tilbisi, 1974), pp. 81-82, gives 1065 as the date for the first major Seljuq incursion into Georgia. The second attack (in 1068) was particularly devastating as the Kaxet'ian kulce, Aḡsart'an, the Armenian king, Kvirike, and Ja'far, the amîr of Tiflîs, had all joined the Seljuqs with the aim of revenging themselves on the Georgian Bagratids.

22. *K'art'lis C'xovreba*, ed. Qauxč'švili, I, pp. 309-22; Lordkipanidze, *Ist. Gruzii XI-načala XIII veka*, pp. 84-87; Javaxišvili, *K'art'veli eris ist.*, II, pp. 160-63.

23. Allen, *Hist. of the Georgian People*, pp. 95-96. Georgians also figure in the larger Turkic world of this period, as recent research on the Bešk'en dynasty of Northwestern Iran indicates, *see* P. T'op'uria, "Masalebi Bešk'eniant'a k'art'uli dinastiis istoriisat'vis" in V. Gabašvili *et alii* (eds.), *Maxlobeli Aḡmosavlet'is istoriis sakit'xebi* (T'bilisi, 1963), pp. 113-31.

24. Lordkipanidze, *Ist. Gruzii XI-načala XIII veka*, pp. 96-97; *K'art'lis C'xovreba*, ed. Quaxč'išvili, I, pp. 335-37; Javaxišvili, *K'art'veli eris ist.*, II, pp. 199-200, and 214-16.

25. Javaxišvili, *K'art'veli eris ist.*, II, pp. 201-10, 216-17; Lordkipanidze, *Ist. Gruzii XI-načala XIII veka*, pp. 101-108, and 112-15. Davit' was especially well-known for his religious tolerance and beneficent treatment of the Muslim population of his realm. A reflection of the Muslim–Georgian

symbiosis (one which underscores the importance of the Muslim urban, commercial population) may be seen in the Georgian coins of the period. Thus, a coin of Davit' 's realm bears an *Arabic* inscription (the formula was: "King of kings / Davit' son of Giorgi / Sword of the Messiah," *see* Lordkipanidze, *op. cit.*, p. 124). This formula was continued by his successors, *cf.* the coin of Giorgi III from A.D. 1174: "Malik ul-Mulûk / Giûrgî bin Dîmitrî / Husâm ul-Masîh," *see* D. M. Lang, *Studies in the Numismatic History of Georgia in Transcaucasia*, New York, 1955, p. 21).

26. Javaxišvili, *K'art'veli eris ist.*, II, pp. 220-95; Lordkipanidze, *Ist. Gruzii XI-načala XIII veka*, pp. 127-34, 152-63, and 166-69; Allen, *Hist. of the Georgian People*, pp. 99-108; O. Turan, *Doğu Anadolu Türk devletleri tarihi* (Istanbul, 1973), pp. 5-21, 93 ff. Warfare with the Seljuqids and their various splinter states was continuous. Major victories were achieved by Queen T'amar in 1195 at Šamxor against the *atabeg* of Azerbayjan, Abu Bakr Pahlivân (*cf., Ahbâr üd-Devlet is-Selçukyye*, pp. 120 ff.) and against the Seljuqs of Rum at Basiani in either 1203 or 1204. M. Lordkipanidze (*Epoxa Rustaveli*, Tbilisi, 1965, p. 27) suggests that T'amar introduced the *atabeg* office to Georgia.

27. J. J. Saunders, *The History of the Mongol Conquests* (New York, 1971), pp. 59, 77-79 S. L. Tixvinskii (ed.), *Tataro-Mongoly v Azii i Evrope* (Moskva, 1970), pp. 159 ff.; Javaxišvili), *K'artveli eris ist.*, III, pp. 14-28, 46 ff., and 324-35. Georgian forces under the renowned Mxargrdzeli military family were in the Mongol army that defeated the Sultan of Rum, Ğiyâth ad-Dîn, in 1243. One of the Georgian princes bore the Turkic name *Ağbuğa* (*see* Aknerli Grigor, *Moğol tarihi*, Turk. trans. H. Andreasyan (Istanbul, 1954), pp. 15-16). Seljuq forces at that time also included an "Abxaz" commander, Dardin/Dardan Šarvašidze (*K'art'lis C'xovreba*, ed. Qauxč'išvili, II, p. 192).

28. This was particularly true of the reign of Demetre II (1269-1289), *see* Allen, *Hist. of the Georgian People*, p. 119.

29. Berdzenišvili—Dondua, *et al., Ist. Gruzii*, I, pp. 257-59; I. H. Uzunçarşılı, *Anadolu beylikleri ve Akkoyunlu Karakoyunlu devletleri* (Ankara, 1969²), pp. 183, and 191-93; Allen, *Hist. of the Georgian People*, pp. 132-33. Important data can be found in Hasan Rûmlû's *Ahsân at-Tavârîx, cf.*, V. P'ut'uridze—R. Kiknadze, *Hasan Rumlus c'nobebi Sak'art'velos šesaxeb* (T'bilisi, 1966).

30. Berdzenišvili—Dondua, *et al., Ist. Gruzii*, I, pp. 260-68; Dukas, *Bizans tarihi*, Türk. trans., V. Kirmiroğlu (Istanbul, 1956), pp. 210-11; A. E. Vacalopoulos, *Origins of the Greek Nation 1204-1461*, trans. I. Moles (New Brunswick, 1970), pp. 221-31.

31. On Russian moves into the North Caucasus *see*: E. N. Kuševa, *Narody Severnogo Kavkaza i ix sviazi s Rossiei v XIV-XVII vv.* (Moskva, 1963).

32. *See* K. Kuc'ia "Kavkasiuri elementi Sep'iant'a Iranis politikur sarbielze," Gabašvili *et al.* (eds.), *Maxlobeli Ağmosavlet'is istoriis sakit'xebi*, pp. 65-75, based on the seventeenth-century Safavid source *Ta'rîx-i 'âlam ârâ-yi 'Abbâsî* by Iskandar Beg.

33. *Idem.*, p. 66.

34. S. H. Longrigg, *Four Centuries of Modern Iraq* (Oxford, 1925), pp. 163 ff., and Silagadze's study, *K'art'veli mamluk'ebi Eraqši* in D. Janelidze—B. Silagadze, *K'art'veli mamluk'ebi Egivipteši da Eraqši* (T'bilisi, 1967).

THE OĞUZ TURKIC ELEMENTS 207

35. S. Jik'ia, *Gurjistanis vilâiet'is didi davt'ari,* I (T'bilisi, 1947).
36. *Idem.,* pp. vii-viii.
37. V. Č'oč'ievi, "Iran–Osmalet'is 1553 clis droebit'i zavi," *Ağmosavluri P'ilologia* 3 (1973), pp. 314-20. The Ottomans periodically held T'bilisi, *cf.* the recently published firman of Sultan Ahmet III to Bak'ar Bagrationi (in Islam: Ibrâhîm) son of Vaxtang VI ("bundan akdam Tiflis hanı olan Vahtân oğlı Ibrâhîm...") S. Jik'ia "Sult'an Ahmed III-is p'irmani Bak'ar Bagrations," *K'art'uli Cqarot'mc'odneob*a 3 (1971), pp. 278-82.
38. *Cf.,* V. Gabašvili, "Sparsul dokumentur cqarot'a publickac'iebi Sak'art'veloši da sparsuli diplomatikis sakit'xebi," *Ağmosavluri P'ilologia* 2 (1972), pp. 160-170; V. P'ut'uridze, *K'art'uli-sparsuli istoriuli sabut'ebi.* (T'bilisi, 1955) and L. Fekete, "Arbeiten der grusinischen Orientalistik und die Frage der Formel *sözümüz*," *Acta Orientalia Hungarica*, VII (1957), pp. 1-20.
39. *See* I. Surguladze, *K'art'uli samart'lis dzeglebi,* I (T'bilisi, 1970) for a critical edition of the *Dasturlamali;* Minorsky, *Tadhkirat al-Mulûk* (cited n. 11). On the information of the latter pertaining to Georgia, *see* K. Kuc'ia, "T'azk'irat' al-Muluk'is c'nobebi Sak'art'velos šesaxeb," *K'art'uli Cqarot'mc'odneoba* 3 (1971), pp. 263-72.
40. D. M. Lang, *The Last Years of the Georgian Monarchy 1658-1832* (New York, 1957), pp. 11 ff,; Allen, *Hist, of the Georgian People,* pp. 143-64; I. H. Uzunçarşılı, *Osmanlı tarihi,* III/2 (Ankara, 1954), pp. 105-10. The notices of the Ottoman chronicler İbrahim Peçuyi regarding Ottoman–Georgian relations in the sixteenth century have been conveniently collected (with Georg. trans. and commentary) by S. Jik'ia, *Ibrâhîm P'eč'evis c'nobebi Sak'art'velosa da Kavkasiis šesaxeb* (T'bilisi, 1964). Ottoman sources give some Georgian lands Turkic appellations: Ismeret'i=*Başı açık/Açıkbaş hanlığı* (Jik'ia, *Ibr. P'eč'evis c'nobebi,* pp. 19-20 of Ottoman text). On the term *Dâd eli, see* K. Tabatadze, "Dad elis ganmartebisat'vis," *Ağmosavluri P'ilologia* 2 (1972), pp. 176-82.
41. *See* P. Oberling, "Georgians and the Circassians in Iran," *Studia Caucasica* 1 (1963), pp. 127-43.
42. Lang, *Last Days,* pp. 12-13, and 17. For Rostom's career, *see*: *K'art'lis C'xovreba,* ed. Qauxč'išvili, II, pp. 416 ff.
43. Lang, *Last Days,* pp. 138-46; Berdzenišvili–Dondua, *et al., Ist. Gruzii,* I, pp. 346-47.
44. *See* Lang, *Last Days,* esp. chaps. 8-14; A. V. Fadeev, *Rossiia i Kavkaz pervoi treti XIX v.* (Moskva, 1961), esp. chap. II.
45. Lang, *Last Days,* pp. 124-26.
46. *K'art'lis C'xovreba,* ed. Qauxč'išvili, I, p. 16.
47. E. Słuszkiewicz, "Über weitere armenische Lehnwörter in Grusinischen, *Rocznik Orientalistyczny,* 37 (1974), pp. 61-78.
48. *Cf.* also Hung. *híd* (<Iranian) "bridge" and Georg. *xidi* "bridge."
49. Z. Alek'sidze, "Siriul-k'art'uli lek'sikuri urt'iert'obis istoriidan (Ramdenime siruli sitqva k'art'ul 'ot'xt'avši')," *K'art'uli Cqarot'mc'odneoba* 3 (1971), pp. 35-39.
50. K. Maxaradze, *Bizantiuri berdznuli p'onetikis sakit'xebi,* I, (T'bilisi, 1965), esp. pp. 81-83 for a listing of such words.
51. G. Alasania "Ori termini ganmartebisat'vis T'amaris meore istorikosis t'xzulebaši," *Ağmoslavluri P'ilologia,* 3 (1973), pp. 205-208.
52. D. Kobidze, "Dašuši," *Ağmosavluri P'ilologia* 2 (1972), pp. 64-69.
53. *K'art'lis C'xovreba,* ed. Qauxč'išvili, I, pp. 225, 249, 250, and 375.

208   ISLAMIC AND JUDEO-CHRISTIAN WORLD

54. C. Cahen, *Pre-Ottoman Turkey,* trans. J. Jones-Williams (New York, 1968), p. 37.

55. V. Gabašvili "Sak'art'velo da t'urk'uli samquaro XI-XII saukuneebši," *Ağmosavluri P'ilologia* 3 (1973), pp. 92-96.

56. *K'art'lis C'xovreba,* ed. Qauxč'išvili, II, p. 70.

57. Gabašvili, "Sak'art'velo da t'urk'uli samqaro..." *Ağmosavluri P'ilologia,* 3 (1973), p. 98.

58. Linguistic criteria are difficult to establish with respect to Osm. and Safavî Turkish. The Central and Eastern Anatolian dialects of Osm. share with Azeri many of the phonetic features found in our Georgian loanwords, *e.g.:* -*q* (Mod. Turk. orthography -*k*) usually changes to -*x* in Cent. and East. Anatolian dialects as well as in Azeri (*cf.,* A. Caferoğlu, "Die Anatolischen und Rumelischen Dialekte," *Philologiae Turcicae Fundamenta,* eds., D. Deny–K. Grønbech, *et alii,* Wiesbaden, 1959, I, p. 251 and A. Caferoğlu–G. Doerfer "Das Aserbeidschanische," *Ph. F,* I, p. 292) and its dialects (*cf.,* M. Islamov *Azärbayjan dilinin Nuxa dialekti,* Bakı, 1968, p. 44). The change *q* > *g* is another feature shared by both, as is *t* > *d* (*Ph. TF,* I, pp. 249-50). The occasional Georg. *z* for *s,* if it is not a native Georgian phenomenon, may point to Anatolian *s* > *z* (*Ph. TF,* I, p. 250). The changes of initial *q* > *g* (*g*) and *t* >*d* so typical of Modern Azeri are not in evidence in any of our Georgian loanwords beyond where this has occured in Osm. as well. Many of the Georgian forms reflect the older Osm. (and probably Safavî Turk.) treatment of vowel harmony: *č'ak'uč'i* (< *čäküč*) ∼Mod. Turk. *çekiç; qut'i* (< *qutı*) ‿ Mod. Turk. *kutu* etc. Thus, the only criteria for distinguishing Osm. from Safavî Turk. are circumstantial (*i.e.* when it can be demonstrated that a given word is used in Georgian with semantic connotations known to one but lacking in the other). Such instances are very rare.

59. B. Ia. Vladimircov, *Obščestvennyi stroi Mongolov* (Leningrad, 1934), pp. 140, and 204.

60. Š. Gabeskiria,"Bağana-s carmomavlobisat'vis," *Ağmorsavluri P'ilologia* 3 (1973), pp. 219-22.

61. St. Stachowski, "Studien über die neupersischen Lehnwörter in Osmanisch-Türkischen," *Folia Orientalia,* 4 (1972-1973), pp. 108-109.

62. L. Ruxadze, "Ramdenime t'urk'iul carmomavlobis sitqvisat'vis k'art'-ul," *Ağmosavluri P'ilologia,* 3 1973), p. 224.

63. *Idem.,* p. 223.

64. *Ibid.*

65. *Idem.,* p. 224.

W. G. Lockwood

LIVING LEGACY OF THE OTTOMAN EMPIRE:
THE SERBO-CROATIAN SPEAKING MOSLEMS:
OF BOSNIA-HERCEGOVINA

There exists in southeastern Europe a living legacy of the over
four hundred year long Ottoman presence—a combined population, excluding European Turkey, of some five or six million
Moslem inhabitants. Of these, the second largest component
(after Moslem Albanians) is the Serbo-Croatian speaking Moslems of Bosnia-Hercegovina (hereafter referred to as Bosnian
Moslems). As of the 1971 census, there are some one and three-
quarter million Bosnian Moslems, 8 percent of the total population of Yugoslavia. They comprise 40 percent of the Republic
of Bosnia and Hercegovina, with a combination of Serbs and
Croats making up nearly all of the remainder.

It is our intention here to present something of a "natural
history" of this important group. The analysis is of two parts,
the first primarily historic and the second, ethnographic. We will
first trace the process of Bosnian Moslem ethnogenesis, the
gradual transformation from religious converts to ethnic group.
We will then look at the relationships between these developments and the cultural and social status of Bosnian Moslems,
especially the Bosnian Moslem peasantry, in contemporary
Yugoslavia.

Bosnian Moslem ethnogenesis was initiated soon after, first,
the Bosnian Kingdom (1463), and, then, the Hercegovinian
duchy (1482) fell to the Ottoman Empire. Over the following
period of Ottoman rule in Bosnia-Hercegovina there were
wholesale conversions to Islam, unlike any other area of Ottoman
Europe except Albania. The source of these converts, and the

reasons for their conversion, are still a subject of debate. The traditional view is that the landed aristocracy of the Medieval Bosnian and Hercegovinian states converted in order to preserve its economic and political superiority under the new regime and that the rank and file of the Bosnian Church, a heretical sect usually identified with the Bogomils, converted en masse in reaction to earlier excesses of Catholicism.[1] Both of these views have long been questioned and recent evidence[2] indicates, not only that the Bosnian Church had been more or less destroyed prior to the Ottoman conquest, but that it was probably not even Bogomil after all. Similarly, the views of certain Croatian and Serbian writers that the converts were predominantly Croatian or, conversely, predominantly Serbian (and hence to be regarded as "Moslem Croats" or "Moslem Serbs" respectively) has little conclusive support in the data. The Bosnian Moslems apparently originated in a combination of all these groups plus others, including Moslems from other areas (e.g., Albanians, Turks, Yürüks) who were subsequently Slavicized. The details of this origin, however, have relatively little significance in terms of what Bosnian Moslems are today. Regardless of what they might have been, the various components have amalgamated over the years into a distinct people.

What I would like to stress here regarding this origin is the individual nature of the conversion process. Except for the *devširme,* or child levy, the Ottomans did not forcibly Islamize. It was not regions, or villages, or probably even families that converted, but individual men and women. Each convert, regardless of his or her previous status, made the decision individually for reasons that were entirely rational at that time and place. Undoubtedly, the tradition of shifting religious affiliations in pre-Ottoman Bosnia-Hercegovina played an important role in this.[3] Changes of religion were a general and common occurrence at this time and, thus, Islamization was only one aspect of a broader phenomenon. The lack of a strong church organization in Bosnia-Hercegovina, either Catholic or Orthodox, made widespread conversion possible. The various material and consumptive advantages afforded Moslems must also have been very important—the special tax on non-Moslems, the restrictions on what a non-Moslem might or might not do. But most important of all, it must be remembered that during the earlier stage of

the Ottoman occupation, the Empire represented the epitome
of civilization, a major center of not only political and economic
power but also cultural and intellectual life. If we can regard it
as such from our perspective, consider how it must have seemed
to Balkan peasants of the period. It was natural to want to
identify with this, and it must have seemed that the easiest way
to do so was to accept the faith that was so fundamental a part
of it. Anthropologists working in Oceania, Africa and elsewhere
during the recent period have frequently noted the same effect
and response upon conquest of a technologically primitive
people by another which is far advanced.[4] In part, religious conversion was an attempt at supernatural identification with an
improved status. Moreover, it was a pragmatic attempt at the
same thing. Whoever wished to get rich quick in the expanding
economic activities of the towns, or to advance in the administrative apparatus of the empire, or perhaps merely to demonstrate that he was a good citizen, converted to Islam. Conversion
was far more common in towns than in the countryside, not only
because the towns were the centers from which Islam was
diffused, but because it was these same towns that provided the
best context for social mobility. It was here that the economic
opportunities lay.

The number of Moslems in Bosnia-Hercegovina increased
steadily until they came to exert a significant influence on the
political and cultural life of the Ottoman Empire. At one point
in the mid-sixteenth century, the Grand-Vizier and two of the
three Viziers were all Moslems from Bosnia–Hercegovina. The
Bosnian influence was so strong in some periods that Serbo-
Croatian became the second language in the Porte.[5]

These converts, taken in the aggregate, did not immediately
constitute an ethnic group in the anthropological sense. It is
appropriate here to sketch just what it is that the anthropologist
means by "ethnicity." As most commonly understood by social
scientists,[6] "ethnic group" designates a population which

1. is biologically self-perpetuating,
2. shares fundamental cultural values, realized in cultural
   forms,
3. makes up a field of communication and interaction, and
4. has a membership which identifies itself, and is identified

by others, as constituting a category distinguishable from other categories of the same order.

In other words, members of an ethnic group are more or less endogamous, marrying others of the group more frequently than outsiders. They participate in a recognizable subculture—with both material and ideological forms—that is identified with the group. They tend to interact with one another more frequently than with others and, because of this, there is an easier flow of information within the group than without it. And they, as well as members of other ethnic groups with which they are in contact, possess a group consciousness, described by some anthropologists in terms of "ethnocentrism."[7]

More and more, we have come to view ethnicity as a form of social organization rather than cultural organization, and as we have done so, it has become more and more obvious that it is this fourth point which is critical.[8] Ethnic groups are circumscribed by boundaries, invisible yet nevertheless recognized by both members and non-members. These ethnic boundaries are established and maintained on the basis of a very limited but critical set of diagnostic features. Most ethnic groups of the Balkans, for example, are defined by a single paradigm of language and religion. Thus, in the Bosnia-Hercegovina context, to be Serbo-Croatian speaking and Catholic is to be Croatian, to be Serbo-Croatian speaking and Orthodox is to be Serbian, and so on. The persistence of the ethnic group depends on the collective recognition and evaluation of these critical traits, although through time or from locale to locale, the remainder of cultural content associated with the group may vary and given individuals may pass from one group to another. This specific cultural content which can vary as to time and place, is nevertheless very important in that it aids the members of a multi-ethnic society in assigning one another within the ethnic boundaries. Thus, distinctive items of costume, dialect, etc., serve to signal one's ethnic identity to all knowledgeable observers.

Within the Ottoman Empire, the Serbo-Croatian speaking Moslems were identified (to the extent they were identified at all) as *Bošnjaci*. Both the derivation of the term and the social group it had reference to were regional, not ethnic, and this accurately reflects the nature of Bosnian Moslem self-consciousness vis-a-vis the central powers of the Empire. Local Christians called them *Turci* (Turks), demonstrating their identification of Serbo-Croatian speaking Moslems with the ruling group. Moslems would sometimes even use the term *Turci* themselves, when it was necessary to distinguish themselves from Bosnian Christians. True, they spoke a distinct language but language was not yet considered a significant criteria of group affiliation. All the less so in this case, since it was shared with the Christian inhabitants and thus not unique to the social category. Because of the international makeup of the ruling Ottoman apparatus (including prominent Serbo-Croatian speakers), there was no official differentiation—no formalization of a Bosnian Moslem ethnic group. A primary explanation for the development of nationalities based on religion in the Balkans is that "the organization of Christian subjects into millets, each a different religious denomination constituting a separate community organized under its own ecclesiastical authorities, stressed the distinctiveness of the various non-Moslem peoples."[9] Undoubtedly, this was so. But note that this did not effectively define the Serbo-Croatian speaking Moslems. They were no different in this respect than other Moslem subjects of the Empire, including the Moslem Albanians, Gypsies, and Turks that they might come into daily contact with. They were considered by both Christians and other Moslems, and thought of themselves, as the establishment, and an integral part of the Empire. The analogy that comes to mind are the WASPs—White, Anglo-Saxon Protestants—of the United States. WASPs are not an ethnic group, though they have all the potential of being one. The objective criteria for an ethnic boundary exist, but it is not recognized. WASPs in the U.S., like Serbo-Croatian speaking Moslems in the Ottoman Empire, are apt to think of themselves as the norm, the standard, which all others deviate from.

The Bosnian Moslems were not, of course, a unified group—socially, culturally, or conceptually. One significant distinction to which we have already made reference was between rural and urban components. Even today, a disproportionate percentage of Bosnian Moslems are urbanites and townsmen, as compared with the Serbs and Croats of Bosnia-Hercegovina. Moslem peasants as much as Christian peasants perceived the predominantly Moslem townsmen, as "a clique which exploited them economically and ruled them politically . . . an opportunistic group of people who had a common response to daily issues and behaved as a class conscious of its own interests."[10]

An even more significant distinction was between the landowning aristocracy, the beys and agas, and the Moslem peasantry, including both the majority of Bosnian free peasants and a much smaller proportion of serfs. In 1878, at the time of the Austrian annexation, there were in Bosnia-Hercegovina from 6000 to 7000 beys and agas in control of some 85,000 serfs. Of the latter, 2000 were Moslem with the remainder either Serbs (60,000) or Croats (23,000). There were also almost 77,000 free peasants, nearly all of whom were Moslem.[11] It is difficult if not impossible to conceive of aristocracy and peasantry as constituting a single, meaningful, social category during the feudal period, regardless of specific context. Social boundaries between aristocrat and peasant were as sharp as between any two ethnic groups. There was little way in which a Moslem peasant could ever become a wealthy landowner in Ottoman society. Each constituted an endogamous group, although the social network for the aristocracy was much more widespread. This reflected a much more dispersed settlement pattern; some beys and agas lived on their own lands in lowland villages, others in the towns, with a gradual shift over time to the latter. The aristocracy also participated in a distinct life style, in their cases much more closely related to the Great Tradition of international Islam than to the highly localized Little Tradition of Moslem peasants. This was true even when inhabiting the same village. But the major boundary between the two groups of Bosnian Moslems was, of course, based on economic status. This was altered somewhat by the expulsion of the Ottomans, but they maintained their privileged position up to World War II. Finally, in the land reform measures enacted after the War, they lost the traditional base of their higher status. It is to be expected that this social differentiation was more pronounced in the past, when the feudal system still functioned. This is confirmed by oral history. It is less expected, but nevertheless true, that the various distinctions between the two groups hold forth in large degree even in modern Yugoslavia. Even today, there is a high degree of self-consciousness among members of the two groups (except in urban, modernizing contexts where it is beginning to break down). Moslem peasants still refer to the descendants of landowning aristocracy as *begovi* ("beys"), in contrast to themselves whom they characterize as *balije* (originally "transhuman herders"). Moslem peasants with whom I have spoken explicitly describe the two as distinct ethnic groups (*nacije*), each possessing its own distinct God-given attributes. Outside of the urban context, at least, there is still little intermarriage beween the two groups. And *begovi*, especially in the smaller market towns, still tend to maintain a well-to-do life style in the Moslem manner. Although no longer large landowners, their advantageous economic position of the recent past allowed them educational opportunities denied to most of the Moslem peasantry. As a result, today they are frequently professionals—doctors, lawyers, teachers, administrators. Others, less fortunate, have used their better education to acquire jobs such as clerks in local bureaucracies. Social relations between Moslem peasants and descendants of Moslem aristocracy tend to be limited to a very few hierarchically structured patron–client relationships. Some peasants have thus perpetuated a traditional relationship to acquire useful leverage with the outside world through the new social positions taken by these descendants of aristocracy in modern Yugoslavia. What is significant about all this is that the contexts in which Moslem peasants and Moslem aristocracy or their descendants act together as a single social group are relatively few, although gradually increasing since the Ottoman decline and, especially, after World War II. There has been an unfortunate tendency for western historians to write of the Bosnian Moslem elite as if they were describing all Bosnian Moslems. We must remember that the considerable Bosnian Moslem peasantry represented (and continues to represent, to a large degree), a distinct group with its own special interests, often closer to those of the Christian peasantry than to their fellow Moslem elite.

With the development of South Slav nationalism in the 19th century, all Moslems came to represent the overlords—Turks and Moslem Slavs, beys and peasants alike. This undoubtedly had the effect of not only emphasizing the boundary between Moslem and Christian, but was also a first step in coalescing the various components of the Slavic Moslem group. After the Austrian annexation, the process of ethnic differentiation quickened. This was a period of heightening ethnic consciousness for the Bosnian Moslems. On the one hand, the circumstances of the Austrian occupation led them to differentiate themselves even further from Bosnian Christians. On the other hand, they also began to think of themselves as a people distinct from the Turks and other Moslems of the disintegrating Ottoman Empire. As a Moslem minority in the Austrian colony, they became more clearly set apart as a distinct group. This was probably aided by selective factors as wave after wave of Serbo-Croatian speaking Moslems immigrated to Turkey. Although evidence is lacking, we can surmise that these emigrants included those Bosnian Moslems most inclined to identify with the Turks, leaving behind those who had reached some accommodation with their new ethnic status.

Ethnic differentiation was also promoted by political developments within the Austrian colony. The Habsburg administration followed their traditional pattern of divide and rule and took care to stress the religious and ethnic differences within Bosnia-Hercegovina. When a parliament for the province was established, the various religious faiths were represented in direct proportion to their numerical strength in the country. But when the Moslem aristocracy and their urban allies tried to organize a Moslem political party, they were unsuccessful. In part, this was the result of the Austrian policy of not disrupting the Moslem elite. Their old economic status had been perpetuated under the Habsburgs and thus their cause continued to lie with the establishment, even though this was now in new hands. Even more important, Moslem peasants were not yet ready to think of themselves as a single group having unified interests with the old aristocracy, especially in view of the continuing economic differences.

This increase in ideological distinctiveness was paralleled by an increase in cultural differentiation as well. From the Austrian occupation onward, cultural differences between Moslems and the Christians of Bosnia-Hercegovina were accentuated, especially in the cities and towns, as non-Moslems more readily accepted elements of western European culture. At the same time, events in Anatolia—the final collapse of the Empire, Atatürk and his reforms—resulted in increased cultural differences between Bosnian Moslems and the Turks. The veil, for example, was legally worn in Yugoslavia until 1950 and the fez is still seen today on many Bosnian Moslem peasants; both were, of course, prohibited in Turkey in 1922, along with many other culture traits which the Turks traditionally shared with the Bosnians.

Beginning with the establishment of an independent Serbia, and increasing after the Habsburg annexation, there was an intensification of competition of Serbs and Croats over Bosnia-Hercegovina. With Ottoman administration gone, the Bosnian Moslems became pawns in this struggle. Up to World War II, both Beograd and Zagreb claimed national kinship with the Bosnian Moslems, this being only one of many bones of contention between the two groups. Thus, it was that certain Bosnian Moslems, nearly all beys or urban elite who perceived their personal interests as lying with one or the other, would declare themselves Moslem Serbs or Moslem Croats, in effect a religious minority of the respective national group. But the great majority of Moslems, particularly the Moslem peasantry, declined from affiliating themselves with either one; whatever they might once have been, they had evolved over the years into yet another ethnic community. One product of the Serbian-Croatian competition was that when the fascist Ustaši government was formed during World War II, Bosnia-Hercegovina was incorporated into a "Greater Croatia."

After World War II, the fact that there were large numbers of nationally undecided Serbo-Croatian speaking Moslems was a major reason that Bosnia-Hercegovina was made a separate republic of Yugoslavia. Although their religious beliefs were tolerated, the Sheriat courts were abolished and Moslem women were by law unveiled. In the earliest censuses after the war, they were given the choice of registering as Serbs, Croats, Yugoslavs, or Undeclared, the official opinion being that they constituted a religious rather than an ethnic minority. It was even anticipated that Bosnia-Hercegovina, with its mixture of three different religious communities all speaking a common language, would provide the earliest development of Yugoslav nationalism. Bosnian Moslems, it was thought, would lead the way. By this time, however, they had come to think of themselves as a distinct people. On the census, nearly all declared themselves "Undeclared." The position of the Bosnian Moslems was altered with the gradual shift in Yugoslavia during the 1960s from an official Yugoslav nationalism to the concept of Yugoslavia as a community of nations. In the 1961 census, they were allowed to register as "ethnic Moslems" (*Muslimani etnička pripadnost*) for the first time, thus conceding that they constituted a separate ethnic category. This status was more formally given them by the Bosnian constitution of 1963 and in 1964, the Fourth Bosnian Party Congress declared explicitly that Moslems had the right of self-determination. Thus, gradually, a Bosnian Moslem nationality was created, or, rather, raised from de facto to de jure status.

Currently, there is something of a nationalist movement taking shape among the Bosnian Moslems. Like past nationalist movements of Eastern Europe and elsewhere, it is almost wholly confined in these early stages to the intelligentsia, in this case mainly from the lower and middle echelons of the Communist Party. The developing middle class of Bosnian Moslems and, especially, the Bosnian Moslem peasantry have so far taken relatively little note. A number of Bosnian Moslem writers[12] have taken upon themselves the task of providing a nationalist ideology. They stress the Bogomil origin of Bosnian Moslems (in order to trace ethnogenesis prior to Islamization), attempt to explain away the fact that the aristocracy was the only politically active Moslem group prior to World War II, and, in general, interpret Bosnian Moslem history so to emphasize vertical divisions based on ethnicity rather than horizontal divisions based on class.[13]

Let us now turn to Bosnian Moslem ethnography and some principal features of Bosnian Moslem life in contemporary Yugoslavia.[14] The Moslem peasantry and the Christian peasantry of Bosnia-Hercegovina are much more alike than either is like its counterpart elsewhere, even within the Balkans. The subculture of any given Moslem village in Bosnia is much more like that of the neighboring Croatian or Serbian village than a Moslem village in Turkey or even Albania or Bulgaria. The obvious exception is in religious practice.

Although religious affiliation is the criterion by which the ethnic boundary is fixed, each religious grouping is also set off from one another by a distinct subculture unrelated to its religious activities. When one encounters a peasant on the trail or in the market place, there is no mistaking his affiliation. And he would have it no other way. Although these cultural differences prevail in almost every aspect of life, they tend to be very small in scale. Differences between different ethnic groups in a single locale tend to be closely related variants rather than totally different traits. Yet the differences, small as they may be, are most significant and are greatly appreciated. They prevail especially in the expressive aspects of culture—dialect, dress, music and dance, cuisine, house type and furnishings, the ceremonial calendar, oral literature, and so on. A particularly graphic example is provided by men's costume in Skoplje Polje, a valley in Western Bosnia with a tri-ethnic population.[15] It is nearly identical for all three groups, differing only in the color of the sash (red for Christians, green for Moslems), the color of a narrow embroidered trim at the cuff of the pants (red for Croats, white for Serbs, and lacking for Moslems), and the style of headgear. Little Tradition (the culture of the village, as contrasted with the Great Tradition or culture of the elite) is, by its nature, very highly localized. Consequently, in the next valley over, the basic pattern changes and while the same degree of ethnic differentiation continues to exist, the code is liable to change as well. In this particular example, the pants are of a slightly different cut, and it is the Croats (in the absence there of a Serbian population) who trim them in white. We have in effect, then, three separate Little Traditions superimposed on a single region, each a slight variant of the regional culture.

It must be emphasized that many of the cultural differences between the Moslem peasant and the Serbian or Croatian peasant do not result from differential diffusion of Ottoman culture. There is in the Balkans a veneer of Turkish culture that extends across the entire area of Ottoman occupation and even beyond. Turkish influence was greatest in the urban centers where the Turks ensconced themselves and in many aspects of culture, Turkish influence follows a rural-urban dichotomy rather than a Moslem–Christian one. This was subsequently obscured in larger urban centers as it was overlaid by western European influences, but it is still the case today in and near the smaller market towns of Bosnia-Hercegovina. Thus, for example, Turkish-style foods are perhaps most commonly prepared in the homes of urban families descended from aristocracy, but they are also more prevalent on the tables of small town Christians than those of rural Moslems.

Such cultural differences between ethnic communities, no matter how minor or insignificant they may seem, have great importance. Most probably, they result from historical differences of origin and contact. Their persistence, however, is due to the interaction of two characteristics of ethnic groups which were discussed earlier in this paper. The first of these is that they exist within relatively closed communication systems. A primary feature of multi-ethnic societies everywhere is an easier flow of information within each ethnic group than between them. With time this inevitably results in unequal diffusion and cultural differentiation. The second important feature of these cultural differences is their conscious maintenance as markers of significant social categories. They constitute, at one and the same time, focal points of in-group sentiment and criteria of out-group identification. Such differences, then, serve an important function, marking the ethnic boundaries.

To illustrate, let us return to the folk costume of the area. Many peasant Moslem men, especially older ones, still wear the fez. But younger ones, most of whom have switched to modern dress, wear a beret instead. Even though this is purchased in the same shop where the Serbian or Croatian peasant gets his own specific type of cap, neither the Moslem nor the Christian would consider wearing the type thought appropriate for the other. Even with modernization of dress, then, the cultural distinctiveness has been preserved. People *want* to be identified.

We've been discussing a process of cultural syncretism—the combination and reinterpretation of elements from both Turkish and South Slav sources. Elsewhere,[16] we have demonstrated that this same pattern extends also to social organization, the very fabric of Bosnian Moslem society. The argument is worth repeating here, very briefly, because it demonstrates an important point.

The basic unit of Bosnian peasant society, whether Moslem, Serb, or Croat, is the patrilocally extended family household. Similarly, in all three ethnic groups the links between these households are based on residency and kinship, including patrilineal, affinal and fictive kinship. But the weight given these various criteria for affiliation varies from one ethnic group to another. Moslem peasants of Bosnia give much less emphasis to patrilineality and to groups based on patrilineal kinship than do either the Croats or, especially, the Serbs. For example, since patrilineal kinship provides a charter for social relations, it is typical for both Croatian and Serbian peasants of Bosnia to be able to recite from ten to fourteen generations of their genealogy. Bosnian Moslems, on the other hand, can almost never provide anything beyond their own grandparents' generation, and are usually very hazy about this. In other words, they are about the same in this respect as modern Americans. Contrary to what one might expect, Bosnian Moslem peasants also give less emphasis to patrilineality than do Turkish peasants. Thus, with regard to emphasis on patrilineal kinship as an organizing principle, they are neither like nor intermediate to the two societies from whom they received cultural influences. The slack seems to be taken up by an increased emphasis on affinal relations, or those formed by marriage.

Fictive kinship (*kumstvo*), in the form of baptismal and wedding sponsorship is an extremely important form of affiliation among Bosnian Christians. Bosnian Moslems have only one type of fictive kinship of much significance, formed on the basis of sponsoring the first haircut of a male child (*šišano kumstvo*). This is used almost exclusively to reinforce and formalize one of those rare social relationships with a Christian or a member of the Moslem elite, in other words, to forge ties across major social boundaries. Bosnian Christians do not practice this form of ritual kinship, except with Moslems, and I know of no precedent in the Islamic world.

Christian patrilineal kin groups are strictly exogamous, even more so in practice than is stipulated by either Catholic or Orthodox church regulations. In contrast, Turks and most Moslems outside of the Balkans practice an endogamous pattern with preferred marriage of one's father's brother's daughter. As in other respects, the Bosnian Moslems have evolved their own marriage system, neither one nor the other. Marriage to kinsmen is permitted as long as the relationship cannot be actually traced. In practice, this means that there is no sanction against marriage between second cousins.[17]

The point I am trying to make here is that the social organization of the Bosnian Moslems—and by extension, Bosnian

Moslem society and culture as a whole—is not Turkish, nor South Slav Christian, not even some intermediate form. Elements from both contributing sources were integrated, in line with the unique history of the Moslems in Bosnia-Hercegovina, to create something new and distinctive.

The cultural differentiation that I have been describing is very pervasive, but it does not extend to the economy of the largest three ethnic groups. This is a highly significant point since it influences the type of interethnic relations that exist in Bosnia-Hercegovina.

Cross-culturally, there are at least two different ways in which multi-ethnic relations can be structured. (Both must be considered as ideal types, since few societies conform wholly to one or the other.) In one case, there is an ethnic division of labor and each ethnic group is strongly identified with a particular occupation or set of occupations. A system of such ethnic groups with interlocking occupational specializations achieves an organic interrelationship. A mutual interdependence is built up between the members of various ethnic groups. Perhaps the best documented examples of this are in the Near East. The Indian caste system of hierarchically arranged, highly structured, occupational statuses seems to represent a specialized case. Some ethnic groups of the Balkans are so organized, at least on a local basis. For example, in Skoplje Polje (the region of western Bosnia whence most of my field data has been drawn), all blacksmiths are settled Gypsies and all settled Gypsies are assumed to be blacksmiths. The term for blacksmith—*kovač*—has come to signify the ethnic group with which the occupation is associated. There is a similar association in this area between coppersmithery and Cincars (a romance-speaking minority of the region), and *kalajdžija*, Serbo-Croatian for coppersmith, is used to denote the ethnic group.

Another possibility is a situation where different ethnic groups compete for the same ecological niche. Such is the usual case with Moslem, Serbian, and Croatian peasants of Bosnia-Hercegovina. In contrast with most other aspects of culture, peasants of all three religious groups practice almost identical economy. All tend to gain their subsistence in the same manner, from the same plants and animals, using the same tools and techniques. Differences that exist are regional rather than ethnic. The primary, if not the only, exception is the absence of pigs from the Moslem complex. Otherwise there is a greater degree of contrast in economy between highland Moslem peasants and lowland Moslem peasants than between highland Moslem peasants and highland Serbian or Croatian peasants. It is a matter of simple ecology. Settlement pattern in Bosnia-Hercegovina is thoroughly mixed; Moslem villages are interspersed among Serbian and/or Croatian villages, with a lesser number of villages having an ethnically mixed population. This means that members of different ethnic groups are in direct competition for the same scarce resources. At the same time, mutually beneficial contact tends to be limited. In a given locale, each village tends to produce the same surpluses and have the same needs. Non-commercialized exchange systems are made up almost exclusively from members of the same ethnic group in different ecological zones. Interaction between ethnic groups is conducted in a relatively small number of contexts—the weekly market, and such overarching institutions as the army and schools. Because each ethnic group is a relatively closed social system, there is almost never any need to interact with peasants of another ethnic group, even though their village is directly adjacent. As a result, each ethnic group tends to be an even more closed social system and opportunities for communication or interaction between them are even more strictly limited than in a multiethnic society where an economic interdependence is the case.

Bosnian Moslem ethnicity, developed gradually over a several hundred year long period, will persist for the indefinite future. The structural relationships based on ecological factors are but one reason that three separate cultural traditions have endured so well, even though they are superimposed on the same geographical region. Cultural differentiation will lessen with continuing modernization in contemporary Yugoslavia. Gradually, a feeling of Yugoslavness will replace ethnic identification in certain contexts, as when thrown together with migrant workers from other regions of Yugoslavia in the factories of western Europe. Even so, the Bosnian Moslems will continue to exist as a distinct ethnic group. There may well be, in fact, a resurgence of ethnic consciousness as presaged by recent nationalist developments among the elite.

NOTES

1. Francis Dvornik, *The Slavs in European History and Civilization* (New Brunswick, 1962), p. 236; Aleksandar Solovjev, "Nestanak Bogumilstva: Islamizatija Bosne" [The Disappearance of Bogomilism and the Islamization of Bosnia], *Godišnjak Istoriskog Društva Bosne i Hercegovine*, no. 1 (1949); L. S. Stavrianos, *The Balkans Since 1453* (New York, 1961), pp. 62-63.

2. John V. A. Fine, Jr., *The Bosnian Church: A New Interpretation* (Boulder, 1975).

3. *Ibid*, p. 386.

4. For examples, see Sylvia L. Thrupp (ed.), *Millennial Dreams in Action* (The Hague, 1962), especially the chapter by Jean Guiart, "The millenarian aspect of conversion to Christianity in the South Pacific," pp. 122-38.

5. Vladimir Dedijer, Ivan Božić, Sima Ćirković and Milorad Ekmečić, *History of Yugoslavia* (New York, 1974), p. 181.

6. *See*, for example, Raoul Narroll, as summarized by Fredrik Barth (ed.), *Ethnic Groups and Boundaries* (Boston, 1969), pp. 10-11.

7. Robert A. Levine and Donald T. Campbell, *Ethnocentrism: Theories of Conflict, Ethnic Attitudes and Group Behavior* (New York, 1972).

8. *See* especially Barth, *Ethnic Groups and Boundaries.*

9. Stavrianos, *The Balkans Since 1453*, p. 89.

10. Wayne Vucinich, "Some Aspects of the Ottoman Legacy," in Charles and Barbara Jelavich (eds.), *The Balkans in Transition* (Berkeley, 1963).

11. Milan Ivšić, *Les problèmes agraires en Yougoslavie* (Paris, 1929). For a general resume of the land-tenure system in Bosnia-Hercegovina during the Ottoman period, *see* Jozo Tomasevich, *Peasants, Politics, and Economic Change in Yugoslavia* (Stanford, 1955), pp. 98-107, or, for a more detailed account, Branislav Djurdjev Bogo, Grafenauer, and Jorjo Tadić, *Historija naroda Jugoslavije* [History of the People of Yugoslavia] (Zagreb, 1959) Vol. 2, pp. 116-20, 130-39, 583-87.

12. Most notably Enver Redžić, *Prilozi o nacionalnom pitanju* [Contributions on the National Question] (Sarajevo, 1963) and *Tokovi i otpori* [Developments and Resistance] (Sarajevo, 1970); Salim Čerić, *Muslimani Srpskohrvatskog jezika* [Serbo-Croatian Speaking Moslems] (Sarajevo, 1968); Atif Purivatra, *Nacionalni i Politički razvitak Muslimana* [National and Political Development of Moslems] (Sarajevo, 1972); Muhamed Hadžijahić, *Od tradicije do identiteta: geneza nacionalnog pitanja bosanskih Muslimana* [From Tradition to Identification: The Genesis of the Bosnian Moslem National Question] (Sarajevo, 1974).

13. I am grateful to Robert Donia for his helpful observations on Bosnian Moslem ethnicity, particularly Bosnian Moslem nationalism. His forthcoming doctoral dissertation, *The Politics of Factionalism: The Bosnian Moslems, 1878–1910* (Department of History, University of Michigan), will shed more light on the subject.

14. This has been described in more detail in William G. Lockwood, "Converts and consanguinity: the social organization of Moslem Slavs in Western Bosnia" *Ethnology* 11 (1972), pp. 55-79; "The peasant-worker in Yugoslavia," *Studies in European Society* 1 (1973), pp. 91–110. "Bride theft and social maneuverability in western Bosnia," *Anthropological*

Quarterly, 47 (1974), pp. 253–269; "Social status and cultural change in a Bosnian Moslem village," *East European Quarterly* 9 (1975), pp. 123–134; *European Moslems: Economy and Ethnicity in Western Bosnia* (New York, 1975).

15. Lockwood, *European Moslems: Economy and Ethnicity in Western Bosnia*, pp. 49–50.

16. Lockwood, "Converts and consanguinity: the social organization of Moslem Slavs in western Bosnia," *Ethnology* 11 (1972), pp. 55-79.

17. *Cf.* Milenko S. Filipović, "Brak izmedju prvih rodjaka (bint 'amm) kod srpskohrvatskih Muslimana" [First cousin marriage among Serbo-Croatian speaking Moslems], *Sociologija* 2 (1960), pp. 55-66.

CONTRIBUTORS

ABRAHAM ASCHER, Ph.D., is Professor of History, Brooklyn College, City University of New York, and Director, Division of Education Programs, National Endowment for the Humanities. B.S.S., City College of New York; Ph.D., Columbia University. Author: *Pavel Axelrod and the Development of Menshevism* (Cambridge, Mass., 1972). Editor: *The Mensheviks in the Russian Revolution* (London–Ithaca, N.Y., 1976).

ÜLKÜ ÜLKÜSAL BATES, Ph.D., is Associate Professor of History, Hunter College, City University of New York, and Visiting Lecturer, Harvard University. Licentiate, University of Istanbul; M.A., Ph.D., University of Michigan. Author: "Anatolian Mausoleums and Their Inscriptions," *Kunsthistorische Forschungen* 1971; "Patronage of Women in Turkish Architecture" in *Beyond the Veil: Women in the Near East,* in preparation; "The Impact of the Mongol Invasion on Turkish Architecture," *International Journal of Middle East Studies,* not yet published; "Turkish Architecture" in *Art and Architecture of Turkey,* not yet published.

ALAN W. FISHER, Ph.D., is Associate Professor of History, Michigan State University. B.A., DePauw University; M.A., Ph.D., Columbia University. Author: *The Russian Annexation of the Crimea, 1772–1783* (New York, 1970); *The Crimean Tatars: A History* (Stanford, 1978).

STEPHEN FISCHER-GALAŢI, Ph.D., is Professor of History and Director, Center for Slavic and East European Studies, University of Colorado. A.B., M.A., Ph.D., Harvard University. Author: *Ottoman Imperialism and German Protestantism, 1521–1555* (Cambridge, Mass., 1959); *The New Rumania: From People's Democracy to Socialist Republic* (Cambridge, Mass, 1967); *Twentieth Century Rumania* (New York, 1970).

PETER B. GOLDEN, Ph.D., is Associate Professor and Chairman of the Department of History, Rutgers University College of Arts and Sciences, Newark, N.J. B.A., Queens College of the City University of New York; M.A., Ph.D., Columbia University. Author: *Q'azar Studies: An Historico-Philological Inquiry into the Origin of the Q'azars* (Lisse–Budapest, in press).

HALÎL ÎNALCIK, Ph.D., is Professor of Ottoman History, University of Chicago. Ph.D., University of Ankara. Vice-president of the International Association of South East European Studies. Author: *The Ottoman Empire: The Classical Age, 1300–1600* (London–New York, 1973); *Studies on the Reign of Mehmed the Conqueror* (Ankara, 1954); *Ottoman Survey Book of Albania Dated 1432 A. D.* (Ankara, 1954); *Tanzimat and the Bulgarian Question* (Ankara, 1943).

TIBOR HALASI-KUN, Ph.D., is Professor of Turkic Studies, Columbia University. Ph.D., University of Budapest. Founder and President, American Research Institute in Turkey; Chief Investigator, Ottoman Domesday Research Group, National Endowment for the Humanities. Author: *Gennadios' Turkish Confession of Faith* (Budapest, 1936). Editor in Chief: *Archivum Ottomanicum*; *Archivum Eurasiae Medii Aevi.*

ALLEN Z. HERTZ, Ph.D., is Assistant Professor of History, McGill University, and Visiting Postdoctoral Fellow, Ankara University and Canada Council. B.A., McGill University; M.A., Ph.D., Columbia University. Author: "Lord and Peasant in the Balkan Lands under the Ottomans, 1400–1600," *Columbia Essays in International Affairs* 4 (1968), pp. 107–125; "Ada Kale: The Key to the Danube, 1688–1690," *Archivum Ottomanicum* 3 (1971), pp. 141–155; "Armament and Supply Inventory of Ottoman Ada Kale, 1753," *ibid.* 4 (1972), pp. 94–171; "The Ottoman Conquest of Ada Kale, 1738," *ibid.* 6 (1974), *c.* 130 pp. (in press).

BÉLA K. KIRÁLY, Ph.D., is Professor of History, Brooklyn College and Graduate School, City University of New York. Member International PEN Club. Ludovika Military Academy, Budapest; War Academy, Budapest; M.A., Ph.D., Columbia University. Author: *Hungary's Army under the Soviet* (Tokyo, 1958); *Hungary in the Late Eighteenth Century: The Decline of Enlightened Despotism* (New York, 1969); *Ferenc Deák* (Boston,

1975). Editor: *Tolerance and Movements of Religious Dissent in Eastern Europe* (Boulder–New York, 1975), *The Habsburg Empire in World War I* (Boulder–New York, 1977). *The East Central European Perceptions of Early America* (Lisse, The Netherlands, 1977), *The Hungarian Revolution of 1956 in Retrospect* (Boulder–New York, 1978).

WILLIAM G. LOCKWOOD, Ph.D., is Associate Professor of Anthropology, University of Michigan. B.A., Fresno State College; Ph.D., University of California at Berkeley. Author: *European Moslems: Economy and Ethnicity in Western Bosnia* (New York, 1975). Editor: *Essays in Balkan Ethnology* (Berkeley, Calif., 1967).

PETER PASTOR, Ph.D., is Associate Professor of History, Monmouth College, N.J. B.A., City College of the City University of New York; M.A., Ph.D., New York University. Author: *Hungary between Wilson and Lenin: The Hungarian Revolution of 1918-1919* (New York, 1976).

JAROSLAW PELENSKI, Ph.D., is Professor of History, University of Iowa. Ph.D., Munich University; Ph.D., Columbia University. Author: *Russia and Kazan: Conquest and Imperial Ideology (1438–1560s)* (The Hague–Paris, 1974). Editor: *State and Society in Europe from the Fifteenth to the Eighteenth Century: Proceedings of the First Conference of Polish and American Historians, Nieborów, Poland, May 27–29, 1974* (Warsaw, in press).

OMELJAN PRITSAK, Ph.D., is Mykhailo S. Hrushevs'kyj Professor of History, Harvard University, and Director, Harvard Ukrainian Research Institute, Fellow of the American Academy of Arts and Sciences. College and university degrees from the Universities of L'viv, Kiev, Berlin and Göttingen. Author *Die Bulgarische Fürstenliste*, Wiesbaden, 1955.

DANKWART A. RUSTOW, Ph.D., is Distinguished Professor of Political Science, Brooklyn College and Graduate School, City University of New York. Ph.D., Yale University. Author: (with J. F. Mugno) *OPEC: Success and Prospects* (New York,

1976); *Middle Eastern Political Systems* (Englewood Cliffs, N.J., 1971); *A World of Nations: Problems of Political Modernization* (Washington, D.C., 1967); (with R. E. Ward, *et al.*) *Political Modernization in Japan and Turkey* (Princeton, N.J., 1964); *The Politics of the Developing Areas* (Princeton, N.J., 1960); *Politics and Westernization in the Near East* (Princeton, N.J., 1956); *The Politics of Compromise: Parties and Cabinet Government in Sweden* (Princeton, N.J., 1955). Editor: *Philosophers and Kings: Studies in Leadership* (New York, 1970).